How to Get Happily Published

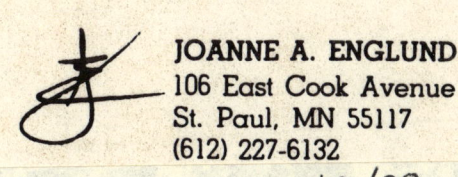

JOANNE A. ENGLUND
106 East Cook Avenue
St. Paul, MN 55117
(612) 227-6132

10/89

How to Get Happily Published

THIRD EDITION
* * *

Judith Appelbaum

A revised and updated edition of
How to Get Happily Published: A Complete and Candid Guide
by Judith Appelbaum and Nancy Evans

1817

HARPER & ROW, PUBLISHERS, New York
Cambridge, Philadelphia, San Francisco, London
Mexico City, São Paulo, Singapore, Sydney

HOW TO GET HAPPILY PUBLISHED *(Third Edition)*. Copyright © 1988 by Judith Appelbaum. Copyright © 1978, 1981, 1982 by Judith Appelbaum and Nancy Evans. All rights reserved. Printed in the United States of America. No part of this book may be used or reproduced in any manner whatsoever without written permission except in the case of brief quotations embodied in critical articles and reviews. For information address Harper & Row, Publishers, Inc., 10 East 53rd Street, New York, N.Y. 10022. Published simultaneously in Canada by Fitzhenry & Whiteside Limited, Toronto.

Designed by Joan Greenfield

Library of Congress Cataloging-in-Publication Data

Appelbaum, Judith.
  How to get happily published.

  Includes index.
  1. Publishers and publishing.   2. Self-publishing.
3. Authorship.   I. Title.
Z278.A56   1988   070.5   88-45008

BOMC offers recordings and compact discs, cassettes
and records. For information and catalog write to
BOMR, Camp Hill, PA 17012.

For Alan

Contents

Acknowledgments xi

What's New, or On Beyond This Book xiii

Initiation 1

*Penetrating the publishing mystique * The friendly editor format * Who wants you * Mistakes editors make * Perfecting your follow-through * The pleasure principle*

Getting the Words Right

Basics 11

*Overcoming fear of failure * Reading like a writer * Where to get story ideas * The procrastination problem * Revising, or getting it right * Criticism, or getting it read*

Formal Instruction 23

*The rip-off factor * Learning by doing: the classroom experience * A correspondence school saga * Evaluating manuscript evaluations * Help from software and the printed page*

A Foot in the Door

Who Do You Know? Agents and Other Connections 41

*Editors' insecurities * How, when and whether to get an agent * The agent's role * Building an acquaintanceship chain * Free admission: writers as sponsors, people in publishing and getting a publishing job * Alliances for progress*

Subject Matter Matters 52

*What editors want * The caring criterion * What readers want * Translations from the technical * Sharing the wealth of experience * Local datelines * Crystal balls * The small-is-seminal syndrome * Guidelines for manuscript development*

Openings, or Where to Submit Your Manuscript 62

*Size places: the pros and cons of larger and smaller publishers * New light on the steppingstone theory * Bonds of affection * Finding the firm that fits you * Keys to timing * Easy-access markets * Vanity presses * High hopes*

Procedures, or How to Submit Your Manuscript 77

*Thinking like an editor * Queries, or this way out of the slush pile * Going one-on-one * Book proposals, or sell your book before you write it * Covering-letter etiquette * Poets' ploys * On writing for children * The multiple-submissions route * Second steps*

A Note on Improving Your Vision 94

The Sale and Its Sequels

Getting What's Coming to You 97

*The outbreak of hostilities * Judging publishers * Doing the contract quadrille: agents, lawyers, the Authors Guild and* *going it alone* ✶ *Payment foul-ups* ✶ *Fringe benefits* ✶ *Power plays for beginners*

Editing, Copy-editing, Design, Production and Part-and-Parcel Advertising   112

How to pre-edit now and avoid trouble later ✶ *Understanding editorialese* ✶ *Conflict management and the anti-snafu checklist* ✶ *The index oversight* ✶ *Free-play period* ✶ *Introduction to the business side*

Why and How to Be Your Own Best Sales Force   124

Small expectations and the bigbook bind ✶ *Increasing your influence* ✶ *Spreading the word* ✶ *Sales strategies* ✶ *The dignity trap* ✶ *Comebacks: coping with orphaned manuscripts and other par-for-the-course perils*

The Self-Publishing Option

The Case for Doing It Yourself   147

Home truths about a writer's real choices ✶ *Quality control, long life, the I-made-it-myself premium and other self-publishing pluses* ✶ *Success stories*

A Complete Starter Kit of Self-Publishing Skills   159

Editing rationales ✶ *Legal rights and obligations* ✶ *Design made simple* ✶ *Setting type* ✶ *A paste-up primer* ✶ *Hiring help* ✶ *Final touches*

Managing Sales   177

The tri-part head start ✶ *How much and how many* ✶ *Winning attention* ✶ *Bookstores, better stores and other routes to readers* ✶ *Selling rights*

Money

Front-end Funding 197

Grants ∗ Room, board and solitude: a run-through of writers' colonies ∗ Field expedients and tax tactics ∗ The salary solution ∗ Institutional angels

Spinoffs 206

Metamorphoses ∗ The excerpt opportunity ∗ Ghosting, packaging, publishing ∗ Talking and teaching

Endnote

Righting the Scales of Success 219

The silent treatment ∗ Behind the best-seller lists ∗ Achievement Awards checklist #1

Resources

How to Use Resources 224

A comprehensive review of the best: Books ∗ Databases ∗ Magazines ∗ Newsletters ∗ Research centers ∗ Schools ∗ Organizations ∗ Advisers

Index 297

Acknowledgments

Hundreds of people in and around publishing provided valuable information and advice for this book, and I'd like to extend my warmest thanks here, both to those who are mentioned in the pages that follow and to those whose contributions the book reflects indirectly, including:

Bob Adelman, Alfred H. Allen, Carolyn Anthony, Robert E. Baensch, Ann Banks, Virginia Barber, Marvin G. Barrett, John Baskin, Sheila Berger, Susan Bergholz, Louise Bernikow, Meredith Bernstein, John Berry, Janice Blaufox, Ruth Brengel, Richard P. Brickner, Selma Brody and Diana Brown.

And Robert Cassidy, Carol Cohen, Janet Coleman, Gay Courter, Page Cuddy, Ginger Curwen, Joann Davis, Kenneth C. Davis, Julia della Croce, John P. Dessauer, Paula Diamond, Paul D. Doebler, Arnold Dolin, Robert J. Egan, Lisel Eisenheimer, Martha Fairchild, Paul Fargis, Jenny Feder, Cheri Fein, John Fischer, Zelda Fischer, Joan Foster and Len Fulton.

And Jonathan Galassi, Elizabeth Geiser, John Gilbertson, David Glotzer, Elizabeth Gordon, Annette Grant, Hannelore Hahn, Elise Hancock, Stuart Harris, Bill Henderson, Susan Hirschman, Hayes Jacobs, Tony Jones, Joan Kahn, Irwin Karp, Laura Katz, Mimi Kayden, Ralph Keyes, Rhoda Koenig, Diane Kruchkow, Mary and Robert Lane, Georgie Lee, Bill Leigh, Tom Lewis and Lydia Link.

And Tom Loven, Miriam Madfis, Rich Marchione, Richard

Marek, Elaine Markson, Peter McCabe, Ken McCormick, Walter Meade, Kate Medina, Lisa Merrill, Robert R. Miles, Tom Montag, Joseph Montebello, Helen Moore, Richard Morris, William Morris, Jennifer Moyer, Julian Muller and Raymond Mungo.

And Jean Naggar, Victor Navasky, William Novak, Carol Ohmann, Don Passer, Christina Paterniti, Molly Peacock, Jean Peters, Ryan Petty, Christine Pisaro, Terry Pristin, Alice Quinn, Eleanor Rawson, Eric L. Reiss, Stephen F. Roth, Pat Rotter, Marc Sacerdote, Richard Sandomir, Karl Schumacher, Eleanor Shatzkin, Leonard Shatzkin, Mike Shatzkin, Robert Shnayerson, Maggy Simony, Ruth Sonsky and Miriam Steinert.

And Helen A. Stephenson, Patsy Sweely, Cindy Taylor, Carl Thorgerson, Linda Triegel, Carll Tucker, Joseph Vergara, Scott Walker, Lois Wallace, Michael Weber, Florence Weiner, Richard Weiner, Sally Williams, Marianne Woolfe, Susan Zakin, Suzanne Zavrian, Mel Zerman and Charlotte Zolotow.

I owe a special debt of gratitude to Leslie Li, to Dan Carpenter and the staff of NADAP and to Stan Taylor and his associates.

Thanks go also, of course, to Nancy Evans, my collaborator on the first and second editions of the book.

And finally, I am enormously grateful to Robert, Harriet, Robert H. and Madelaine Pilpel, to Alan, Lynn, Alec and Edith Appelbaum, and to Florence Janovic and Berenice Hoffman.

Thank you all.

What's New, or On Beyond This Book

MY FELLOW speaker was a famous agent, and when the moderator said I'd written a book called *How to Get Happily Published,* the famous agent raised one eyebrow and snickered. "It's not possible," he said. "To be an author is to be unhappy."

That was way back, ten years ago, when the first edition of this book appeared. Although I didn't believe him then, I was a little shaken. After all, he'd been working with writers longer than I had. Maybe I too would become cynical as time went by.

But I don't believe him today either. In fact, now I know he's wrong, and I've got plenty of proof, thanks to writers who read earlier editions of *How to Get Happily Published* and writers I've talked with at conferences, at courses and at the consulting company that the book spawned.

These people sell articles, short stories, poems and books to publishers large and small; they publish their own books and magazines, their own newsletters and newspapers. They write full-time to make a living or part-time because of commitments in other fields. And when they get their work published, that makes them happy.

In voices brimming with pleasure, they report: "*Travel and Leisure* bought my piece about going home to China"; "Six editors asked to see my proposal on custody battles, and one offered me a $20,000 advance the day she got it"; "You won't believe how many foreign countries bought rights to that guide I published for expectant mothers"; "I have to show you these letters I just got. Imagine readers saying I changed their lives!"

Of course, the writers I talk with aren't always in good spirits. I hear publishing horror stories too, an astounding variety of them.

But when publishing gets people down, it doesn't necessarily get them out. Energetic writers who believe in their work learn to recover from bad breaks and to create their own good ones.

They learn, in other words, that getting happily published is an activity, not an award, something you do rather than something somebody does for you. Since the second edition of *How to Get Happily Published* appeared in 1982, more and more writers have decided to be active players in the publishing process, and more and more resources have appeared to help them win.

In the "Resources" section of this edition, therefore, you'll find hundreds of new listings—things to read, places to go, people to contact.

New information also appears throughout the body of the book. Readers asked for more specific advice about selling poetry and work for children; it's in here now. Publishing and bookselling patterns have changed drastically over the past decade; the text takes recent developments into account. Writers keep finding new ways to reach readers; these pages highlight their discoveries.

Because reaching readers is a vital ingredient in this book's recipe for happiness, it covers the full spectrum of publication possibilities. Unlike guides that focus either on writing for periodicals or on writing books, unlike guides that deal either with selling to the publishing establishment or with becoming a self-publisher, *How to Get Happily Published* assumes that you need to know about all your options so that you can use different forms and different routes for different purposes.

You may find, for example, that the article you wrote and sold is germinating into a book, which you'll need to place and promote. Conversely, you may find that the book you wrote and sold can be publicized best through articles you write and sell.

What's New, or On Beyond This Book xv

Furthermore, just as you're apt to want to switch between books and shorter works, you're likely to benefit by placing some projects with publishing giants, submitting others to small, specialized companies and maybe even handling some through a tiny company of your own.

All these options are viable today, all of them figure in the pages that follow and any or all of them may help you reach the readers who'll be most receptive to your work.

If you ask me, the best part of getting published is getting comments from those readers. Fame and fortune and well-turned phrases are rewarding too, of course, but nothing beats hearing from people who've read what you've written and who tell you they're better off as a result.

Nothing except hearing from people who tell you that, having read your work, they got people to read their work, and those people, in turn, wrote to them to express appreciation. When you write a book about getting published, that kind of compound pleasure can come your way.

My thanks to readers across the country and around the world who've made me happy by responding to *How to Get Happily Published* in the past. I'll look forward to hearing from those of you who have comments, criticisms, stories to share or quick questions to ask after you've read the new edition.

Judith Appelbaum
P.O. Box 8290
New Fairfield, CT 06812

Initiation

TO BEGIN WITH, an announcement for writers, would-be writers and people who have important things to say from time to time and want to say them in print: It is largely within your power to determine whether a publisher will buy your work and whether the public will buy it once it's released.

That having been said, two questions naturally arise: Why do so many people who try to place articles, stories and books with publishing firms get rejected time and again? And why do so many people who succeed in placing articles, stories and books with publishing firms then find that their work never attracts a sizable audience?

The answer is surprisingly simple. Failures abound because hardly anybody treats getting published as if it were a rational, manageable activity—like practicing law or laying bricks—in which knowledge coupled with skill and application can ensure success. Instead, almost everybody approaches the early phases of the publishing process, which have to do with finding a publisher, by trusting exclusively to luck, to merit or to formulas. And when later phases come along, bringing production and marketing problems, writers too often opt out.

Such behavior is thoroughly counterproductive, but it's entirely understandable at the same time, and on several grounds.

In the first place, people who write are as reluctant as the rest of us to expose themselves by asking questions. Seeking

2 Initiation

information is an intimidating task in this day and age. We've all been raised to believe that, since knowledge is power, ignorance must be impotence, and it's shameful, therefore, to admit it when there's something we don't know.

And in the second place, we tend to proceed on the assumption that mastery of any field is the exclusive province of specialists and experts. The lay public, so the theory goes, can't expect to understand how to fix a leaky pipe, let alone how to get a manuscript from writer to reader, so that people who aren't prevented from finding out by the fear of looking silly are hindered by the fear that the information they'll receive will be unintelligible anyway.

But even those who are brave and energetic enough to go in search of knowledge about getting published have not, in most cases, found the effort worthwhile. What all aspiring authors really need is an editor who has the time and the inclination to sit down with them and show them the industry ropes. What a writer gets, however, is more likely to be a handful of books from the oppressively large canon of works on breaking into print (which usually tell only parts of the truth and may not tell the truth at all) or a handful of books from the somewhat smaller canon of works on subsequent aspects of the publishing process (which tend to explain the way the business works without focusing on the flesh-and-blood men and women who run it and who inevitably alter the rules to fit personal and practical demands).

This book is a substitute for the friendly editor. It offers a full and frank description of the contemporary publishing picture—complete with fallible human beings in the foreground and annotated guides to hundreds of available resources at the back. Anyone who reads it intelligently should come away with a good general idea of the way the publishing process normally works, some valuable specific information on the ingenious tactics assorted individuals have devised to make it work for them and easy enough access to additional information about the full range of publishing options to be able to create effective publishing strategies for particular projects.

More than twenty-five years of personal experience in editing books, magazines, newspapers and newsletters have gone into the advice you'll find here about getting through the publishing labyrinth. And so have myriad experiences other publishing professionals shared, all of which help explain each phase, introduce the people in charge, define the unfamiliar terms, set forth the basic unwritten rules that govern progress and tell you how to discover more about whichever aspects of getting published interest you.

But at every step the main focus of attention will be on you—what you want, what you need, what you'll have to contend with to get it, how wide your options are, and how you can reach your goals most expeditiously.

This book, in other words, is designed as a launching pad for individual writers and writing projects, and its overriding purpose is to help you improve your improvisational skills so that you'll be able to switch gears when you need to, no matter what the rulebook experts say. The idea is that once you understand the query letter in context (for example), you'll see that it's a valuable tool for you and not just a time-saver for editors, and you'll choose to use it to maximum advantage. Similarly, once you've gained the confidence to obey other people's dictates only when they fit your situation, you'll draft a covering letter to an editor at *New Age* that's quite different in tone—and perhaps in content as well—from the one you'd send to the *New York Review of Books*.

New Age may return your material, of course, and so may the *New York Review of Books* and Bantam and the Globe Pequot Press, but please don't let yourself be discouraged if getting what you want involves a few false starts. To keep your spirits up on darker days, you may find it useful to dwell on three important facts:

✻ *Publishers need you at least as much as you need them.* Despite widespread suspicions of conspiracy, there's little truth in the theory that an elite circle of editors and writers concentrated in

Manhattan and doing business on the cocktail-party circuit reserves every printed page for itself.

Editors do, no doubt, know established writers, and established writers do, no doubt, know editors, and, unquestionably, a lot of assignments are given out at New York cocktail parties and at opulent New York publishing lunches as well (they still exist, those lunches, somewhat subdued by current conditions but worth angling for if you find yourself with a big-city publisher interested in you).

On the other hand, (a) even the deputed leaders of the New York Literary Establishment are wary of accepting too much material from fellow NYLE members; in spite of long and liquid lunch hours, editors are always aware of the dangers of provincialism; and (b) no matter how many authors editors know, they never have enough first-rate material. In publishing firms on both coasts and in between, the quest for new ideas and new writers is considered so vital that editors-in-chief frequently chide—and sometimes threaten—their junior colleagues about it. "Unless you have three projects to propose, don't come to the editorial meeting this week; and if you miss three meetings, don't come back to work," a particularly stern taskmaster is in the habit of telling his staff.

One editor's nonstop search for fresh talent led straight to a hardworking man named John Robben. After many abortive attempts, Robben, a toy manufacturer during normal business hours, had finally had a piece accepted for the Op Ed page in *The New York Times*. He wrote about breaking away from what he called his programmed past, and the day his article appeared an editor from a large New York publishing house tracked him down. Had Robben, he wanted to know, ever thought of writing a book? "Writing a book!" Robben said. "I have seventy-two journals in my basement."

Undaunted (or at least not fatally discouraged) by this revelation, the editor went on with the conversation, and eventually, over the course of the next several months, he helped Robben fashion material from his journals into a book titled *Coming to*

My Senses, which was, in essence, an expanded version of the *Times* piece. None of the major review media paid any attention to the book when it appeared, but it got some nice mentions in a handful of small magazines and papers, and word of mouth coaxed sales to a thoroughly respectable level.

This writer happened to get a big break because he'd gotten a small piece into *The New York Times,* but editors doggedly scan far less eminent publications looking for promising material. And of course they spend hours each day paging through the manuscripts and outlines and proposals that arrive on their desks in the hope of discovering a new writer who will boost their status with their colleagues and improve their employer's standing in the marketplace.

✶ *Editors make mistakes.* Publisher after publisher turned down *Zen and the Art of Motorcycle Maintenance, Lolita, The Peter Principle,* and Roger Tory Peterson's *Field Guide to the Birds,* for instance. And John Fischer, for many years head of the trade (i.e., general) book department at Harper, used to tell—with the aplomb made possible by his otherwise admirable record—of spurning a book that went on to make publishing history.

"I hate to remember," Fischer confessed in one of his "Easy Chair" columns in *Harper's Magazine,* "the time when James R. Newman first told me his scheme for a history of mathematics.... He wanted to gather all the basic documents of mathematical thought and arrange them into an anthology which would trace the development of the science in the words of the masters themselves. It would be a big book—perhaps five hundred pages. What did I think of it?

"I told him it was impossible. Nobody would buy it; its subject was too specialized—in fact to most people (including me) downright repellent—and it would be far too costly to manufacture."

Newman's *The World of Mathematics* was subsequently issued by Simon & Schuster, having grown to four volumes from the originally contemplated one, and Fischer noted drily that before long the publisher had sold over 120,000 sets, in addition to those distributed by two book clubs. Just recently, the book was re-released by Microsoft Press with considerable fanfare and a $75,000 advertising and promotion budget.

The point, clearly and comfortably, is that a rejection (which in any case is directed to your work and not to you as a person) may well reflect more unfavorably on the editor's ability than on yours.

✴ *Perseverance pays.* Outlets for writing are multiplying rapidly nowadays, as new technology makes small publishing ventures economically feasible. And at large houses as well as small, editorial tastes are always so varied that there should be an editor somewhere who's looking for what you have to offer, as Judith Guest discovered when she tried her now famous, but then rejected, novel *Ordinary People* on a new pair of editorial eyes.

After the book was turned down by Random House, Ms. Guest sent it on to Viking, where an editorial assistant named Mimi Jones picked it out of the slush pile and passed it along to her colleagues with enthusiastic comments. Viking accepted the book, whereupon it was published to good reviews, selected by the Book-of-the-Month Club and sold to a paperback house for over half a million dollars, after which it went on to make the bestseller lists and win four Oscars in its film version.

The author was delighted, for obvious reasons, that she hadn't quit while she was behind, but Mimi Jones won a full measure of joy from the novel's fate too. "It was exhilarating," she explained, "to have one of my cherished ideals finally borne out just at the point when I was about ready to abandon it: that real talent will always eventually be recognized, that a good first novel does have a chance."

Precisely because so many people inside publishing companies share Mimi Jones's desire to get valuable pieces of writing the attention they deserve, it makes sense for an author to persevere even after the acceptance stage. In fact, a wise writer will shepherd his or her work all the way through production and distribution until finally it reaches its readers, realizing that when the pros are prepared to do their part, it would be a shame to have a project founder because the writer didn't pitch in.

Please understand: there's no need for the author to actually perform every publishing chore, but authors who make it their business to know what should be done to give their work its best shot—and when it should be done and why and by whom and how they themselves can participate—stand by far the strongest chance of winning attention from the critics and purchase money from the public. Moreover, they figure to escape the frustrations that so often arise to plague people who rely on the specialists in a big and busy organization to handle important matters for them.

In publishing, as in practically every other field of modern endeavor, "success" is a term that each individual must ultimately define for him- or herself. But if you set your goals wisely, with full comprehension of the framework that surrounds their realization, you can find an unprecedented degree of fulfillment in getting published, and you should encounter serendipitous pleasures at several points, for using your own wits and your own energies provides an especially satisfying way to ensure that the profoundly personal act which writing constitutes comes finally to fruition.

Getting the Words Right

Basics

A GREAT MANY successful authors have never taken a writing course or read a writing manual, and they wouldn't want to. Instead, they rely on common-sense measures to improve their writing skills. Realizing, for example, that reading offers one good way to learn about using words, they are apt to go through several books and magazines a month and to pick up pointers on style, organization, point of view and the like from each one.

Sometimes the learning process that takes place when you read is virtually unconscious. For instance, you may barely sense that steeping yourself in Henry James novels causes you to be more careful about nuances in your own prose; but the effect will have occurred nonetheless and, at a minimum, it will have taught you something about your options in selecting language.

To make learning from reading a more deliberate act, writers often stop to examine each powerful passage they encounter in order to figure out how it achieved its impact (through a succession of startling images, a change of tense, a panoply of facts?). And to further advance their educations, many authors turn to behind-the-scenes books like Virginia Woolf's *A Writer's Diary* and the diaries left by Chekhov, Hawthorne and Thoreau, which deal directly with how a writer creates and organizes material, how private reading feeds constantly into present and future projects and how to deal with writer's block, self-doubt and the other psychological hazards of the trade. Similar subject matter characterizes anthologies like the *Paris Review Interviews,* in which writers not only talk about their craft but also reveal whether they write reclining nude on a sofa or standing up in an A & P parking lot.

Because analyzing and explaining how they do what they do appeals strongly to many writers, the common-sense approach to writing has given rise to a body of teachings based on personal experience and handed down over the years in print and through word of mouth. It's from this legacy that the following suggestions derive. For additional guidance, see "Getting the Words Right Resources."

Story Ideas—Files . . .

Writing well for publication demands, first, that you pick a subject that excites you and will attract others, and, second, that you flesh it out with examples, images, anecdotes, facts and characters. Many writers meet these requirements with the help of the pack-rat process, which involves hoarding printed materials that interest them along with scribbled notes about ideas, snatches of conversation and nuggets of information they find provocative.

In the beginning, these bits and pieces may not mean much but as they accumulate they'll start to form patterns, and eventually a number of items may cluster around a subject like (for example) building your own house. At that point, the next step is easy: label a folder with that heading and stock it with all the makings for an article or book: notes on background reading, research materials, people to interview, associations to contact, relevant data from the *Congressional Record,* preliminary reflections and angles of approach.

Any subject, it's important to understand, can be treated in numerous ways, so that even before you begin to write you have vital choices to make. Whom shall I write for, and how should I address them? What style will I use? What tone? What do I want to say, and how will I arrange my material for optimum effect?

To get a concrete idea of the range of choice that confronts you, take a subject you're curious about and look it up in the *Readers' Guide to Periodical Literature* and the *Subject Guide to Books in Print* at your local library. Then look up related headings and read around in the materials you discover. You'll find that although the topic is unchanging, each treatment of it highlights a different aspect for a different audience, and you'll come away more alert to the decisions you must make at the start of any writing project. (Furthermore, by way of bonus, you'll get a leg up on your research.)

In making these preliminary choices, some writers consult style folders in which they've filed samples of the short, pithy, anecdotal piece; the first-person report; the informal essay in social criticism; the investigative story; and other forms available to authors today. If you start such a folder for yourself you can use its contents as a checklist each time you begin work on a new topic. Perhaps that will prevent you from propping a sprightly personal reminiscence on a scaffolding better suited to *War and Peace*.

. . . and the Free Space

Some of the nicest people we know turn pompous when they write, probably because they've been saying to themselves, "Who wants to read what I, a nobody, have to report about marriage? I'd better write like somebody people ought to listen to." Unfortunately, and for obvious reasons, the attempt to impress is usually counterproductive; just as people at a party groan when someone comes in putting on airs—that old standby defense against the social jitters—readers will be put off by a manuscript that's written with pretension rather than warmth and sincerity.

To build confidence in your writing ability to the point where you can drop your poses, you might try keeping a journal. Ideally, a journal is a free space, inaccessible both to the self-critic and to the critics lurking in the great out-there. In your journal you can experiment by writing whatever comes into your mind without censorship and by following your thoughts wherever they lead, because it's not polished work you're after now, but loosening up to feel comfortable with the written expression of your thoughts and observations.

If you also use your journal to jot down quotes and facts that appeal to you, to try out different writing styles, to test and develop story ideas and to phrase your reactions to current events, you should find that it serves as a healthy complement to research, reporting and the more structured writing you produce when you begin to draft your manuscript.

Drafting

No matter how extensive your preparation, you may be struck by panic and confusion when you finally sit down to write. The best way to handle the performance jitters—however devastating they seem—is to recognize the fears as normal and then take a simple step. Get something down on paper. It doesn't have to be perfect; it just has to exist so that you will have the beginning of a rough draft to work with, and not merely a pile of notes.

The impetus to get that initial group of words out of your head and onto your paper will be strong if selling what you write is the only way you're going to pay the rent. Otherwise, though, writing all too often strikes people as an activity that can fit under the heading "Important But Not Urgent" devised by Edwin C. Bliss in his *Getting Things Done*. To make sure you really do get started, both Bliss and other writers suggest that you reserve substantial blocks of time for writing each day, or three times a week, or at whatever intervals are practical in the light of your other commitments and priorities.

You may finish a full morning's stint having completed one sentence; on the other hand, you may become inspired once you're involved in the work of figuring out what you want to say and saying it. But keep trying. "Many times, I just sit for three hours with no ideas coming to me," Flannery O'Connor once said. "But I know one thing: if an idea does come between nine and twelve, I am there ready for it."

Particularly for people working on book-length manuscripts, making the best use of writing time takes practice. When she was drafting her book about crime victims, writer Dawn Sangrey recalled, "Making lunch dates was good for me at first. They served to get me out of the apartment and gave me some contact with the outside world. As I got more involved in the book, though, lunch dates became an interruption. Now I see people either for breakfast or in the evenings and I keep my days completely free for writing."

Other people work best by interspersing sessions at the keyboard with periods of physical activity (one accomplished writer gets up and dances madly around his apartment whenever he's stuck for a word or a phrase). And still others function most effectively when they think in terms of deadlines. Two professors in this last group, both of whom were carrying full teaching loads and under pressure to publish, found that a deadline buddy system ensured productivity. On target dates, each teacher was required to deliver a chapter to the other; both had finished manuscripts ready for a publisher within a year.

Just as optimum time schedules vary from writer to writer, so the physical situation an author works well within may range from a book-lined cabin on the top of a mountain to a corner of a cramped, urban kitchen. Susan Brownmiller, author of *Against Our Will: Men, Women and Rape,* found ideal working conditions inside the New York Public Library in "a very special place called the Frederick Lewis Allen Room, where I was given a desk for my typewriter and a shelf for my books. I was also given the companionship of a score of writers who became my own private seminar in how to get the job done. The interrelationship of my Allen Room friends and me is too complex to detail; suffice it to say that each of us struggled together, respectful of one another's progress, in a supportive environment dedicated to hard work and accomplishment, a writer's Utopia or close to it." A set-up like that can be created by any group of writers who arrange to share some working space.

Every so often, people who want to write discover that they simply can't manage the task under any available circumstances, and in such cases finding collaborators or ghosts may be a good idea. (A ghost, by the way, should always be given corporeal existence through a shared by-line or, at the least, through an explicit acknowledgment at the front of the book.)

"Getting the Words Right Resources" offers leads to writers who'll work with nonwriters on book and magazine projects. And even editors have been known to function as ghosts by reworking clumsy prose completely in order to get important ideas to an audience. But for most people ghosting isn't necessary. Almost anybody can put words together in a serviceable fashion provided they're not hampered by believing that they must compete with the great stylists. So just remember that if you know fully what you want to say you will find a way to say it, and write as you speak, or rather, in the words of Northrop Frye, use language that "is not ordinary speech, but ordinary speech on its best behavior, in its Sunday clothes, aware of an audience with its relation to that audience prepared beforehand."

Revising

The printed materials you buy at the bookstore or newsstand have generally gone through numerous revisions. "I rewrote the ending of *Farewell to Arms* thirty-nine times before I was satisfied," Ernest Hemingway once told an interviewer.

"Was there some problem there?" the interviewer wanted to know. "What was it that had stumped you?"

"Getting the words right," said Hemingway.

Thirty-nine rewrites are several more than most writers will want—or be fully able—to attempt, but you should count on revising your work up to half a dozen times before you consider it finished. To make revision easier, be generous with spacing from the start. If you write longhand on a yellow legal pad, double space so you can insert words and rearrange sentences without totally destroying legibility. If you use a typewriter or a word processor, triple spacing might be best.

Instruction in the self-editing process that revision constitutes is available in several good books (see this section's "Resources"), most of which explain, sensibly enough, that it makes sense to begin with the beginning. This is the time to look with a critical eye at those first few paragraphs. Did you breeze through the start just to get up some steam? Do they read just as they were written—as a preliminary clearing-the-throat exercise? If so, X them out and find the spot where you really begin to address your subject in a way that will capture a reader's interest.

Devising a good lead is worth all the craft and inspiration at your command. For it's with your first few sentences that you must convince people to read what you have to say. If you're not sure what constitutes a good lead, look hard at writing you admire. And during all your reading, be on the alert for openings that grab your attention. Try to figure out why they attract you and compel you to read on. If you can determine the causes behind the effect—a catalog of precise details, a bold question, a colorful anecdote—you will be better equipped to fashion an exciting lead of your own.

Though the lead is the single most vital section of your manuscript, each word counts, and each should be designed not to dazzle but to communicate. Keep your critical eye sharp as you continue through passages now familiar to you by reading silently in a monotone or aloud to yourself. Both methods will help you spot places where a reader may stumble.

Finding the precise word that says what you mean is not, of course, a luxury; it is a crucial necessity. Sometimes the best choice doesn't come to mind right away, but when that happens you can leave signals for yourself as you draft: circle a word you're not sure about; bracket a choice of two phrases; put a question mark in the margin; write in TK in a circle (it's a printer's abbreviation for To Kum); then come back later and get the thing right.

As you pencil in your changes, you may notice that entire sections should be scrapped or reshuffled, or that you shortchanged a point and need to elaborate. Maybe, for example, you left out the illustrative material that would make your point clear on page 6; maybe the paragraph at the end of chapter four clearly belongs with the discussion toward the beginning of chapter two. Don't be alarmed. This kind of reworking is the norm, not the exception, for experienced writers, so you should move material around with some abandon. And if the first move doesn't work out as well as you thought it would, you can always try another arrangement until you get a smooth, effective draft.

Deleting material is, of course, psychologically harder than moving or adding it, but abridgment is frequently necessary in revision. Although you may have grown fond of a passage, if it duplicates an earlier one, something has got to go. The freedom you allowed yourself in drafting now requires that you be ruthless in pruning the redundant, the irrelevant, the gratuitously showy. And that may mean cutting your first draft by half.

Getting Criticism

To get critical feedback before you send your manuscript to an editor—from whom, by the way, you shouldn't expect a critique—you can approach a variety of people. The most obvious source for constructive criticism is another writer, either one who is at your stage of development, or a professional whose work you've read and admired.

"If you really like someone's work, why not write them?" asks Elliot Figman of Poets & Writers, an organization of professional writers sponsored by federal and state arts councils. "The worst thing that could happen is that they won't write back." Most writers are accessible to some degree (see "Resources" for directories that include addresses and phone numbers), and James Harkness found Annie Dillard, Pulitzer Prize–winning author of *Pilgrim at Tinker Creek,* to be very accessible indeed.

> I had just finished reading *Points for a Compass Rose* by Evan Connell—about four times, without coming up for air—and I was rushing around to all my friends, clutching them by their coat sleeves and crying, "My God, read this!" Of course no one was paying the slightest attention. I wanted to share my enthusiasm, and I was frustrated. Then Annie Dillard published an essay/review about the book which was rhapsodic and well-written.
>
> I sent her a note via the publisher to tell her I enjoyed the piece and agreed. She replied. We spent several weeks whooping and hollering "Connell! Connell!" and eventually moved on to other topics.
>
> Although Annie knew I was ghost writing for the president of the university where I worked, I kept quiet about the stuff I was grinding out privately. By then I had seen essays from what came to be *Pilgrim at Tinker Creek,* and I had no burning desire to send a bundle of my mawkish scribbling to this obviously brilliant and talented writer who was knocking them out in the aisles.
>
> I don't recall exactly how it came about that I finally did allow Annie to see a manuscript of something or other. She wrote me back an ecstatic paean to the effect that I was "obviously the best writer alive on the planet," a composer of "muscled prose," and on and on. I replied proposing marriage. Too late.
>
> As far as the sort of comments went, they were general and supportive. Mostly she stroked my ego and let the verbs take care of themselves—a strategy, I'll add, that seems to me now not only humane but pragmatically wise. For anyone who has a certain innate potential, the most difficult aspect of learning to write is the long, dreary, often desperate silence that greets early efforts. What is needed there isn't so much criticism, constructive or otherwise, as encouragement. Sooner or later you will begin to get close analysis from editors or critics, if your manuscripts are promising enough, but not many editors or critics will hold your hand and tell you how wonderful you are in the face of much evidence to the contrary. Annie instructed me to try not to be the subject and object of my own prose, an idea I've thought about a lot and

attempted to put into practice. But she told me I was the best writer on the planet first, and I suspect the hyperbole was more sustaining, hence more valuable, than the bits and pieces of "objective" commentary.

At various points in their lives, a surprising number of writers knowingly and graciously accept the responsibility of encouraging beginners. "For ten minutes of time and postage costs (they never send return envelopes), I can restore a person's faith in humanity," one established essayist says. "Lots and lots of people write me and send manuscripts. I try to read and comment on all of them."

Nevertheless, asking for criticism is a hard thing to do, primarily because everyone is afraid of being told their work is downright rotten. And this fear often makes beginning writers just as skittish about seeking comments from peers as they are about approaching literary lights. Friends can be helpful, though, even if they're not writers or editors or professional critics. In fact, when he won the Nobel Prize for Literature, Saul Bellow declared that nonprofessionals may have an edge when it comes to critical comment. Many letters from readers, he told *The New York Times Book Review,* "are very penetrating; not all are completely approving, but then I am not completely approving of myself. In recent years, I would say that I have learned more from these letters than I have from formal criticism of my work."

So consider asking friends whose intelligence you respect to act as critics of your work in progress, not by passing final judgment on it but by pinpointing strengths and trouble spots. As Cynthia Buchanan, playwright and novelist, has explained, "It's a matter of being clear to other people. What I want to find out from friends is, first, can they follow what I'm saying. Then I want to know if it's boring and where it's boring. And third, I ask whether they feel that the language is too baroque and unrealistic in places. In the long run I choose what I want to do, but I need this consensus." Buchanan maintains that her fine track record in getting her work published is due in large part to the informal consulting system she's developed for herself.

To initiate a productive feedback system, first formulate specific questions. You might begin, for example, by asking people which passages they had to read twice; which sections they remember best; and which parts they would eliminate if someone were to insist the manuscript be shortened.

If you've written a story for children, the most obvious testing ground is the children's story hour at your local library. And if you're eager to get ongoing criticism of your work, you may want to join or organize a writers' club, whose members will be a ready source of reactions.

It's not hard to do that, as Linda Triegel discovered. In her case, as it happens, the impetus to act came from the first edition of this book, which she read just about the time she decided she was serious about her writing. Realizing that the author lived nearby, Triegel got together with a couple of other beginning writers she knew and arranged for the library in town to host a Q-and-A session.

"We thought there must be more would-be authors around who would come to hear you speak and, lo and behold, dozens turned up," she remembers. "We had them all sign a guest book with their addresses and a few weeks later invited them to a meeting to organize a writers' group. We read our work to one another and critiqued it as best we could. We also, right off, decided to put out a collection of our work just for the sake of seeing it between covers, and this has become an annual event."

The New Fairfield (Connecticut) Creative Writers Workshop, which Triegel headed for several years, was and still is a source of moral support for its members. To get "down-to-brass-tacks advice" on markets and contacts and writing techniques, she eventually joined a more advanced writers' group in her area. Today, she's the author of five published books under the name Elisabeth Kidd, she writes a column for her local paper under her own name, and she's thinking of joining still another writers' group she's just heard about.

Meeting with other people engaged in writing has several advantages. Frequently, you'll get useful pointers. Sometimes a collaborative project will be sparked. And always your morale will be strengthened by a feeling of support and community—by the knowledge that other people understand and care about what you're doing and what you may be undergoing—as you progress through the process almost nobody likes, writing itself, to the point nearly everyone enjoys, having written.

Formal Instruction

MAYBE IT'S BECAUSE of the glamour—write and you too may hobnob with the rich and the famous; write and one day they'll all look at you with respect. Maybe it's a simple semantic confusion—writing, after all, is something you learned back in first grade, so of course it will be easy to bring your prose up to publishable level. Or maybe the explanation is that people are just naturally communicative. In any case, millions of Americans are regularly seized by an urge to write. Naturally—in a culture that believes in advancement through education—lots of would-be writers immediately look for courses and manuals that will start them writing and get what they've written into print. And just as naturally—in a culture of entrepreneurs—there's no lack of individuals and institutions prepared to provide what the public wants.

The goods and services on sale can be summed up under a short list of headings—courses, criticism, computer software and books. But within these categories variations in quality are enormous. A few of the writing aids on the market promise a great deal and deliver next to nothing, while others make modest claims for themselves and then yield surprising benefits. Many, it's a pleasure to report, will honestly reveal what they offer, but only to those who carefully interpret their ads and investigate their operations.

Before you spend your first penny on any form of printed,

computerized or personal instruction, you should be able to answer these four questions:

1. Is this necessary for the successful development of my written work?
2. What exactly am I buying?
3. What value will it have for me?
4. How much will it cost, both in money and in psychological wear and tear?

The answer to Question 1 is no, and you may therefore wish to go directly from this sentence to the beginning of "A Foot in the Door." But because "unnecessary" is not synonymous with "ineffective," and because much of what's on the market can be valuable if it's skillfully selected and used, here's a guide to instructional aids.

Classes

Good teachers of writing will tell you that writing cannot be taught; it can only be learned. The teacher's role, they will explain, is to create and capitalize on opportunities for learning so that the students can develop faster and more efficiently than they would on their own. Or, as Lawrence Durrell put it in the catalog description of his course in California's International College Independent Study Program, "While nothing can be taught, the presentation of notions and ideas with precision and enthusiasm can hatch out the talents in people and thus develop them." Word it any way you like, the point is that no writing course can be worthwhile unless you exercise initiative and work hard on follow-up.

First among your required course activities will be writing, setting words down on paper until they form a structured whole. Having written, you will then be asked to submit your work to your teacher and your fellow students for criticism. And after they've commented, you'll have to rewrite, accepting those of their suggestions that your emotions and intelligence can approve and rejecting the rest. Moreover, you will probably be called upon to offer constructive criticism of your classmates' work—which means you will have to figure out where their strengths lie and how their weaknesses can be corrected.

None of this is easy; much of it may be agonizing. And what do you get for your pains?

Motivational energy, for one thing. Whether you call it writer's block or procrastination or just plain fear of failure, the difficulties that many writers experience in getting started can be eased by the presence of an instructor who assigns, expects and encourages the completion of a manuscript.

And despite instructors' protestations, you may actually get some traditional teaching during class discussions, for good teachers will seize on particular pieces of student writing to illustrate important aspects of literary technique. They may focus on dialogue, transitions, point of view, narrative exposition, plot structure or even basic rules of grammar, but whatever the subject, it will serve to sharpen every student's critical perceptions and thus to improve the value of any comments on classmates' work and the value of changes in her or his own.

Most conscientious teachers not only discuss students' writing in class and with each student individually; they also turn manuscripts into teaching tools by jotting comments as they read. As director of the Iowa Writers Workshop, John Leggett edited and copy-edited each piece of student work he read, just as he used to edit books when he worked for large publishing firms. And at Yale, William Zinsser, author of *On Writing Well,* marked up student manuscripts in memorable letters of red. Katie Leishman, one of Zinsser's many appreciative pupils, describes the consequences of his technique for learning:

> In the opening lecture Mr. Zinsser asked for a five-page account of "My First Day at College." I still have my notes: Writing is a craft. Good writing is very difficult. One word is better than two. Unnecessary words = CLUTTER. In the margin I've written, "This is all *very* obvious."

All that was obvious a week later was that I had a twenty-two-page draft when Mr. Zinsser wanted five pages. No amount of frenetic snipping and repasting of paragraphs made it any shorter. So I did the only thing I could do. I put the draft and my typewriter in the car and started driving. I suppose I thought that somewhere along the road I would have a vision of the sections I could trim from the article. Then I would stop in a coffeeshop and rewrite.

Five hours later I was still driving. At midnight I checked into a motel in the Berkshires and lay in bed wondering, in the middle of winter, in the middle of nowhere, which were the 1,000 critical words of the 6,000 words I had written. I spent the weekend in the bathtub, writing on an upside-down drawer which I laid across the rim of the tub. Saturday, I rewrote ten pages and threw out the rest. By Sunday afternoon I had what I thought were five pages of flawless prose. Satisfied and very clean, I drove back to school.

When I got that paper back it was bleeding—bleeding badly. Mr. Zinsser's red arrows, red question marks and red slashes were everywhere; he had excised entire paragraphs. I slunk out of the classroom, crestfallen, resentful.

That evening, when I could bear to look at it again, I retyped the piece, simply leaving out what Mr. Zinsser had cut and clarifying expressions he'd found vague. As I typed I realized that he hadn't robbed me of my say. Though the edited version ran only one and a half pages, it retained every point of the original twenty-two-page draft.

So "clutter" and "craft" and "the difficulty of good writing" suddenly became real, personal problems to tackle. In later assignments if I used a gratuitous or vague expression, I could almost see a slash or question mark welting over it. Eventually I developed my own sense of what was essential or expendable, of what was my own style and what was imitative. By the end of the course, when Mr. Zinsser joked about students in his "red pen orbit" I knew what he meant. Because, though his principles remained a crucial point of reference, each student was spinning off on his or her own path.

The fact that writing well is a path, not a destination, a process more than a goal, is perhaps the most important truth a writing course can divulge. The ongoing give-and-take with the teacher and the other students makes it clear, as nothing else can, that the effort has no end; it is possible to make progress; it is necessary to accept defeat and go on. Because teachers of writing are themselves writers they can comfort students as fellow sufferers while providing living examples of at least limited success. They are people who have won the right to take themselves seriously as professionals, and they can help you earn that privilege, too.

Carol Lew Simons, having spent three terms in Richard P. Brickner's "Free-Style" Writing Workshop at New York City's New School, sums up the benefits of writing courses this way:

> I am not, strictly speaking, a beginning writer. All my life I have written essays that loyal friends and my mother have dutifully praised; as a literature major at Antioch College I wrote very well-received critical papers; for the past four years I have been writing for a medical magazine. I decided to take a writing course, however, because I felt a gap existed between these slender accomplishments and the claim I sometimes made, more often than not to myself, that underneath it all I was a *real* writer. So far my attitudes have undergone more revolution than my writing, but this fact may suggest the major advantages of workshop courses.
>
> One attitude that has begun to alter rather remarkably is my view of writing as an activity, which has come about largely through the nature of the workshop discussions. What makes a workshop different from the scores of good literature courses I have taken is that the author is there in the room; the work is being regarded as a thing in process rather than as something that has, as doctors say, passed "into the literature"; and the people considering the work are involved to some extent in trying to do a similar task.
>
> I think, though I would never have admitted to this had I been asked, that before the workshop I regarded writing as an either/or proposition; you wrote something, revised it a little, and it succeeded or not. The workshop has made it clear that writing is something to be practiced very diligently, like the piano. One might never write as well as one wishes, but one can learn to write as well as one *can*—although only with considerable time and concentration. The workshop has given me a much greater respect

for writing as a craft and a process, even as it has made me see it as an endeavor more accessible and less mystical than I had once thought it.

To find a course that's as good for you as Brickner's has been for Simons, decide first—and honestly—how big a commitment you are willing to make. Depending on your age and station in life, as well as on your financial and emotional wherewithal, you may want to choose anything from a full-scale, two-year creative writing program leading to an MFA degree and a career in writing, to a journalism course or a weekend workshop (though a very short course is likely to be more useful for making contacts than for learning to write; see "A Foot in the Door"). Then, if you're contemplating a sizable investment of time and/or money, consult "Getting the Words Right Resources," read catalog copy and works by your prospective professor, talk with fellow students, and look for these hallmarks:

* A commitment from the teacher to comment individually, in detail and in person, on each student's work.
* An indication that your classmates will be at approximately your level of writing ability, so that you will be able to respect their comments without developing feelings of inferiority or superiority.
* An instructor who has published, who intends to publish again and whose work you admire.
* An absence of dogma in the course description. Teachers should be loath to mold you in their image and eager, instead, to point you toward what Brickner calls "that language which is most yours and which is yet to be made available to a readership, to help you impose your specialness in a way that's beneficial to the outside."

Correspondence Courses

Despite the fact that almost every big university now has a writing program, that more and more colleges are opening their undergraduate courses to part-time students and that continuing education centers exist throughout the country, many people who would like to get instruction in writing find it hard to attend classes.

In some cases geography is the problem; there's simply no appropriate course within a reasonable radius. In others, the stumbling block is time; personal or job responsibilities can make it impossible to show up anywhere at the same hour each week. And in still other instances, psychological difficulties arise; taking criticism in front of a group—no matter how similarly situated and how sympathetic the members—may be a terrifying and repellent prospect. In these situations, among others, a correspondence course can be worth considering as a source of motivational energy and critical reaction.

No doubt, you will do your considering skeptically, because anyone who reads the papers knows that education by mail in America today is not only a big business, but also sometimes a bad business. State departments of education usually regulate refund policies, and any school that actually lies about its faculty's credentials or its graduates' achievements is likely to find itself in legal trouble—when and if somebody institutes an action against it. But for the most part, nobody monitors the quality of correspondence-school offerings. So skepticism is entirely in order.

Fortunately, however, you can size up a correspondence course before enrolling. As proof, consider a personal case history in which the protagonists are Judith Appelbaum as the Aspiring Author and the Institute of Children's Literature in Redding Ridge, Connecticut, as the Eager Instructor.

Our story began in an urban supermarket where a flyer on display at the exit trumpeted, "We're looking for people to WRITE CHILDRENS [sic] BOOKS!" Under the subhead "If you ever wanted to write and be published this is your opportunity," a lengthy copy block explained how lucrative the market for children's literature was and invited all comers to send for the institute's free (no obligation) aptitude test and descriptive brochure.

The aptitude test proved sensible, if hardly grueling. Starting with True/False questions ("Young people don't have any serious problems and don't want to read about any"), it proceeded through a varied series of short assignments ("Write a step by step instruction for a child on how to fly a kite, cook an egg, or plant a seed") to a request for a two-hundred-word piece about "something that happened during your childhood."

Without trying to do either badly or well, the Aspiring Author filled out the form, sent it off and sat back to study the accompanying brochure, which offered hard sell—but hard information, too—about faculty credentials and curriculum.

A flurry of activity then ensued. The institute fired off a form letter accepting Judith Appelbaum as a student (and then more form letters counseling prompt enrollment). Judith Appelbaum asked for additional information about course content and for the names and addresses of graduate references. The institute responded with a lengthy, informative and personally typed letter. J.A. called the ex-students (all three of them liked the course and said it helped them develop discipline and self-confidence). And the final step was checking to see whether ICL was listed in the *Directory of Accredited Home Study Schools* (which it was).

At this point the Aspiring Author was satisfied, having learned enough about the school to discount the tone of hucksterism in its ads and in its programmed correspondence (letters offering new and improved incentives to enroll kept coming for months) and to conclude that ICL presented a conscientious and apparently effective program of instruction. Because J.A. never did enroll—not even when an offer of a "Special Publishing Course" at a vastly reduced cost arrived in the mail—this case history can't end by recommending ICL specifically, but it can and does serve to recommend these methods of investigation.

To find a worthwhile correspondence course, send for the *Directory of Accredited Home Study Schools* (you'll see full information in "Resources") and then explore the programs that interest you by carefully reading their brochures. It's a good sign if a school belongs to the National University Continuing Education Association, but you'll also want answers to questions like:

* What's the refund policy?
* How much is the total cost of the course—including any and all finance charges?
* What promises do they make about selling your work?
* Who's on the faculty?
* Are academic credits earned here accepted anywhere else?

Ask to talk or correspond with students; check consumer and government agencies for complaint histories; write faculty members to inquire about how actively they participate in instruction and how much individual attention you'll receive.

Though you won't, of course, need to know who your fellow students are, you should see to it that the other three hallmarks of good writing courses (see page 28) characterize your correspondence course too. Careful evaluation before you sign up can prevent crippling blows to your psyche and your pocketbook.

Paid Critics

Both classroom teachers and correspondence-school faculty may offer advice and assistance on marketing, but as a rule they emphasize writing well at least as much as writing to sell. This is generally not the case with criticism services, which tend to stress marketing above all else and which, as a result, can be dangerous. As you read their ads (they appear regularly in writers' magazines and sometimes in general-interest periodicals too), keep the risks in mind.

Chief among the dangers, perhaps, is the possibility that your whole approach to writing will suffer if you heed the comments of agency critics. For what they're selling is not continuing advice on improving a work in progress but, rather, a one-shot assessment of an allegedly finished manuscript couched primarily in terms of its salability. Confronted with this emphasis, you may be tempted to stop concentrating on saying what you have to say as well as you can say it, and to focus instead on giving the public what it supposedly wants. From there it can be a short step to hack writing if you're glib and to writing garbage if you're not.

Of course, hired critics may not know what the public really wants; the chances are, however, that they'll say they do, and that, furthermore, they'll have a particular "public" in mind—big-name commercial book and magazine publishers. Now, commercial publishers may very well be the wrong audience for your work, and even if they're right for it their reactions to a given manuscript simply cannot be accurately predicted. Editors themselves are so aware of the variety of tastes in their ranks that they often refuse to comment on a book or article (even if they think it has merit and promise) unless they themselves can buy it; each is afraid to suggest changes that might be anathema to another editor.

Your money, in other words, may be ill-spent on a criticism service (though the fact that you've actually spent it will provide a powerful and destructive impetus for thinking well of the advice that it bought). And your money may also be stolen. The field is full of charlatans, people who will take what you pay and then vanish where the Better Business Bureau cannot follow. For every grateful writer who praises Scott Meredith, say, there must be scores who are bitter about the hundreds of dollars expended for bootless or nonexistent critiques.

Consider, as a warning, this portion of a letter from Great Novels, Inc., to writer Wayne B. George: "There is not enough emotion in your book. Instead of the storm in Boston clearing up right away you could have a snowdrift blocking your home in the suburbs. You are slowly starving, and the young lady who is your guest gets sick and needs a doctor. Finally you are both saved from death."

The advice may strike you as insultingly simple-minded on the face of it, but it is downright infuriating when you realize that Wayne George had paid $50 for strictures such as this when the manuscript he'd submitted had no snowstorm scene.

If it's criticism you want, try the approaches mentioned in the preceding chapter; if it's marketing advice, turn to "A Foot in the Door," which comes next. But if you're determined to pay for comments on your completed work, take these precautions:

* Ask your chosen critic for a current client list, and call or write some of the people on it to discuss the quality of the critic's services.
* Ask prospective critics for lists of editors who've bought their clients' work recently, and get in touch with them.
* Consult government and consumer agencies about complaints.
* Get a written explanation, in advance, of charges and services.
* And don't forget that the substantial sums you can pay for advice have no logical connection with what that advice is worth.

Computer Software

Computer software for writers comes in two primary varieties, one that's supposed to spruce up your spelling, vocabulary and style, and one designed to "process words." Ironically, the second sort is far more likely to improve your writing than the first.

As writers by the dozens have now testified, word-processing programs let you be remarkably flexible, experimental and demanding as you draft and revise. Several good programs are on the market. You can get specific recommendations from writers you know, from nearby computer stores and/or from computer periodicals.

Unlike word-processing software, "writing software" tends to make you less flexible because it holds you to simple-minded rules. In essence, each program has a finite storehouse of words and patterns to approve or criticize, and when those words or patterns show up, it spews out prescribed responses. Some of these are undoubtedly helpful, as, for example, when a program takes you to task for overusing certain words or writing interminable sentences. But some of them can be harmful, too; given the Gettysburg Address to critique, one program faulted Lincoln for using the passive voice.

The best advice, therefore, is: Get yourself a computer and a good word-processing program if you can afford to do that; buy a spelling checker to go with your word-processing program if spelling is a real problem; and pass up other software that tells you what to do instead of enhancing your ability to do whatever you decide makes sense.

Books

Relax now. It's hard to make a bad mistake with a book, both because books are inexpensive (as instructional aids go) and because their influence for evil (if any) is far weaker than that of either awe-inspiring technology or a human being who claims to be talking exclusively to you.

Though they tend to be similarly titled, books about writing divide into three classes: those in which the author becomes your partner in the task of learning to choose and combine words; those in which the author imparts formulas; and those in which the author explains how to find things out.

Partnership books, like good writing courses, see learning to write as an unending process in which the teacher's role is to provide fertile ground for growth. Though the authors here are often men and women of considerable literary distinction, they tend to talk humbly of their work and to speak unblushingly of frustration and failure. As a rule, they concentrate on the development of skills in four primary areas:

Reading: "What the writer wants to note, beyond anything that concerns even the critic, is how the story, its language, and all its parts have been joined together" (R. V. Cassill, *Writing Fiction*).

Creativity: "To begin with, you must teach the unconscious to flow into the channel of writing. . . . [L]ess elegantly and more exactly, we might say that the first step toward being a writer is to hitch your unconscious mind to your writing arm" (Dorothea Brande, *Becoming a Writer*).

Diction: "You will never make your mark as a writer unless you develop a respect for words and a curiosity about their shades of meaning that is almost obsessive" (William Zinsser, *On Writing Well*).

And construction: Or learning "how to put words together . . . so that the reader not simply may but must grasp your meaning" (Jacques Barzun, *Simple and Direct*).

Obviously, this approach involves steady hard labor. You can expect to be stimulated by a partnership book; to be satisfied you must experiment with its teachings (preferably in a playful, almost childlike way), and you must also absorb them, so that they color your perceptions as you work. And rewrite. And rewrite some more.

Few formula publications dwell on the importance of painstaking revision. Instead, they offer to make writing easier. Almost always the authors are professionals setting forth the fruits of their experience as a series of instructions, and they tend to utter commands with great confidence.

Generally, these writers are most trustworthy when they discuss their own activities (by outlining, for example, how they keep records or conduct interviews), and they are least to be believed when they deal with the effects of their systems on editors (beware, for instance, of detailed directions about the physical appearance of a manuscript; if you follow them, you'll signal most publishing people that you're a fledgling writer trying to be slick).

Essentially, formula publications constitute a grab bag for authors in which some of the goodies are much better than others; some may not suit you at all and none is a major gift. For, where learning to write is concerned, tips on technique and on industry mores, and gimmicks and shortcuts and nuggets of knowledge can be no more than peripheral aids. The central job—developing your individual style, substance and purpose—demands independent, innovative work.

To the extent that gathering data is part of the writing assignment you set yourself, your burdens will be eased by a knowledge of research tools and techniques. As you'll see if you explore your local public library, the current range of informational materials is astonishing; running from the *Guide to Reference Books* and the *Encyclopedia of Associations* to the *Directory of Chinese Scientific and Education Officials* and the *Minerals Yearbook,* the assortment casts a sweeping light on the infinite targets of human curiosity and provides starting points for anybody in search of facts.

Research manuals provide starting points too, and most of those that get published offer solid information and analysis in lively prose (since they can't depend on the glamour of their subject to attract readers, they almost have to be good).

Manuals on interviewing procedures tend to be less meaty. In fact, many of them are chatty, anecdotal discussions that illustrate nothing so well as the art of padding article-length copy into book-length size. But they do serve as useful reminders that people can be excellent sources of new knowledge. And the best of them offer serviceable pointers on how to get human beings to tell you what you want to know.

Wherever you get your information, you may need help in evaluating it because, as this single example from William L. Rivers's admirable *Finding Facts* suggests, the plainest of factual statements can bear a highly complicated relationship to the truth:

> [Consider] varying news stories about a simple report on gifts to Stanford University during one fiscal year. The university-published *Campus Report* headed its story:
>
> HIGHEST NUMBER OF DONORS
> IN STANFORD HISTORY
>
> *The San Francisco Chronicle* headline said:

Formal Instruction 37

STANFORD AGAIN RAISES
$29 MILLION IN GIFTS

The *Palo Alto Times* story was headed:

DONATIONS TO STANFORD
LOWEST IN FOUR YEARS

The student-published *Stanford Daily* announced:

ALUMNI DONATIONS DECLINE;
BIG DROP FROM FOUNDATIONS

These headlines accurately reflect the stories they surmounted—which were also accurate.

Clearly, one lesson here is that the way a writer presents a piece of data determines its meaning in the reader's mind. Which brings us around once more to the reason for learning to write. You can teach yourself by following the suggestions in "Basics" or by devising others or by muddling through. You can take courses, contact critics, plug into computers and study books. But your fundamental goal must always be the same—full absorption (to such an extent that both your conscious and your subconscious choices are informed as you work) of a crucial principle: What you communicate is a function of how you communicate. Or, as Northrop Frye has explained with exemplary clarity, "The words used are the form of which the ideas are the content, and until the words have been found, the idea does not fully exist."

A Foot in the Door

✳ ✳ ✳

Who Do You Know?
Agents and Other Connections

THE CHARGE THAT the publishing game is fixed, that you've got to know an insider if you're ever going to break into print, is part myth, part truth. The myth arises because the easiest response in the face of repeated rejection is to say that everyone but you is pulling strings left and right. It's not a large step from this interpretation of bad fortune to a full-blown conspiracy theory of an entrenched literary establishment. Those who've written superb (and fairly conventional) prose, however, are all but sure to get published by a major house—even if they don't know a soul remotely connected with publishing—for the reasons indicated in the "Initiation" section.

As for the truth: there's no doubt that it helps to have personal contact with people in a position to make editorial decisions, particularly when your work is good rather than great. The point is not that editors will publish you because you're friendly with them (that would not be a good way for them to keep their jobs); the point is that they will be more likely to take a chance on you if they see you as a known quantity. Editors are as insecure about their own judgments as most other people, and therefore they always find it easier to back a pre-tested, pre-approved author. Anything you can do to provide trustworthy testimony to your skills will help reassure editors that by gambling on you they'll be running a fairly small risk.

The idea of a connections approach to publishing shouldn't

repel you, since, in the first place, connections are not necessarily insidious and artificial, and, in the second, most sources of connection to publishing insiders are not only generally accessible but also worthwhile cultivating in their own right.

Agents

The first question everyone asks is about agents—How do I get one?—the assumption being that you've got to have an agent if you're going to place your work. Well, agents aren't necessary, though they certainly can be useful (explanations follow); and, furthermore, looking for an agent may not even be smart. If you're a beginning writer with only a handful of publication credits or a relatively unknown teacher or scientist with one book you want to write, no agents are likely to welcome you to their client lists; your agent-hunting efforts will simply waste time and energy that could more profitably be devoted to writing and marketing your own work.

Agents take on people who give them enough evidence of past accomplishments and future potential to assure regular income from writing over a long period of time, because agents, after all, are in business. Although an appreciation for good writing may have initially attracted them to this line of work, they can't keep going on literary love alone.

Virginia Barber, an agent committed to work hard for any writer she believes in, illustrates the economics of the situation like this:

> For a year and a half I sent out a novel and a bunch of short stories by a woman I think is brilliant. She had won literary awards and she has great talent. The book was rejected fourteen times and only one of her stories sold—for $550, which left me with $55 [the 10 percent commission] for eighteen months of work. It was clear to me that I wasn't doing her any good, and when a small press expressed interest in her book, it made sense to both of us that she withdraw as a client.

Because literary agents must live on commissions of 10 or 15 percent, they have to aim at major markets. (If you find one who's charging a fee up front instead of living off commissions, cross that one off your list.) It's simply not worth an agent's while to send manuscripts to the kinds of small publishers that can't pay advances or to small-circulation magazines with tiny budgets. In fact, most agents won't even do large-magazine placement because there's not enough money involved; clients are encouraged to deal with periodicals on their own.

The bulk of the money that agents stand to make comes from books, so that if, and only if—by applying your efforts intelligently to placement—you eventually succeed in getting a firm offer from a book publisher, you'll probably have no trouble getting almost any agent around.

Of course, finding just any agent to represent you should not be what you're after. Instead, you need to find an agent who's specially suited to you, someone with whom you can have a healthy, constructive relationship. "My concern as an agent is to develop an author's overall career," says Jean Naggar, whose clients include Jean Auel, author of *The Clan of the Cave Bear* and its sequels. Ideally any agent you hire will have the same goal in mind for you.

You can get information about agents from directories (see "A Foot in the Door Resources") and from organizations like the Society of Authors' Representatives and the Independent Literary Agents Association in New York, but the best way to find out about an individual agent's interests, strengths and idiosyncrasies is through word of mouth. Long before you're in a position to hire one, you might begin investigating agents by asking published writers you know whom they'd recommend, or by calling a local author you've just read about in the paper for suggestions. Alternatively, you might contact the local writers' club, talk to your librarian, scan prefaces for comments on agents' contributions and browse through the book trade's organ of communication, *Publishers Weekly*.

Or, when you finally find an editor who expresses interest

in your book, you can ask for names of good agents; since someone who has already taken a liking to your work should be particularly well suited to single out an agent who would be congenial. (A note of warning here: if you want an agent to negotiate your contract, don't agree to a specific sum of money before you get the agent into the picture; once you've verbally agreed to a dollar figure, there's nothing anyone can do to get you a better monetary deal.) For advice about how to query an agent when you're ready for that step, consult "Procedures."

One important part of an agent's job is sending a client's work to the editors who may be especially apt to warm to its subject, approach and style. A good agent who's been in the business a while knows dozens of editors well enough to estimate their reactions to a given manuscript, and this knowledge is obviously an asset any writer can use. But no agent can have contacts at every one of the hundreds of viable publishing houses that exist today, and even when agents select editorial targets sensibly, they can't ensure that the particularly receptive editors they addressed will be the people who actually read what they've sent. Because of other demands on their time, many editors turn all submissions, even those from agents, over to junior colleagues for a first reading. And to balance those editors who respect and rely on agents' recommendations, there are others who declare themselves disgusted by the generally low level of agented offerings and loath to read any submissions with certain agency imprints. Manuscripts that come from an agent will be read—or at least skimmed—by someone at the publishing house where they've been submitted, but that, frankly, is the only guarantee most agents can make about placement.

During the placement process, agents maintain files of all correspondence and records of all submissions and their outcome. Most agents try to keep their authors abreast of the manuscript's status. But don't expect a weekly progress report; with dozens of clients, agents find it impossible to pay constant attention to each. In any event, some writers prefer not to know every detail of a flat-out rejection letter, and your agent can serve as a buffer between you and potentially devastating comments. If you get frantic for word of what's happened to your book, write a note and ask (most agents don't take kindly to a barrage of phone calls). And rest assured that when something sells, you'll hear about it.

It's when your manuscript is accepted at last that an agent's most valuable skills come into play, for at this point a book publisher will usually offer you an advance against royalties, and an agent will know (as a writer probably won't) how much money that advance should consist of (according to a survey conducted by the Authors Guild for titles scheduled for publication in 1985, the advance on most general-interest books was $5,000 or more, with many authors reporting between $10,000 and $40,000).

Furthermore, as your business representative, an agent can sell your talents and potential to a publisher in a way calculated to get you the best possible terms throughout your contract (see "Getting What's Coming to You" for additional advice on contract negotiations). Most writers who feel uncomfortable about singing their own praises and unqualified to argue over the details of a deal clearly need either an agent or a literary property lawyer at this stage.

As a book progresses through production to sales, good agents perform other intermediary functions. For one thing, they can explain terms and procedures that may irritate or puzzle you; and for another, they can act as gadflies to get your book as much attention as possible (though they probably won't without prompting).

In executing all these services an agent's effectiveness depends in large part on his or her place within the matrix of publishing. The friendships agents have cultivated with editors help them to help you, but those friendships also exert pressures of their own, which may be contrary to your best interests. Like all intermediaries, agents sometimes have trouble keeping both sides happy without short-changing either. And the author-agent-publisher relationship is not the only one that's hard to handle; agents are often whipsawed by the author-agent relationship as well (if a manuscript doesn't sell, that's the agent's fault, and if it does sell, authors think they could have placed it themselves and saved the commission).

But for all the wavering allegiances and disputed powers, an agent who understands and is enthusiastic about your work may very well become a friend, a supporter and a trusted adviser as well as a skillful business manager. And when you're hoping to make a lot of money writing books, those are all good things to have around.

Writers

Any way you can associate with writers is bound to be to your advantage. Taking a writing course will put you in touch with at least one published author, the teacher (there may be others among the students). Ask instructors for the names of people you should send your work to, and ask if you may use their names in the covering letters. (Michael Chabon, whose first novel, *The Mysteries of Pittsburgh,* sold for $155,000, placed it with the help of Macdonald Harris, his adviser at the University of California at Irvine, and although the dollar figure is unusual, the pattern is common.) In addition or instead, go to readings and nerve yourself to talk with the writers after their presentations. Tell them who you are and what you're working on; they could be valuable links between you and a sympathetic editorial ear.

Some writers make it a point to share their contacts—"I know an editor at the *Atlantic;* I'll write and tell him you're sending an article in." Others you meet may recommend you for assignments they hear about but don't want for themselves.

One of the best ways to meet a large number of writers is by going to one or more of the hundreds of conferences and weekend workshops organized each year (see "Resources" for advice on finding those nearby). When professional writers and editors and would-be writers gather to share marketing tips and critical evaluations, exciting developments sometimes occur.

Who Do You Know? Agents and Other Connections 47

This is most often the case for writers who come to conferences with manuscripts in hand. Anne Rice, for instance, brought the manuscript of her first novel to the Squaw Valley writers' conference. An editor from Knopf who was there to lecture read it and was impressed enough to bring it back to New York for consideration. Rice's *Interview with the Vampire* was subsequently published by Knopf and brought in large sums from paperback and movie sales.

To forge a valuable connection at a conference, you may have to do more than plant yourself on fertile ground and hope to be discovered. You may have to boldly bring your work to the attention of others. Christina Baldwin's story illustrates the snowball effect that one step of initiative—taken in a mood of nothing lost, nothing gained—can have.

> When I saw an announcement of the Second Annual Women in Writing Conference, on women's personal writings, I wrote the director, Hannelore Hahn, of my work teaching and my intention to write a book, and she invited me to be a panelist at the conference. I headed for it in early August with my third-draft manuscript, and a twenty-minute presentation entitled "The Rituals of Journal Writing." After that everything felt like a hurricane.
>
> I gave my presentation, and was astounded and delighted with the energy and response it generated. I was asked to do a mini-workshop later in the afternoon and agreed to invite anyone interested. Fifty women crowded into that space, journals in hand, and we shared avidly all we could for the next three hours. Published authors came up to me with advice and referrals for breaking into the New York publishing world. The next day someone introduced me to Meredith Bernstein and told me she was a book agent.
>
> Monday, August 9, Meredith and I had lunch, discovered we liked and trusted each other. I gave her my manuscript copy of *One to One*. She read it that night and called me the next morning saying she loved it, and I agreed to have her handle it. That afternoon she hand-carried it to Herb Katz at M. Evans, who promised that he would read it Tuesday night. Wednesday morning he called Meredith, said Evans was highly interested in it, and he wanted some other staff people to read it and wanted us to meet him on

Thursday afternoon. Thursday I met with Evans and found them supportive and helpful about revision. Only one more week passed before Meredith had negotiated the contract and the advance.

It's possible that all you'll get from a conference is a rudimentary suntan and a dent in your bank balance, but it's also possible that you'll come away having found (1) encouragement from peers and/or professionals; (2) references you can use later in submitting manuscripts or applying for grants or jobs; (3) a demystified view of the publishing business; and (4) proof at first hand that unknown writers do get published. The overwhelming response of many conference-goers is joy, because they discover that the publishing world is not as sealed as they had thought.

Publishing Personnel

If you don't want an agent (or you don't want one yet) and if close association with writers doesn't appeal to you, perhaps you'd like to make your connections through people who work in publishing.

First, reach far and wide among your acquaintances to see what leads you can turn up. Maybe your brother-in-law's sister's friend or one of your high school classmates is a production assistant at a national magazine. Well, that one name is enough to get you read by somebody and rejected with a letter signed (if not written) by an editor. The same strategy works for book publishing; Peter Tauber, for example, got entrée to an editor's office for his first book, *The Sunshine Soldiers,* through an introduction from a mutual friend who'd worked with Tauber on a newspaper.

Another effective strategy involves turning a rejection from an end into a new beginning. Call the editor who returned your manuscript with an admiring note to ask politely for suggestions about colleagues at other houses who might like your work. A covering letter mentioning one editor's opinion sends powerful signals to the other editors who read it.

A third promising approach lies in making friends with a sales representative. Reps from all publishing houses travel the country constantly. You can find out from your local bookstore manager which ones will be in your area when, and then you can arrange to meet some of them. It would do you no harm to learn as much as you can about their work in general, and if you find that one of them likes what you've written, you've gotten yourself an influential sponsor. (Since sales work is often a route into editorial positions, sales reps will be just as pleased to "discover" you as you will be to have made contact with them.)

In case none of these methods attracts you, there's a still more direct way of building publishing connections: go to work in the field, either informally—by offering editors reliable assistance with clerical chores during your free time; or formally—by getting a job.

Obviously, there's no point undertaking a job hunt in a crowded (and poorly paid) field just to gain connections. But if you're genuinely interested in becoming an assistant editor, say, or a publicity department trainee, and if you manage to get yourself hired, you'll find making connections among the fringe benefits of your work. Lisa Smith explains why:

> At college I told every teacher and student I knew that I wanted to go into magazines and that I was interested in finding out about an internship program so I could see what magazines were like without the pressure and commitment of a permanent job. A teacher told me about the American Society of Magazine Editors internship program and I applied and was accepted. During my internship I made extremely good contacts. In addition to the people I met at the two magazines I worked on during the summer, I got to meet editors from other magazines who came each week to participate in discussions at the ASME offices. A lot of the editors I met face to face were editors I later submitted story ideas to.
>
> After graduation I was offered a job at *Mademoiselle*, where I worked for two years. Because of my work there, I know how to shape ideas and who to direct them to. I know why manuscripts are accepted or rejected because I've been on the other side of the

desk. As far as I'm concerned, going into magazine work is one of the best ways to prepare the ground for a writing career.

The same encomiums can be applied to jobs in book publishing, no matter how lowly they may be to begin with. Crossovers from editing to writing are frequent (Toni Morrison, Michael Korda and Richard Marek are current examples of the phenomenon), and all knowledge gained on one side of the spectrum is clearly relevant to success on the other.

Collaborators

Connecting yourself to people with good connections is a fine way to win readers and influence editors. You might try quick canvasses of celebrities on assorted subjects (What's the most terrifying event in your past? How do you think we should deal with the federal deficit?). And deeper patterns of collaboration may ease entrée to publishing houses too.

Consider, for example, the experience of Victoria Y. Pellegrino, a freelance writer and career consultant who had been depressed for some time without fully understanding why. Realizing that lots of other women were feeling the same way, she decided that an analysis of the problem could help them all, and she began to read with an eye to finding an expert who might be interested in collaborating with her on a book.

Research done by Dr. Helen DeRosis, a psychoanalyst and psychotherapist, best addressed Pellegrino's concerns, she discovered, and so it was DeRosis she approached with her idea. "The important thing about collaboration," Pellegrino reported, "is to find someone whose work you respect and whom you personally like and trust." In an atmosphere of mutual admiration, the writer and the doctor decided to work together on a manuscript about overcoming depression, and with the benefit of DeRosis's professional credentials, Pellegrino found a publisher fairly quickly.

Endnote on Priorities

Regardless of who its members are, an acquaintanceship chain in publishing (as in any other industry) simply greases the wheels. The final verdict on your manuscript will be determined by its perceptible merits. For guidance in making those merits show to best advantage, please move on through the next three chapters.

Subject Matter Matters

THE MAIN TROUBLE with writing for a market is that editors can't know for sure what they want until they've read it. They know what they wanted in the past, of course (and so will you if you study back issues of magazines at the library or this year's book catalogs in *The Publishers' Trade List Annual* at your local bookstore). And they may think they know enough about what they will want in the future to fill out the questionnaires sent by annual marketing guides (though the statement that a magazine is looking for fiction "on contemporary life and its problems" is not likely to help you much, no matter how accurate it is). But what editors really want is something they can't describe because it doesn't exist yet—the untold story, the fresh perspective, the new idea.

Editors spend a great deal of time trying to think up article and book topics. Once they finally agree on a subject, they spend still more time talking about how to narrow it, how to focus it, what facts to go after and what purpose to serve. After that they'll confer about which writers might handle the project effectively. And when they eventually find a writer willing and able to do the article or the nonfiction book they've been discussing, as often as not the project fizzles (obviously, good fiction cannot result from this process, though popular fiction sometimes does). Bearing in mind that this is what frequently happens when professionals try to create prose that will sell, you may be inclined to abandon the effort yourself. If men and women who are not only intimately familiar with the character and needs of their own publications but also knowledgeable about marketing trends and literary talents can't get it right, how can you?

Quite simply, by following where your enthusiasms lead. When the individual who has an idea he or she finds exciting is the same individual who develops that idea for publication, the chances of pleasing an audience (including an audience of editors) shoot way up.

Thus, if you're a lawyer who's eager to propose a new legal status for couples who live together but are not married, or a commercial fishing boat captain who longs to write a novel exposing the corruption in the industry, or a corporate vice-president who's desperate to know whether other highly paid executives feel useless too, you don't have to go looking for a strong subject. All you have to do is write up the one you care about and then figure out how and where to get it into print.

Suppose, however, that you can't think of a story you're determined to tell. Given that the best criterion for choosing a subject is your own enthusiasm about it, and that you feel no enthusiasm for any subject at the moment, it may look as though you have a serious problem. For enthusiasm clearly cannot be legislated; neither technique nor willpower nor patient craftsmanship will suffice to create it.

Fortunately, the real problem can't be that there's nothing for you to be enthusiastic about. Instead, it's probably that you've failed to provide an environment in which your natural passions can reveal themselves and that, as a result, you simply haven't recognized your natural subjects. One good way to correct this situation is by beginning a program of clipping and filing, as outlined in "Basics." And another is by developing an awareness of readers' motivations and your relationship to them. (What needs could you fill for the reading public that nobody else has filled yet? What needs could you fill that nobody else could fill better?)

Why people read what they read is an endlessly interesting

question with plenty of sensible answers. If you keep a list of theories in the back of your mind as you examine events occurring around (and within) you, you should soon find your energies engaged by an idea for a poem or a story or a book.

From the multiplicity of readers' motives, here's a selection to get you started.

Readers Want to Learn . . .

Everyone has some knowledge that would be useful to other people. Perhaps, for example, you could write a manual about financial planning or cooking Lithuanian delicacies or even getting published. Eric L. Reiss had always been interested in old phonographs and "thought that maybe it was time someone wrote a book about them" so he tried the idea out on a small publishing house that "specializes in books for oddball collectors." Reiss's *The Compleat Talking Machine* not only got great reviews, he reports; it sold about 3,000 copies in less than a year, which necessitated a second printing and led the publisher to ask for a sequel.

Or perhaps what you know—and ought to transmit knowledge of—should serve as the basis of what's called a service piece. Can you explain how to find your way through a complicated morass of information? Could you prepare a *Complete Guide to Home-Swapping Programs* or *A Directory of Occupational Diseases,* for example? Have you discovered a scientist whose studies of genetic engineering excite your interest or a musician who's created a startling new system of notation? By all means, consider making valuable technical data accessible to the general public, and explore collaborating with an expert so that new findings that otherwise would be couched in trade jargon and buried in the voluminous literature of a specialized discipline can reach a wider audience.

To find current research that may be grist for a story, make it a habit to browse through special-interest and academic journals in your library. If a title intrigues you, read the article, and if the article meets your expectations, consider writing the author (in care of the magazine) to ask about other good material on the subject; later perhaps you can interview the author/expert.

Interviews offer a good form for communication between experts and the rest of us because Americans today are coming more and more to value the authentic personal voice, the individual mode of expression, the first-hand, eyewitness testimony. But traditional narrative and expository approaches are fine too.

The most complicated kind of knowledge you can relay to an audience involves not just knowing something but knowing what that something signifies. With practice, you can develop the perspicacity and skill necessary for asking revealing questions about apparently commonplace events. What's behind the movement back to the kitchen and the resurgence of affection for the smell and taste of homemade pasta, for instance? Economics? A recommitment to family life and the home? A diabolical plot by a handful of women's magazines and food manufacturers? The answers may provide fresh material that concerned Americans will value.

. . . to Amass Experiences

Twentieth-century men and women are avid consumers of experience. What we can't do in fact we're usually eager to do vicariously, so that reading matter which can serve either as a trial run or as a substitute for activity has definite attractions.

Thus if you can reveal what it's like to cross the Alps on a bicycle, to experiment with a new method of childbirth or to serve on the jury in a murder trial, you have an excellent foundation for the kind of I-was-there-and-this-is-how-it-really-was kind of piece that the media are fond of nowadays.

And if you haven't already had an experience worth sharing, you can set one up. Twenty-two-year-old Mark Rasmussen, for instance, deliberately got himself seduced into attending one of the Reverend Sun Myung Moon's Divine Principle three-day workshops; Rasmussen's edited diary entries appeared in two national magazines. And anthropologist David K. Reynolds arranged to be committed to a veterans hospital as a potential suicide. Reynolds spent two weeks as a mental patient and then wrote a book with suicidologist Norman Farbow about what happened to him and how his experiences jibed with current research findings.

Even when they don't involve this degree of subterfuge and risk, inside stories always appeal to readers' natural curiosity, and there's nothing to stop you from using the form. If you're not an insider by right, you can make yourself one.

. . . to Read about Themselves

It's always exciting to see a movie made in your neighborhood; somehow your own life takes on luster after that and you feel almost as if you'd been featured in that film yourself. A similar pattern of identification probably lies behind the substantial sales of written work with a local focus.

What with diaries and oral histories and natural wonders and the unnatural acts of the couple next door, enough raw materials exist in everybody's town or region to create innumerable poems, novels and works of nonfiction. If you become fascinated by a subject of local interest, you're in luck, because gathering the kind of concrete data that make a lively manuscript is no problem (most of the facts are right before your eyes), and selling your work will be relatively easy too, since editors are well aware that Americans love to read about where they live (or where, in this rootless age, they used to live in younger days).

Just as we flock to read about our neighbors because proximity makes us identify with them, we reach eagerly for material about people we recognize as psychological kin. The widening stream of feminist literature results in part from the fact that most women identify to some extent with all women, and therefore feel personally drawn to any discussion of the sex in print. So if you can write as a member of any clearcut group, you can expect other members to form a readership.

. . . to Be Up on the Latest

Check the shelves of your supermarket if you doubt the attraction of the *new* for the American public. Where books are concerned, though, being new means living a year or two in the future because it will take roughly that period to get a manuscript from the idea stage to the bookseller. Since even periodicals usually have lead times of several months, bestseller lists and other conventional hit-parade compilations aren't much use as tools for keeping up with the times; though they seem to reflect the present, they actually portray phenomena that will be in the past by the time you get your manuscript out.

A crystal ball of sorts does exist, however, in the bible of the book trade, *Publishers Weekly* (unfortunately, although there are periodicals about periodicals, *PW* has no counterpart as a channel of communication among editors and publishers of newspapers and magazines). *PW*'s circulation is small (roughly 36,000), but its influence is enormous; almost everyone involved with book publishing reads it and reacts to it, so that when the magazine repeatedly covers books about money, for example, you can bet (a) that books about money are a big item on current publishers' lists, and (b) that they'll continue to be welcomed by editors, who naturally like manuscripts apt to interest an influential journal.

The pleasure of glimpsing such motives behind the dignified façade of publishing is one of the auxiliary benefits of reading *Publishers Weekly*. As you skim through the magazine, you can begin to feel yourself a member of the gossipy publishing fraternity, listening as hard as the next person for the first sound of a new bandwagon getting ready to roll.

Like its treatment of publishing trends—which it covers in

reportorial articles as well as through information tidbits—*PW*'s coverage of forthcoming books provides an outstanding resource for keeping current. Its Spring and Fall Announcement issues present annotated lists of upcoming titles, and throughout the year the magazine prints items about manuscripts that are still somewhere in the idea or rough-draft stage; books, in other words, that will be published a year or more later. If you can discern a pattern among the new titles, you're on to something that will be hot just when you get your discussion of it off the presses. Similarly, conclusions you can draw from studying *Small Press* magazine or the Bowker directory *Forthcoming Books* (see the Subject Guide section) are likely to foretell subjects that will keep readers up to date in the near future.

To capitalize on current trends in publications more transient than books, you can begin by noting what's selling on the newsstands. Look at the cover lines on view at a variety of locations over a period of several weeks, and see if you can get newsstand dealers to talk with you about what's selling and why. Then, if one of the subjects now drawing customers captures your interest, you can do a piece about it for a periodical that has a very short lead time—a daily paper, perhaps, or possibly a weekly.

. . . to Be Prepared for the Future

If you have to look a couple of years ahead to see the publishing present, it follows that you will have to be even more farsighted to spy its future. Confusing though this seems, it is worth puzzling out because the demand for previews of what's coming next is huge. Looking hard for handholds in a maelstrom of accelerating change, people today are greedy—and will be grateful—for anything that helps them predict, and therefore prepare for, tomorrow.

The trick can be done by anyone who realizes that small is seminal. When you think about it, you will see that almost without exception cultural, political and intellectual movements of note start small—with one ardent individual or a small group of impassioned people. At first these initiators are unknown to the rest of us. As they begin to focus attention on themselves, we may well regard them as nuts. But gradually the ideas they've championed catch on, often becoming so widely accepted after a time that new small groups form in rebellion against them.

It's through little observations, which anyone can make, that large changes first become visible. When Mary McLaughlin edited the "Right Now" department of *McCall's,* she spotted a new attitude toward children among a sizable group of parents before it came to national attention when one friend and then another confided in her that, if they had their lives to live over, they'd stay childless.

And it's through small, specialized publishing companies that seminal thinkers and doers are usually first able to address an audience. You can get a leg up on embryonic movements by reading special-interest periodicals and books in fields you care about. Check *The International Directory of Little Magazines and Small Presses* to see which publishing companies specialize in them. Then skim any titles of theirs that your library carries and/or send for their book catalogs or for sample copies of their magazines.

As you study special-interest material, you may develop an ability to sight coming movements long before the general public has any inkling of them. Then you can be the one who introduces evidence for self-healing or schemes for redesigning our school systems to the wider world as soon as the time is ripe.

Two cautionary notes:

* Gauging the moment of ripeness is far from easy, because if the future you're describing is too far off, most audiences will see you less as a forecaster than as a fool. Perhaps, like Margaret Kavanagh-Smith, who writes out of Waynesville, North Carolina, you'll decide to do a piece whenever you come upon a portentous subject and then put what you've written away in a drawer until you can see indications of a general

readiness to accept its content. (For more on timing, read "Openings.")

* While it's true that what's seminal is small, it is not equally true that what's small must be seminal. Again, your own passions are probably your best guide; what you feel strongly about, other people may respond to as well, or at least they may respond to it once you have explained it to them. That way, you'll not only have helped prepare for the future, you'll also have helped create it.

Development

Have faith. Let's assume that one stimulus or another or several in combination have triggered the degree of excitement necessary to launch you on a writing project. As you begin to flesh your subject out, use the following suggestions to help ensure that your readers will respond with an enthusiasm to match your own.

* If you're writing nonfiction, start by conducting a small, informal survey among your acquaintances to see which other people really would like to know what you're planning to tell, and what their general level of ignorance is. It's as important to avoid boring readers by dishing up background they already have as it is to avoid confusing them by beginning your discussion on too advanced a plane.
* Unless you think you're the sort who'd make talking a substitute for writing, tell all sorts of people about your project. You may be surprised to see how many of your friends and associates will present you with valuable ideas or data. Moreover, you'll make new discoveries about your own ideas as you listen to yourself talk.
* Figure out what special sources might exist for the information you need by following the practice Alden Todd outlines in his masterful *Finding Facts Fast*: on any given matter, ask yourself (a) who would know, (b) who would care and (c) who would care enough to have put it in print.

* Keep tugging on the informational chain. You might want a map as background for a short story, or an anecdote to liven up a piece of social criticism, or some word on who could help you understand black holes in space, but whatever you seek you should find if you press each person you talk with for the names of others who could help you end your search.
* Refer back to "Basics" in the "Getting the Words Right" section, and consider using some of its resources.
* Narrow your focus. "Prison Reform" won't work as a subject, but "Why Halfway Houses Are the Best Hope for Prison Reform" probably would. If you can't phrase a good working title, chances are your subject isn't adequately defined yet.
* Be as graphic as you can. Don't tell if you can show. Specifics are much more interesting than generalities, so round up generous collections of anecdotes, illustrations, descriptions, dialogue and quotes.
* Don't be afraid to put yourself in the picture. Who you are and why you're writing this and what makes you think anyone should listen to you can be important elements of your story.
* Bring the wisdom of your lifetime to your task. Writing from experience does not, of course, mean transcribing experience. You have a responsibility to sift and shape your material until it makes sense as a unit and until that unit can be fitted into the context of the reader's life.
* Stay flexible, expect changes and setbacks in the normal course of development and abandon all rules—including those propounded here—if ever some combination of gut feeling and dispassionate analysis tells you to try something outlandish. Maybe it's just what the world needs now.

Openings, or Where to Submit Your Manuscript

WRITERS TODAY HAVE thousands of markets for their work. Both magazines and book publishing companies keep springing up, and the book publishers are multiplying fast enough to make your head spin (R. R. Bowker's *Books in Print* database now includes titles from approximately 21,000 firms; roughly 6,000 to 7,000 new publishers join the ranks annually while fewer than 1,000 go out of business).

Although some of today's small publishers put out scruffy little periodicals every so often (when time and funds permit) or issue books they themselves write (and then can't figure out how to unload), many run viable, professional, profitable operations, which experienced writers find increasingly attractive. They like the personal attention small publishers give them; they like the way small publishers market their books year after year, so that sales curves rise over time; and they like the fact that small, specialized publishers get written work to readers who share the authors' special interests.

Large publishing operations may still offer advantages, of course, especially for prose that's directed to a very sizable general audience. Since everybody's heard of big companies, their imprint on your writing tends to confer prestige; also, they often pay higher advances than small firms (but, please note, a good small firm will probably net you more over the course of a book's life), and they frequently have more clout with general-interest media.

On the other hand, big firms may offer you little or nothing in the way of promotion unless you're a celebrity or about to become one. Furthermore, large companies are often—although by no means always—impersonal, and they have an irritating habit of getting tangled up in red tape.

Fledgling writers are frequently advised to start with small companies and work their way up to big ones, on the theory that competition for editorial space is less keen in the so-called minor markets. And sometimes it's true that sales to small publishers will establish a record of achievement that will persuade one of the giants to want you on its list. No press or periodical is designed to be a steppingstone, of course; each has its own independent dignity of purpose. But evidence that one editor thought your work worth printing can serve to embolden another editor to back you, in much the same way that an endorsement from a mutual acquaintance might confirm an initially shaky editorial judgment.

One good reason not to invest heavily in the steppingstone theory is the fact that some smaller publishers are every bit as fussy about accepting manuscripts as any larger firm. And another is this: at heart, effective marketing of your work has less to do with choosing between big and little or top and bottom than with finding the particular publishers who are going to want the particular manuscript you're trying to place right now.

In some cases, it will make sense to aim at Simon & Schuster or *The New Yorker;* in others, the best targets may be Pelican Publishing or *Entrepreneur;* under a third set of circumstances you might consider trying a special-interest quarterly first and then using a clip of your piece as it appeared there to boost your chances at a slick mass-market magazine.

Because the paths to publication are so numerous, you can probably discover a variety of promising markets for every manuscript you have to place. And if you use the strategies outlined below and the "Foot in the Door Resources," you should be able to concoct a thoroughly workable (if not an entirely watertight) solution to any placement challenge you face.

The Affection Approach

"An editor's enthusiasm is the fuel that makes the project go," says Kate Medina, vice-president and senior editor at Random House. "Unless you have somebody who's nuts about a book you don't get a fire lit under it." It's a view most book and magazine editors would endorse. Despite moanings and groanings in the press about how bottom-line managers are running the publishing show, editors still base acquisition decisions more on excitement than on sales forecasts. In fact, Herman Gollob—who's held senior editorial positions at Atheneum, Doubleday, Simon & Schuster and the Literary Guild—has predicted "an unending chain of disasters, financial as well as psychological, for houses that publish books no editor feels strongly about."

The emphasis is undeniably attractive. Unlike the outdoor grill manufacturer or the automobile designer or the orthodontist, an editor can—and should and frequently does—allow passion to rule, at least where acquiring manuscripts is concerned, with the result that publishing doesn't suffer as much from homogenization as most other industries.

Unfortunately, the reverse side of this coin shows a less pleasant picture, partly for reasons to be discussed in "The Sale and Its Sequels," and partly because it's extraordinarily difficult for writers to figure out which editors, among hundreds, are going to respond passionately to them. "Love" is a word even the gruffest editors like to use in high praise—"I loved this story," they'll scribble on the back of its envelope without embarrassment—but, as when boy meets girl, the chemistry is hard to predict and impossible to manufacture.

Fixing yourself up with a promising editorial partner—which is the best possible way to ensure a happy publishing future—is

Openings, or Where to Submit Your Manuscript   65

largely a matter of learning a lot about individual editorial tastes; try one or more of the following tactics.

* Compile a data bank, using a separate index card for each editor's name and filling each card with as much information about that editor as you can glean; perhaps eventually you'll be able to sell a piece about smokers' rights because your files led you to somebody who'd run two pieces on minority power.

One good way to get information about editors without actually meeting them is by reading about them in a publishing memoir. You'll find dozens of lively portraits in books like Peter Schwed's *Turning the Pages* (consult the *Subject Guide to Books in Print* for other current titles), and once you've made allowances for bias and for that striving after color which afflicts editors as diarists no less than other people, you can use acquaintanceship through print to facilitate acquaintanceship in person.

Publishing memoirs get published a lot (for obvious reasons), but they're by no means the only things that editors write. Poems, novels and nonfiction by editors appear often, and should prove revealing, so that skimming reviews and ads and biographical notes to find writing by working editors may be worthwhile.

Other good data for your files can come from comments about particular editors that you collect at writers' conferences or from friends; from *PW* items about which editor is responsible for which new title; from dedications and prefatory notes that express gratitude for an editor's work; and from the assorted across-the-editor's-desk jottings you'll find sprinkled through magazines.

* Break through editorial anonymity by investigating personal publishing, which is flourishing today on two fronts. Within the large houses, it's becoming common for editors to arrange to acquire and issue lines of books under their own personal imprints. Pioneers in this system, like Joan Kahn and Seymour Lawrence, have been joined recently by new recruits. Moreover, the number of independent, one-person publishing operations is growing outside the establishment too.

Brief descriptions of one-person publishing outfits appear in the "Book Publishers" listings in *Literary Market Place* and in the *International Directory of Little Magazines and Small Presses*. (Naturally, publishers are not formally categorized as one- [or two- or 112-] person operations, but you can tell which houses are an individual's property by checking staff rosters for number of employees and similarity of surnames.) When a company's description attracts you, write to the head of the firm and ask for a catalog; from the catalog you'll be able to infer a great deal about the personality in charge and about your own potential relationship to him or her.

* Discover an editor through a book you feel passionate about. One young writer who greatly admired Robert Pirsig's *Zen and the Art of Motorcycle Maintenance* figured there might be an emotional affinity between him and Pirsig's editor. He therefore placed a call to the publicity department of *Zen*'s publisher, William Morrow, and asked who had edited Pirsig's book. They told him—no questions asked; he got in touch with the editor, and his book proposal was subsequently accepted at Morrow.

Though it takes considerable nerve, this approach will undoubtedly put you on a good footing with editors at the receiving end. They'll be impressed by your effort to find out something about them, and perhaps their pleasure in learning that you enjoyed books that they helped create will lead them to greet your submission with a small prejudice in its favor.

* Advertise. Paid ads may put publishers off, but indirect advertising is worth thinking about, especially since it can be obtained easily and without cost. One method of indirect advertising entails using the biographical notes that run with work you're currently getting published. If you ask the editor who's printing your study of utopian theory to run a line saying, "The author is halfway through a novel called *Bravest New World*, about a messianic cult in Washington State," you may hear from far-flung editors who want a chance at the book.

✻ Find a receptive editor by checking the "People" column in *Publishers Weekly*. Editors who have recently changed houses probably had to leave some of "their" authors behind. As they set up shop at new firms, they'll be especially eager to sign up new books and develop new relationships with as many good writers as possible.

Matching Exercises

For a straightforward approach to manuscript placement, nothing beats matching the subject matter of your work with the subject matter that appeals to a particular publisher.

Perhaps, without fully realizing it, you've already formed a mental image of what attracts the editors of magazines you read regularly, in which case you'll know almost instinctively whether your work belongs there. Though your sense of a book publisher's range of interests is likely to be hazier, you can bring it into equally sharp focus by studying the *Publishers' Trade List Annual*, where current catalogs from close to 2,000 firms are gathered. Lists from small houses and from subsidiaries of large houses and regional or special-interest publishers are easiest to categorize, but even a general-interest publishing giant has a personality of its own, and whatever you can conclude about the likes and dislikes of any size firm will help you with placement.

To supplement impressions formed through study, you can turn to descriptions in *Literary Market Place* (which is commonly referred to as *LMP;* see "Tools" in this section's "Resources" for a full description) or to the other directories you'll find in the "Resources" pages. Moreover, you can read the publisher profiles in *Small Press* and get hold of the newsletter published by COSMEP (aka The International Association of Independent Publishers) to see whether any of the publishing companies its pages mention are likely to welcome your work (again, see "Tools" in "Resources"). Have you, for instance, written a travel book, an autobiographical poem or a report on a new development in psychology? Not long ago, publishers who belong to COSMEP were looking for just such material.

Furthermore, you can try the *Subject Guide to Books in Print*, a four-volume directory listing more than 600,000 books under a galaxy of subject headings. Start by looking at the titles under several headings that are relevant to your work. You'll probably discover that certain publishers' imprints appear again and again, and you may be tempted to conclude that the editors there are now surfeited with the subject. That's possible. It's at least as likely, however, that they're still hungry for more. They wouldn't have done a second book on exercise for the elderly, after all, if the first hadn't sold well, and the fact that they issued a third or a fourth indicates that they've tapped a lucrative market they'll be eager to supply with new reading matter. Specializing in non-fiction about sports, the outdoors and the environment, Sierra Club Books even branched out into publishing fiction when they got an allegorical novel about fishing. That book, *The River Why* by David James Duncan, was then picked up for reprint by Bantam, which is still selling it.

Matching your subject to a company's demonstrated strength may be the single best placement strategy, but matching it to a company's obvious weakness can make sense too. Is one national magazine you read short on profiles, when the form is clearly fashionable? Are there no gardening books in the publisher's catalog you've been studying, even though *PW* has just announced an unprecedented boom in their sales? If so—like a high school student who recently accused the editor of the local paper of ignoring the kids' point of view and got himself hired to write a column—you've found a gap in need of filling.

Once you've made good matches between your work and publishers' needs, go one step further and try match-making with businesses or other kinds of organizations that aren't publishers yet although they perfectly well could be. Thanks to new technology, all sorts of groups—including corporations, associations, governmental bodies, schools and fraternal societies—can, and do, now publish articles and books of interest to the people they serve. Look for likely candidates to approach in the *Encyclopedia of Associations*, the *Thomas Register of American Manufacturers* and other directories you'll find in "The Self-Publishing Option Resources."

Tips on Timing

Consider "How to Heat Your Home by Burning Wood." Way back, before the energy crisis hit America, only counterculture papers and perhaps a few rural periodicals would have bought such a story. As prices for oil, gas and electricity soared, however, big-city dailies, national magazines and book publishing firms might have gotten interested. And today, it's likely that the market for material on this subject has dwindled nearly to the vanishing point.

The point, clearly, is that each moment creates and destroys publishing potential, so that sensitivity about timing is an enormous aid in placement.

If you are alert to passing events you can sometimes hang an already completed manuscript on a news peg to attract editors. A much-rejected book about Big Foot, for example, might suddenly become salable the instant that new evidence of the monster's existence turned up. Similarly, if an article about the unquenchable desire for war has been repeatedly turned down on the grounds of familiarity, a timely new lead might help. Perhaps, for instance, the piece could be sold to a newspaper for the June 25 issue if it began by pointing out that June 25 marks not only the anniversary of Custer's Last Stand and of the invasion that began the Korean War, but also the occasion of the National Skillet Throw Championship (this celebration, along with hordes of others that delight and inform, is listed in *Chase's Annual Events;* see "Tools" in this section's "Resources").

People unprepared with manuscripts can also take advantage of propitious moments for getting published. Was it your town the tornado hit? Your aunt who gave the governor a ticket for jaywalking before the speech at the travel agents' convention? Your college that voted overwhelmingly to reinstitute curfews? When you're involved in any way in a newsworthy event, it makes sense to offer an eyewitness report to interested publications that have no representative on the scene. If you can plan ahead for the story, query selected editors about it beforehand (see "Procedures"); otherwise make a few phone calls to see if you can get an expression of interest.

Either way, you might consider parlaying the temporary position of on-the-spot reporter into an ongoing job as a stringer for one of the national newsmagazines or large metropolitan papers that like to keep up with news breaking locally around the country; get in touch with the nearest bureau chiefs (you'll find their names on mastheads) if the prospect appeals to you. Stringers' assignments are sporadic; their copy is generally rewritten beyond recognition; both their by-lines and their pay may be virtually invisible. But think of it this way: magazines like *Time* and *Newsweek* make nice additions to anyone's list of credits, and being even partly responsible for what millions of people get to read has its charms.

Not every story needs, or should have, explicit links with current events, but no manuscript can be sensibly submitted unless targets are selected with timing very much in mind, because every publishing enterprise has a definite position on a temporal spectrum. As noted in "Subject Matter Matters," special-interest publishers tend to congregate near the leading edge, getting to the future way ahead of most mass-market, general-interest publications. Thus a piece that *Medical Self-Care* might like this month probably won't be suitable for *Self* until sometime next year and might not be welcomed at the *Reader's Digest* until long after that (for tips on making several sales with the same story, see "Spinoffs").

Art Harris, a prep-school teacher turned freelance writer, learned his lesson about timing the hard way: Years ago, "having three sons and a wife who was reading all these articles on 'How Safe Are Birth Control Pills?' I had a sterilization operation—the vasectomy. What a great idea for an article, I thought. It even tied in with another subject—zero population growth. 'You're a nice fellow,' the editors said, 'but frankly nobody wants to hear about your operation. Forget it. It's too personal a subject.' So I put the idea aside only to see a whole crop of articles on the subject a year or two later. If I were to approach an editor today with 'My Male Sterilization,' I would get laughed out of the office; the subject has been well covered, thank you."

However painful Harris's education, he learned enough in the end to write a piece called "Timing the Submission" that he sold to *The Writer*. The advantages you'll derive from developing timing skills may not be quite as direct, but they're sure to aid your progress nonetheless.

Easy Access

"We regret that we are unable to consider unsolicited manuscripts" is a sentence that causes a lot of needless anguish. It's true, as enraged would-be authors are quick to point out, that many publishers make it a rule to return unsolicited material unread. But that policy can't debar anybody's work as long as editors respond to queries and proposals with invitations to submit the manuscripts described (see "Procedures"). And besides, no matter what rejection slips may say, the periodical press is increasingly open to contributions from unknowns, as witness the following rundown.

Reader-Participation Departments. Magazines and newspapers of all sizes and sorts are now actively soliciting material from the general public. Like the physicists and politicians of the mid-twentieth century, publishers have recently discerned that our deepest sense of reality demands some confluence of subject and object, of actor and acted upon. The results of this realization—which is especially powerful because it's not entirely conscious—vary among disciplines, but in publishing it has led editors to try making writers of readers. "The magazine game has tended to look on readers as spectators," editor Tony Jones explained when he sparked the trend with *Harper's Weekly*. "We think they should be players, and we're looking for ingenious ways around the limitations on how many can play."

Not long ago, the only place open to readers as players was the "Letters to the Editor" column, but today ordinary folk are cordially urged to contribute to "Viewpoint" in *Glamour,* the "My Turn" column in *Newsweek,* the "Living" section of *The New York Times,* the Op Ed pages of innumerable newspapers, and the gazette pages of *McCall's* and *Ms.*—to name a few items on the steadily expanding list of reader-participation departments.

In all these columns, and in the letters column too (which remains a good launching pad for an idea and/or a writing career), short pieces that emphasize specific, significant experience rather than abstract theory are most likely to succeed. Editors can use writers with reputations when they want opinion and analysis; it's for the small wisdoms of everyday life, the personal stories that will resonate in readers' minds and lives, that they have to turn to you.

Book Review Columns. In addition to sections that solicit contributions from readers, there are a good many periodical departments that are entirely open to the public, though they seldom proclaim that fact. One of these, as Robert Cassidy discovered, is the book review section. Cassidy, who got his start with a review, is the author of *What Every Man Should Know About Divorce,* among other books. You can follow his example by checking publishers' catalogs and *PW* for forthcoming titles you'd be able and eager to write about, and then querying editors to see if they'll either let you cover a book you'd like to discuss (mention title, author, publisher and publication date) or try you out on one they have up for grabs. Book review editors' names are listed in *Literary Market Place,* and their preferences as to style and substance can be inferred from the reviews they ordinarily run; try your library for copies. Book reviewing doesn't usually pay much (in fact, the book itself may be your only payment), but the rewards in terms of exposure and contacts and credits and pride of performance can be considerable.

Other editors who are especially receptive to newcomers include those who work on:

Community Newspapers. Applying to a neighborhood weekly for a particular beat is a fine way to begin a career as a published writer; once you've regularly covered dance, say, or home repairs for a small periodical, you've got credentials to present to a big one. And if you've written anything with a local focus, you should find a ready market among community weeklies.

Company Magazines and Newsletters. Both profit and nonprofit organizations need people to discern and relay ideas relevant to their concerns. Here again, the pay may be low or nonexistent, but the audience will consist of anything from a couple of hundred employees to thousands of sympathetic members of the general public, so that you can expect high dividends in the form of exposure.

Campus Publications (Including Alumni Magazines). The connection between you—or your subject—and the school will give you an edge here, and though the pay scale varies widely, most editors in this field—like their counterparts on other small publications—are generous with assistance. "We have to scratch harder for good stuff," said Elise Hancock, editor of *Johns Hopkins Magazine*. "So if something has possibilities we'll work on it rather than turn it down because the possibilities weren't quite realized. I once published a piece called 'Bald Is Beautiful,' a magnificent parody on radical manifestoes that maintained (quite rightly) that bald people *are* discriminated against. The author was urging the *Ten Commandments* be refilmed starring Woody Allen. It was a great piece, but *Esquire* had turned it down. I think they just weren't willing to spend the hour required to cut it by two-thirds, which was all it needed. So that's a plus of working with alumni magazines if you're starting out."

Contests. Both book and periodical publishers use assorted competitions to attract new talent and, not incidentally, to generate publicity. Announcements about them appear from time to time in trade journals, in a firm's own publications and in the directories listed in "Resources."

It would be misguided to treat the easy-access openings with less respect than any others; what you've written must be right for the specific publisher you send it to in terms of subject matter, style, tone and timing. But if you submit to the most hospitable editors with the same care you'd use for the most forbidding, you can anticipate better results.

Vanity Presses

With one exception, any publication opportunity you can seize is worth seizing; ever-widening ripples move out from even the smallest of splashes. Something more like a self-contained plop is all you're likely to get, however, if you resort to a vanity press. Vanity publishing is not the same as either subsidy publishing or self-publishing, though the terms are often used as if they were synonymous. Subsidy publishing is best defined by its guaranteed audience (see "Front-end Funding"); self-publishing is partly defined by its realistic efforts to find an appropriate audience (see "Managing Sales"); vanity publishing frequently involves no audience at all.

You can recognize a vanity press by its come-hither ads. "An invitation to authors of books," they'll say (or words to that effect). And they'll offer a free (no obligation) manuscript evaluation and a free (no obligation) brochure about the publishing operation. Usually vanity houses wait until you've begun corresponding with them to mention their fee. Be advised, though, that a vanity press is likely to charge you several thousand dollars to handle publication processes that you'd be far better off directing and/or executing yourself. (Please don't decide you lack the necessary skills before you've read "The Self-Publishing Option" chapters.) And don't be dismayed if you recognize vanity as one of your own motives for getting published, as long as it's not the only one you see; virtually every writer is seeking glory to some extent.

Most vanity houses issue impressive-looking pamphlets that explain their operations with varying degrees of candor and detail. These booklets generally fail, however, to stress two crucial points:

* The press has no stake in the success of your book; it takes its money up front by getting you to pay all the costs of editing, typesetting, proofreading, printing, overhead and the like—plus a sum that's pure profit for them; then, if the edition actually earns anything they'll take a cut of the revenues from sales too (and they'll charge you for any copies you buy over and above the allotment mentioned in your contract).
* Distribution efforts by vanity presses can be worse than useless because vanity books bear a stigma. Most libraries, bookstores and book reviewers won't touch them; and while some titles do manage to rack up sales, it's virtually certain that most vanity press successes could have been easily equaled by writers on their own.

Testimonials from happy authors are a regular feature of vanity press catalogs, which don't, of course, print any litanies of complaint. The complaints are a part of the picture, though ("I never realized that binding all the copies in the first printing wasn't included in the deal" commonly heads the list). Anyone who's considering vanity publishing should, first, send for a reprint of "Does It Pay to Pay to Have It Published?" (*Writer's Digest*, January 1975). Second, become familiar with "The Self-Publishing Option." And third, consider taking a short course in calligraphy; your book will be prettier, cheaper and less aggravating to produce if you letter it by hand than it will if a vanity press puts it out, and probably no less practical for marketing purposes.

High Hopes Department

No matter how long and rough the road to publication, somebody somewhere wants your work. Just remember that marketing manuscripts is a two-step process. Step one is recognizing and reminding yourself that tens of thousands of outlets exist. Then, once you've learned how enormous your range of options is, Step two is using the tools in "Resources" and the pointers in this chapter to narrow it sensibly, so that you end up sending what you write to the particular publishers and editors who figure to be receptive to it and enthusiastic about it.

Procedures, or How to Submit Your Manuscript

A LOT THAT'S written about the fine points of submitting a manuscript not only can be disregarded, it should be. Editorial etiquette is mainly a matter of common sense; for obvious reasons, your copy should be neatly typed, free of misspellings and coffee stains, consecutively numbered page by page, clearly labeled with your name, address and telephone number and accompanied by a stamped, self-addressed envelope. Those rules that have no common-sense basis will only divert your attention to minutiae when it ought to be focused on your primary purpose: getting editors to publish what you write.

Any pieces of paper you send editors—from three-paragraph queries to thirty-page proposals—will persuade them either to move your manuscript one stage closer to publication or to reject it right then, depending on whether they've been led to answer yes or no to the two all-important questions that echo in editors' heads:

* Will this article (story, book), if it's skillfully handled, add to my company's prestige and/or profits (and therefore to mine as well)?
* Can this writer handle it skillfully?

If your idea comes across in the beginning as a half-baked notion jotted down in a spare moment, no editor is likely to take it more seriously than you apparently have. It's best, therefore, not to think of any approach to an editor as a preliminary move designed merely to feel out the situation before you submit your "real" work. Even the shortest introductory note, though it should look effortless, probably ought to be the end result of several drafts.

Essentially, what you're doing when you first make contact with an editor is applying for publication, much as you might apply to college or for a job. And just like a director of admissions or of the personnel department, the editor you apply to will be only the tip of a decision-making iceberg. Almost always, a group rather than an individual has the power to accept or reject, and if your proposal succeeds in winning one editor's vote, that editor in turn will have to convince several colleagues that your project is worth backing.

Queries and proposals generally circulate among editors, with more and more people becoming involved when the risks of commissioning a project are high; some book publishers insist that every manuscript under consideration be reviewed by two or more sizable committees before an editor gets clearance to buy it. No matter how many people participate in the process, however, what you've set down on paper is all they've got to go on.

To give yourself every advantage in approaching editors, you'll need a working knowledge of the forms of communication they've developed over the years. Here's a roundup.

Queries, or Don't Get Stuck in the Slush Pile

On the surface, a query is simply a letter that asks editors whether they'd be interested in work you're planning or have already produced. It's an introductory move, used to pave the way for submitting articles to periodicals and proposals or finished manuscripts to book publishing houses (and to agents too). With magazines, queries may also function as proposals, in the sense that they can earn you an assignment—complete with guaranteed minimum payment (but they're not likely to do that if you're an unknown). And in all cases they obviously make for efficiency; evaluating a letter takes a lot less time than reviewing the entire manuscript it describes, so the winnowing process is speeded up. But the query's most important function is often—and oddly—ignored: a query is a tool for steering your manuscript clear of the slush pile.

Judging from the number of unsolicited submissions that reach editorial offices daily, most writers either don't know this or don't believe it. The fact is, though, that queries get manuscripts solicited status, with benefits all around.

Queries about nonfiction offer editors the opportunity to become involved in shaping your material at the outset. When the subject you've suggested is one they're interested in pursuing, they'll welcome the chance to share thoughts on how the story should be approached, what length it merits and what information should be included. Their suggestions will improve your manuscript, at least for their purposes. And to come closer to what an editor has in mind—as long as doing that doesn't violate the basic premises of what you want to say—is obviously desirable.

With fiction, phrasing a query is more difficult, but if you write an intelligent letter in which you explain what led you to tell your story or why you think its subject is important and timely, you should succeed in building up a backlog of editorial interest in you and your work that will help it over the final decision-making hurdles.

Whether or not an editor offers specific comments, a go-ahead means that your submission will land in his or her in-basket rather than in the unsolicited-manuscripts bin when it arrives. Expressing interest obligates editors to read, or at least to skim, what you send. That's all it obligates them to do, however, unless they've agreed to commission your forthcoming work; when editors say they'd be delighted to see your manuscript on speculation (or "on spec," to use the common jargon) they mean they think it has promise but they're guaranteeing nothing.

"A magazine writer shouldn't expect to get an assignment the first few times out," Rona Cherry, executive editor at *Glamour*, explains:

> And anyway—at *Glamour*, at least—the only difference between an invitation to submit on speculation and an assignment is that with the latter you get a kill fee [generally a couple of hundred dollars] if the piece doesn't work out. We usually give formal assignments only to writers with good track records who bring us good ideas, but if an editor expresses real interest in your article and would like you to send it on spec, then go ahead and give it everything you've got. That may mean investing two months of your life; still, when you want to be published that damn much, that's what you have to do. If, after all that time and effort, the piece doesn't succeed, at least you'll have impressed the editor by the work you put in. And that means on the next try you'll have a sympathetic, receptive audience.

To get a positive initial response to your query you need to do more, of course, than ask to be invited to submit your manuscript. The question "Would you be interested in my story about snowmobiling being hazardous to health?" can call forth only one reply: "Well, it depends." It depends on what, exactly, your point is and how you're going to express it.

"A query letter is really a sales letter without the hype," says Lisel Eisenheimer, the managing editor of *McCall's*. "It should show that you have our market in mind, indicate the kind of color and life you can bring to your subject, and represent your best writing efforts. That's important even if you already have a relationship with an editor, because that editor probably can't make an assignment unilaterally."

Remembering that a query must do double duty—by selling your idea to the editor it's addressed to and then by helping that editor sell it to colleagues—makes it easier to compose a good one. The following guidelines summarize most editors' advice for drafting a one- or two-page query letter about a nonfiction manuscript; if you adapt them in a creative fashion, they'll serve for fiction as well.

* *State your specific idea* (as opposed to your general subject). A title that conveys the essence of your story will be useful here; perhaps skimming magazines will help you come up with one.
* *Explain your approach* (how-to; first-person experience; a canvass of opinions), *and give some sense of the style you've chosen for this project* (will it be informal and chatty or scholarly and critical?). One editor who had received dozens of queries on the subject of teenage tensions rejected them all as bloodless until she got one from a young woman who wrote, "I'm twenty and have survived adolescence to tell the story." That was worth encouraging, the editor thought, because the writer clearly had both a personal stake in her subject and enough psychological distance from it to give her findings value.
* *Show how what you have to say is fresh and different from other things already in print.*
* *Cite your sources* (will you conduct interviews; use case studies; work from historical documents?).
* *Estimate length.* A figure that's appropriate to your topic and to the publishing concern you're writing for gives an editor a clue that you do your homework.
* *Provide a tentative delivery date for your manuscript.*
* *Mention your connections and qualifications.* If you have any relevant expertise, let editors know, and tell them, too, about your publishing credits, even if they're minor. A young writer who's worked during the summers on a newspaper or won honorable mention in a high school short-story contest has credentials worth mentioning; in fact, some editors ask their first readers to direct manuscripts from anyone who lists such credits to their personal attention. Include clippings (two at most) only if they're relevant to the piece you're proposing or if they're outstandingly good samples of your work.
* *Convey some sense of your enthusiasm for the project.* Enthusiasm is infectious and, as noted above, editors are inclined to encourage writing that obviously has conviction and energy behind it.

It should be needless to say (but experience indicates it's not) that you should enclose a stamped, self-addressed envelope with your query; that you should direct it to a specific editor, not to The Articles Editor; that you should spell his or her name correctly; and that you should remember that the editor-in-chief isn't the only one on the staff. Associate editors, assistant editors, department editors and others still lower in the ranks may give your manuscript more personal attention than the higher-ups who get most of the mail.

To find your target editor, consult the latest edition of *Literary Market Place* or the most recent issue of the magazine you're aiming at. Then, because editors are notorious job-hoppers, call and ask the switchboard operator whether the one you've chosen is still with the company before you write.

Some writers shy away from queries for fear that editors will steal their ideas. Well, in the first place, they probably won't. In the second place, they may well get similar stories from other writers, so if it looks as if they stole something of yours they probably didn't. And in the third place, what alternative does an aspiring author have? You can't sell your work sight unseen. So conquer your paranoid tendencies. The grain of truth that may lurk behind them in this instance is a rotten reason to give up one of the best door-opening tools you have.

Person-to-Person: Calling Up and Calling On

Occasionally, telephone calls or personal visits to editors will provide the best way to acquaint them with your idea for a piece. Long before she wrote *How to Eat Like a Child,* for instance, Delia Ephron dropped in unannounced on the editor of the magazine supplement of the Providence *Journal* to propose writing about sports from a woman's point of view. He said sure, on spec, and bought the first piece she did. Ephron then used that clip to get an assignment from a national magazine.

Once you've got an editor listening, you're in a make-it-or-break-it situation, so be 100 percent sure that you've formulated what you have to say in the best way possible. Boiling your story down to three or four sentences or coming up with a descriptive title beforehand will help you arouse an editor's interest during the few minutes of time you've requested.

Perhaps, following the lead of successful freelancers, you'll want to equip yourself with three or four well-developed story ideas before you enter conversations with editors. Then if all those fail, two other tactics will remain to be tried. You can turn the tables and ask editors whether there are any weak spots on their lists of upcoming titles that they'd like you to work on; maybe after they tell you their editorial problems you can mull them over and return in a week or so with a list of ways in which you might help solve them. Or you can see if editors will suggest other markets or other topics that might work for you.

Like the written query, a well-planned phone call or visit gives receptive editors the chance to help shape your idea and ensures personal attention to your manuscript once they've encouraged you to send it in. Established writers approach editors in person all the time; and for beginners who are effective in one-to-one situations, it offers an exceptionally good means of entrée.

Book Proposals, or Sell It Now, Write It Later

In essence, what you're asking when you send a query to a magazine editor is, Will you buy my manuscript (or at least tell me you think it sounds promising and ask to read it)? When you send a query to a book editor, though, what you want to know is, Will you look at my book proposal? (See pages 84–86 for a checklist of what a proposal should contain.)

It then becomes the book proposal's job to give editors the information they need to answer the harder question, Will you buy this book (or at least ask to read it)?

Editors routinely bid for nonfiction books on the strength of a proposal alone (the payments can be made half on signing, half on delivery of a satisfactory manuscript or in thirds or even quarters), and although it may be hard to convince them to buy a first novel if they haven't seen the whole thing, it's by no means impossible. With second and subsequent novels, the proposal becomes a more powerful selling tool.

If publishers are to advance money for books, however, they must generally be convinced that the book they're buying will be a book they can sell. (Some small presses and, on occasion, certain large houses will pay more attention to literary merit than to sales potential; if your book has no future as a commercial property, you'll be better off stressing the virtues it does have.)

Book proposals can be submitted to agents (who will take you on—or not—having read them) as well as directly to editors, and the basic principles that contribute to the success of a query apply to proposals too: because it's much shorter than a full manuscript, a proposal can be considered more quickly and easily, and because it represents raw possibilities, it has the power to ignite editors' imaginations and get them involved in what you're trying to do.

Editors commonly define a book proposal as "an outline and a sample chapter," but what they really want is anything on paper that will give them some sense of how you write (which several unrelated passages may demonstrate better than a chapter in a book's early stages) and some reason to believe that your subject, when developed, will interest a large group of readers (which no rigid I, II, III, A, B, C outline of contents is likely to convey).

The following checklist for organizing a complete and effective proposal will keep you from omitting elements of importance to editors, but it won't serve as a guide to phrasing or arranging your presentation. Only you can figure out how to mesh your proposal and your earlier query so that together they do justice to the book you hope to write.

* *Describe your book* well enough so that editors can say to their colleagues, "I have a great proposal here for a book about

how television has smashed the barriers between men and women, adults and children and politicians and the rest of us." Later, this same pithy description will be useful in acquainting sales people with the book, an eventuality the editor already has in mind. Your title, if it's catchy or compelling, can be a strong selling point.

* *Give an anecdote or example that illustrates your theme and its significance.* Take whatever space you need for this—a paragraph, a page or more.

    Ralph Keyes, for example, used the following paragraph in the proposal that won him a contract for a book called *The Height of Your Life* about the problems of being tall and small. "Just to see what would happen, a newspaper recently had two reporters converge on various public servants and simultaneously ask for help. One reporter was 5'6" tall, the other 6'2". In every case the larger reporter was helped first. 'Your height seemed to demand that I speak to you first,' explained a Hertz clerk to the taller newspaperman."

* *Identify the audience to whom the book is addressed* (coin collectors; people in rebellion against impersonal bureaucracies; everyone who loved *To Kill a Mockingbird*). Sometimes you can direct editors' attention to several possible markets and thus inspire them to think of still others.

    Since salability is a vital consideration for most editors, it's a good idea not only to identify your markets but also to suggest ways of reaching them. If you're planning to write about St. Louis architecture, for instance, you might mention that you're game to approach architects about your book at their upcoming convention and that you're planning to write some articles for publication in their professional journals around the time the book comes out.

* *Talk realistically about the competition and how your book is different,* so that both editors and sales reps will understand why it needs to be written and why it will be read.

* *Show how you plan to develop your book.* Indicate the breakdown by chapters and sketch your primary sources of infor-

mation (where will you go; whom will you talk with; what statistics will you gather?).
* *Explain your credentials.* Cite publishing credits as evidence of your ability to write, and any experience or training that qualifies you especially well for this project.
* *Enclose a sample of your text* (twenty pages is about the norm). Send whatever chapter or excerpts will reflect your book's content and style most accurately and most favorably.
* *Express any passion and excitement you may feel about the project.*

To see one author's unconventional response to an editor's request for an outline and a sample chapter, consider the following book proposal. Then tailor a fresh and individual approach for yourself.

Ann Banks, who wanted to write a book about women and children who live on military reservations, had herself grown up on army posts, so she chose to begin with a reminiscence about her regimented childhood. After her personal foreword, she explained:

> I propose to write a book about the women and children who are the official "dependents" of U.S. military men, about what life is like on a "reservation" where young wives are expected to master an elaborate social protocol as well as a series of plans for the proper evacuation procedures in the event of enemy attack. Military posts are self-contained communities, portable small towns whose residents have little connection with life outside. (Military personnel who reside off the base are said to be living "on the economy.")
>
> I will approach the book as an ethnographic journey, a report from the interior of a little-known country. Little-known, but not little: all told, there are nearly 3 million military "dependents." To provide a structure, I will do my research on the five Army posts where I lived as a child: Ft. Sill, Oklahoma; Ft. Bragg, North Carolina; Carlisle Barracks, Pennsylvania; Norfolk, Virginia; Frankfurt, Germany.

The primary focus of the book will be investigative, although it will also have a strong autobiographical motif.

Having thus covered many of the elements a good book proposal requires, Banks continued with a description of her book's seven chapters, noting what each would include and how its material would be treated ("My narrative will blend profiles of families, descriptions of the milieu, vignettes, mythology and fables, statistical information, autobiographical sketches and expert testimony").

Then, following a space break, she reinforced the thesis of her book by listing topics to be covered, with a paragraph devoted to each; this, she explained, "is not an outline; rather, it is intended to suggest directions for research."

In eight pages, Banks obviously provided sufficient material to convince editors that she knew her subject and that it was worth writing about. The proposal was sold to a large New York house, and although the book that will eventually grow out of it will no doubt depart from Banks's plan in several significant respects (books always do develop in surprising ways), both publisher and writer know enough about what they're getting into to anticipate success.

Poetry

Certain guidelines will serve you well no matter what kind of manuscript you're trying to place. It's always a good idea, for example, to address an editor by name and to triple check for typos. But what makes sense for poetry submissions does differ in some respects from what makes sense for prose.

In the first place, poets don't need to use query letters since the material they submit won't run to dozens or hundreds of pages. Instead, it's best to start by sending roughly half a dozen poems ("five has always felt comfortable to me as an editor," says

Diane Kruchkow, editor of *Small Press News*), along with a brief covering letter that shows you're familiar with each publisher you approach and tells publishers about your credits if you have them.

Poets often aim their work at magazines first because, as Alice Quinn notes, "In general, poets enjoy and require the reinforcement magazine publication provides." Quinn, who edits poetry for Knopf and fiction for *The New Yorker,* says some of the poets she knows use a lazy-susan system. Instead of agonizing when something is returned, they send it right out again; "the three poems *Grand Street* turned down go straight to the *Atlantic;* the two that *Poetry* didn't want go straight to *Southwest Review.*"

A lazy-susan system can, of course, also cover magazines that aren't devoted to poetry. The poet Judson Jerome has found that "specialized publications are a wonderland for those of us swamped in the miasmic plains of literary magazines." Jerome was particularly taken with the notion of submitting some poems about horses to *Arabian Horse* in Waseca, Minnesota, which says it pays $10 to $75 for poetry, and to *Toys "R" Us Magazine,* which says it pays handsomely—$200 to $700.

Going to the other extreme, certain literary magazines have lately begun to demand payment from poets by charging what they call "reading fees" for considering submissions. The practice is common, and conceivably defensible, for contests. But the consensus among poetry editors is that no self-respecting magazine charges to screen manuscripts for publication, so steer clear of those that do; credits from them aren't likely to count for much.

Having poems appear in reputable magazines gives you credibility with book publishers, as Jonathan Galassi points out. Galassi, editor-in-chief at Farrar, Straus & Giroux, thinks magazine credits are a poet's most important credential when the time comes to try for a book.

Should that time come for you, consult the preceding section on book proposals, and bear in mind that "in almost all instances it is better for poets to publish with a smaller house, if only because the smaller house will keep their work in print longer." That advice comes from Scott Walker, head of the distinguished Graywolf Press, who adds that a small house is more likely than a large one to "consider poetry books as its meat and potatoes, so it will give them more attention and more marketing energy."

Children's Book Channels

The main difference between children's books and adults' books in terms of procedures is that, in the words of Greenwillow's editor-in-chief, Susan Hirschman, "any unsolicited children's book manuscript will be looked at." If you're working on a lengthy book for older kids, you should still approach editors first with a query letter, but if what you've done is a picture book, you can just send it in as soon as you've figured out which publishers and which editors are right for it.

To target publishing houses and editors, browse through the children's books sections in nearby bookstores (they're increasingly popular nowadays). Study the children's books on your library's shelves (although they don't dominate the market the way they used to, libraries are still big buyers). And if you're in New York, familiarize yourself with the Children's Book Council collection (see "People, Places and Programs" in this section's "Resources"). Then use any applicable "Foot in the Door" tactics to make your approach.

Unless you want to illustrate your book yourself and you're as good an artist as you are a writer, do not send illustrations along with your manuscript. "Children's book editors are trained to see the illustrative possibilities in text," Elizabeth Gordon explains, and editors spend a lot of time looking at artists' portfolios. Gordon, publisher of the Harper Junior Books Group, sees choosing the right artwork as "one of the value-added pieces of expertise a publisher brings" to a book project. "Sometimes," she adds, "we can do things that are unusual, like matching a well-known illustrator with an unknown writer."

Covering Letters

Several marketing manuals suggest dispensing with a covering letter when you mail your manuscript, on the theory that if the thing's going to sell, it will sell on its own merits and that a letter saying simply "Here is my manuscript" only wastes an editor's time. There is, however, more than that to say.

You can use your covering letter to reestablish personal contact with editors by reminding them of previous exchanges between you (or to establish personal contact if you've decided a query won't convey the strengths of your short story and opted for just mailing it in). You can use it to convey thoughts or information of the sort that might have appeared in your original query but didn't. And you can use it to indicate that you're eager to improve your work even now, after you've tried hard to do your best.

Listen to an editor vacillating about a submission: "A very interesting idea, I think—'romanticizing the Holocaust.' It's good. But he is heavy-footed, repetitive and clumsy in places. Excessively wordy. It could be helped by a few passages of quotations, to refresh our memories if not to make the point. Is it worth sending back for fixing?"

In a case like this, the fact that your covering letter proclaims an openness to criticism and a willingness to make changes might be enough to keep rejection at bay. Although major revision is a headache and a gamble for both editor and writer, it is also a much-traveled route to publication.

Authors of magazine pieces are regularly asked to revise on speculation, but most book editors say they wouldn't think of requesting that a writer make substantial changes without offering to pay for the labor, and without fully intending to buy the improved version of the work. Since one editor's idea of an improvement may be another editor's idea of a change for the worse, you'll have to assess your own position carefully before you decide whether the risk/reward ratio is reasonable enough for you to proceed.

The Question of Multiple Submissions

Only a few years ago, everyone who sent out a query, a proposal or a full manuscript could anticipate one of two fates. Either they'd wait several weeks—or months—and then be rejected, in which case they'd have to start all over again. Or they'd wait several weeks—or months—and be accepted, in which case they could take whatever terms they'd been offered (perhaps with minor modifications) or start all over again. Now, however, thanks in large part to innovative agents, all that has changed, and the vehicle of change has been the so-called multiple submission.

Although the manuscript auction, which is a related form also pioneered by agents, is still used most frequently for big-budget projects, multiple submissions can be used by all. To offer your idea to several editors (or agents) simultaneously, you need to observe only one rule: tell each of them that's what you're doing.

In book publishing, where long periods usually go by between the time you present your work and the time you get a response to it, multiple submissions are now standard operating procedure, and anyone who receives positive responses from more than one publisher may be able to play them off against each other a bit before picking the one that's best. (See "Getting What's Coming to You" for a further discussion of choosing among offers.) For periodicals, one submission at a time is still common, but by no means the rule. The fact that magazine editors respond more quickly than book editors makes multiple submissions less necessary and less usual where they're concerned.

Follow-up

Queries normally elicit a response within a few weeks; book proposals can have you checking the mail for months. It's a good idea, therefore, to keep records of everything you've sent out and to follow up on magazine pieces after about six weeks and on book outlines after roughly twelve. Editors do get bogged down, go on vacations and sometimes even lose manuscripts (this is as good a place as any to remind you always, *always* to keep a copy). Furthermore, delays may result when a project hovers on the borderline between acceptance and rejection. A polite letter of inquiry is a reasonable and perfectly proper way to find out what's holding things up.

If and when you do get a positive response from an editor, acknowledge it with thanks and with some word on when you expect to deliver your finished manuscript. Be as realistic as you can about the due date; then if you find it impossible to stay on schedule, let your editor know.

Any rapport that you establish with particular editors obviously works to your advantage, and can be strengthened by simple gestures of courtesy—saying thank-you for comments, for example, or expressing gratitude for encouragement offered along with rejection.

And speaking of rejections—well, everyone gets them, even the best of writers. And everyone feels the same way; rotten and hurt. But bear in mind that it's probably true if an editor says that he or she really liked your piece even though other editors didn't, or that everybody liked it except the editor-in-chief (whose no means no). And remember, too, that the roots of rejection are infinite: an editor who had a marital spat last night bristles at your piece about how to achieve a blissful relationship through yoga; a story like yours just came in from a house author and, while it isn't any better than the one you wrote, it isn't any worse either; your book just doesn't strike the sales manager as a good bet; or your article sounds too much like one that just came out in *Business Week*.

What this variety of causes signifies is that one editor's rejection may be another's acceptance, so continue to circulate your material. If you've followed the advice in these chapters without garnering a single encouraging word from the forty-six editors who've considered your manuscript, then it's time to take stock. Perhaps your logic is not as sound as you first thought, or your point is not so fresh and crisp after all. Sigh one sigh, file the manuscript away, and get on with something new. (Unless you're still convinced of its merit, in which case you might consider publishing it yourself; see "The Self-Publishing Option.")

If, heaven forbid, you receive nothing but printed rejection slips without so much as a personal note scribbled at the bottom, go back to the beginning of this section and start rereading.

A Note on Improving Your Vision

The next two sections present complementary perspectives on the same set of processes. "The Sale and Its Sequels"—which approaches publishing from the point of view of authors who want someone else to take charge of producing and selling their work while they assist—should provide self-publishers with valuable information on the standard operating procedures that have helped conventional firms succeed over the years. And "The Self-Publishing Option"—which approaches publishing from the point of view of authors who want other people to assist in producing and selling their work while they take charge—will prove a good source of innovative ideas for conventionally published writers.

Therefore, whatever role you want to play, please read both.

The Sale and Its Sequels

* * *

Getting What's Coming to You

RECEIVING WORD THAT a publisher is interested in buying your work is just cause for celebration. What follows, however—the business of talking money and rights—can be (and usually is) an ordeal, especially where books are concerned, because although you and your publisher share many goals, your aims diverge on the division of profits and risks.

With magazine pieces, areas of contention are relatively minor. You can ask to be paid on acceptance rather than on publication; you can ask for a kill fee; you can ask to be reimbursed for expenses; you can ask to retain everything but first serial rights. Your publisher can then refuse any or all of these requests. If your wishes are largely ignored, though, it may not matter much, and in any case, relations between you and your publisher are likely to be amiable.

The situation is quite different with books, as a quick glance at the average contract will convince you. Book publishers, who must sink substantial sums of money into each title they issue, have developed complex, formal mechanisms for minimizing their losses and maximizing their gains, which tend to put burdens on—and take rewards away from—authors.

Authors, understandably, resent this, and many of them are tempted to vent their anger on their editors, whose earlier support may now seem suspect. You'll be better off, though, if you can manage to treat yours with kindness. After all, the editor has just assumed the unenviable role of mediator between you and all the publishing people who will be handling aspects of your book; and besides, you'll probably never have a better friend at a large house. With everyone else there, you might as well gird yourself for an adversary relationship; expect the worst and be prepared to fight for the best.

Comparing Offers

If, having made multiple submissions, you've attracted two or more interested buyers with your book proposal, your first task is to decide which one to accept. The house that offers the most money? Maybe not. Although the size of an advance does provide a tangible index to the publisher's level of commitment, as well as an all-but-guaranteed income, you should investigate each publisher's abilities to prepare and sell your book in addition to each one's proposed down payment on it before you make a decision. These are the areas to explore:

* *Distribution* (i.e., sales to booksellers). Does the house have its own sales force? How large is it? What territories does it cover and how often does a sales rep visit each one?

    Houses that can't afford to maintain their own sales departments depend either on sales reps from larger firms (who handle books from a number of houses besides their own), on commissioned sales representatives (who sell books for lots of different publishers) or on independent distributors (whose interest in selling books is likely to coincide neatly with that of their clients, so that they may do as good a job for the titles they represent as any salaried, in-house sales force could).
* *Backlist policy.* Many houses actively market brand-new books only, paying no attention to older titles—aka backlist—even though a small sales push can make a big difference. Carol Cohen, who's in charge of Harper & Row's trade reference titles, points out that sales of many older books will rise with

updating and/or repackaging and/or continual promotion in special sales outlets and through direct mail. So ask about expectations for—and commitment to—your book over time.
* *Foreign rights.* A house with its own foreign rights department and/or its own international department is most likely to maximize whatever potential your book might have for sales abroad, whether in English or in translation.
* *Other rights.* Would people like audio tapes of your book? Video tapes derived from the book? Dolls, toys or clothing inspired by characters in the book? When you think there's a real chance for rights sales like these, find out whether prospective publishers think so too and whether they're eager and able to market those rights successfully.
* *Library sales.* Since libraries account for a big chunk of trade-book sales, look for an active library promotion department or, at the least, a dynamic library sales specialist.
* *Mail-order sales.* Authors who have concluded that their books can be sold easily through the mail should find out which editors agree and which houses have mail-order departments.
* *Special sales.* If you've written a book about cross-country skiing, perhaps sporting goods stores would do a good job selling it. Ask publishers whether they're equipped to distribute to sales outlets of this sort.
* *Pecking order.* The importance of your book in relation to others on a publisher's list is significant because you will be competing with every other current title for the time and money budgeted to all departments in the house. Perhaps your book would not be considered a "bigbook" by any publisher, but even second-rank titles get appreciably better treatment than those on the bottom of the heap, so try to feel editors out about their expectations for yours; most will be quite frank about the prospects.
* *Personal compatibility.* Don't be ashamed to ask a lot of questions; naïveté coupled with an eagerness to learn may prompt an editor to talk with you at length, and the longer you

converse, the stronger will be your sense of how well the two of you would work together.

Contracts, or the Agent's Hour

Because a book publishing contract is a complicated legal agreement in which the commitments of both author and publisher are defined (by the publisher) and the financial terms of the partnership are set forth (by the publisher), it's smart to hire either an agent or a literary property lawyer to represent your interests as soon as you've decided to accept an offer for your manuscript (once more, a warning: don't agree to any dollar figures until your representative is in there fighting for you).

If you hope your first book will be only the beginning of a long writing career, you probably ought to get yourself an agent at this point (you're a desirable client now, remember, with a firm offer from a publisher that guarantees an agent a commission). If, however, you don't plan to write much (or if you intend to make subsidiary sales yourself or leave them in your publisher's hands), then a lawyer with expertise in publishing may be what you need (ask your editor to recommend a couple). While an agent will receive a 10 or 15 percent commission not only on your advance but also on all subsidiary sales of your work, a lawyer can be hired simply to negotiate your contract for a fee.

There's only one case in which you'd be wise to proceed without the help of either an agent or a lawyer who's familiar with publishing, and that's when you're signing up with a small house that uses a simple, straightforward contract to buy rights that are strictly—and appropriately—limited. If all they have to deal with is a short memorandum of agreement and a one-person publishing operation, assertive authors can probably handle negotiations themselves.

Authors who are represented are not, of course, relieved of all responsibility for shaping a contract that's acceptable to both sides; at the least, you should be familiar enough with your publisher's contract form to know what changes you'd like to make. You'll have to read the thing, therefore, and probably more than once.

Much of it, you'll find, is intelligible, and what you don't understand you can ask about (consult your editor and/or your lawyer and/or your agent). But comprehension of a contract's basic provisions is about all writers can hope to achieve on their own. For the use of common sense (which this book has touted before and will encourage again by and by) has no place in the highly stylized negotiations of the usual contract quadrille. And that's where the agent's or the lawyer's expertise comes into play. Almost as if there were annotations throughout the contract that were visible to authors' representatives but invisible to authors themselves, your champion will X out and add in and modify clauses, acting a part that's as predetermined as the patterned figures of a dance.

Each house has a different contract—Simon & Schuster breaks the record at over sixteen pages—so that standard changes vary a bit, but both sides always know which moves are about to be made; in fact, even your editor will know (and might tell you in advance if you ask) roughly what terms the whole maneuver will produce in the end.

Why, you may well wonder, go through the motions? If every expert is aware that an author with clout can get the paperback split changed from 50-50 to 60-40 (author's favor) this year, and that clauses A, D and Z are always deleted by authors' representatives, who regularly add identical riders to paragraphs 4, 7 and 12, wouldn't it make sense to amend the forms before issuing them and skip the back-and-forth that comes afterward?

Well, arguably, no. For one thing, although the initial round of demands and counterdemands about changes in a publisher's standard contract is pretty well determined by custom, its outcome and the outcome of all subsequent rounds can be influenced to some extent by an astute and aggressive bargainer. For another thing, no matter how generous the form contracts were, authors would always want more. And for a third, publishers still scent the possibility that unrepresented writers may swallow the package as printed.

Don't you do it. If you decide for some reason to conduct contract negotiations yourself, apply for membership in the Authors Guild (see the "People, Places and Programs" segment of "Resources") so you can get a copy of its recommended tradebook contract. It's an excellent document, designed—with full knowledge of the contract quadrille's choreography—to get every author a fair deal, and even writers who are represented can use it to assist their agents in arranging for the best possible terms.

Payments

Controlling payments from periodicals is fairly simple, the idea being to collect once, for a single use of your material by a magazine or newspaper, and then, if any other use of your article, story or poem occurs, to get paid again by the second user. Thus, you have only two things to watch out for:

* *Get the going rate.* To learn what a magazine or paper normally pays its contributors, read its guidelines sheet (if it has one) and check to see if it's listed in *Writer's Market;* then multiply any figures you find by roughly 150 or 200 percent (because they're directed to neophytes, published prices almost always fall at the low end of a periodical's payment scale).
* *Don't sell more than you must.* When you receive a check from a periodical, be sure to examine it front and back for fine print before you endorse it. Otherwise, you may sign away all rights to your piece, with the result that the periodical will get the fee if it's reprinted in an anthology, say, or sold for use on TV, and you won't.

   Periodical publishers don't try to buy all rights from anyone with an agent or from any writers who can be presumed to know their business as well as their craft, mostly because the publishers realize they'd never get away with it. They shouldn't get away with it where you're concerned, either. Speak with your editor and see if management will issue you the same voucher they use for sophisticates. If that fails and the magazine insists on purchasing all rights, then you should insist right back that they sign a letter promising to give you an assignment of copyright in the piece as soon as you ask for it. Do this even if you have no plans at the moment to reissue your material in any other way.

Payments for book manuscripts are, predictably, far more complicated, and consequently far more likely to provoke and prolong aggravation.

The first money you get for a book will probably be your advance; as much as a half or as little as a fifth of that may be paid when you sign your contract, with the remaining payments coming due per contract specifications, usually on delivery of satisfactory sections of your manuscript. Occasionally, a publisher can be persuaded to pay the entire sum up front (this is worth angling for if you need the money to pay back bills or to keep a roof over your head while you write). Sometimes, in the case of a small publisher perhaps, no advance at all will be forthcoming. And all too often, collecting turns out to be a chore because of sloppy bookkeeping on your publisher's part.

Payments that are slow in arriving are no rarity in modern publishing circles, and the first thing to do about them is write a polite letter of inquiry to your editor; then nag as necessary. Payments that must in the end be returned are a somewhat less frequent phenomenon, but if you fail to deliver a manuscript that's satisfactory to your publisher (or if you fail to deliver any manuscript at all), you may be obliged to repay any advance you've received.

Nowadays, partly because advances have escalated into five, six, and even seven figures and partly because publishing houses are being pounded into financial shape by their new corporate owners, it's increasingly common to find a publisher demanding its money back when a book project doesn't pan out. If your advance was relatively small and if you tried your best to write a good book and if you're poor and starving anyway, your publisher probably won't pull out all the stops to try to get money back from you. But don't count on it.

Assuming that you turn your manuscript in on time, or nearly so (editors grant extensions on due dates much as professors do, although here too they are getting stricter), and assuming further that it's found acceptable and subsequently published, the next money due you will be paid after your advance has been earned out, and it will come in the form of royalties.

If you have an agent, your contract probably takes some subsidiary rights out of the publisher's hands and puts them in yours; among them, you'll usually see first serial rights (for excerpts in magazines and newspapers before book publication) and motion picture rights, but you'll almost never see reprint or book club rights, which are too lucrative for publishers to part with.

All monies from subsidiary sales effected by agents go directly to them; they subtract their commission and forward the rest to their clients. When writers are not represented by agents, their publishers can sell all subsidiary rights and will keep the monies received until they've been reimbursed for whatever advance they paid. Thus, if *Sports Illustrated* bought an excerpt from your book for $3,000, $300 would go to your agent, if you had one who charged 10 percent, and $2,700 would go to you; if you had no agent and were represented by your publisher, approximately 10 percent would go to your publisher no matter what and the remaining 90 percent would go to the publisher until such time as your advance had been earned out, unless your contract specified otherwise.

The sooner your advance has been earned out through one sort of sale or another, the sooner you begin earning royalties. For a typical hardcover, you'll get 10 percent of the retail price on the first 5,000 copies sold, 12½ percent on the next 5,000 and 15 percent on all copies sold thereafter (make sure that you're getting a percentage of list price, not of wholesale price or of the publisher's net receipts, both of which will yield substantially lower dollar figures). Royalty rates may differ a good deal from the ones mentioned here, depending on the book's format, the publisher's financial situation and the author's clout.

Essentially, royalty figures represent your cut of the money a customer pays for your book. But if you get $2 per copy on the first 5,000 sales of a $20 book, where does the other $18 go? One big chunk is for bookstores and wholesalers, who will buy your book at a discount of roughly 45 percent, which gives them their margin of profit and means that all they actually remit to the publisher is $11. After your $2 has been subtracted, the $9 balance must stretch to cover the costs of editing, manufacturing, advertising, selling, shipping, warehousing and, of course, the publisher's normal overhead (rent, utilities and payroll).

Taking all this into consideration, it's easy to see why large publishing houses maintain that they must sell thousands of copies of a book just to break even, and why they may sometimes engage in a variety of shenanigans to hang on to whatever money finally comes in. One author who suspected that his publisher was keeping cash it owed him was lucky enough to discover an interview in which his editor bragged about sales of his book. Since sales figures quoted in the interview far exceeded those indicated on his royalty statements, the author called at once to discuss the matter; it was then settled in his favor.

The point of this story is not that all publishers will try to cheat you or that if you read widely enough you will catch the ones who do; instead, it's that you may need to take the offensive not only to get the money you're entitled to, but also to find out how much it is. Royalty statements don't divulge a great deal (few note, for example, how many copies have been printed and how many are still on hand), and the way in which they're issued makes the data that do appear hard to grasp.

Twice a year the income generated over the preceding six-month period is supposed to be reported in a royalty statement. Usually, there's a lapse of three to four months between the closing date of the royalty period and your receipt of that period's statement, which means that money for a serial sale consummated in February will show up not on the statement you get in April but on the one you get the following October, some eight months from the date of sale. To make matters worse, money earned just before a given closing date is sometimes not included in the statement where it belongs; instead, it's held for the next statement because a publisher "forgot" to list it (and thus gave itself an interest-free loan at your expense).

"Statements are practically always incorrect, some more than others," remarked Georges Borchardt, president of his own literary agency, to a meeting of the Authors Guild. If yours seems wrong, you or your agent should ask your publisher for complete, accurate and up-to-date information about your book; how many copies were printed (it's unlikely that the print order mentioned at the outset will be the print order scheduled at publishing date); how many are still in stock; what subsidiary sales have been negotiated, with whom, for how much and when payment is due. If necessary, put your questions in writing and add a request to examine the accounting department's records. The Authors Guild, which is lobbying along with agents and authors for more detailed royalty statements, has a useful form for soliciting royalty data that it will supply to members.

Fringe Benefits

Authors who know the ropes routinely ask their publishers for a host of extras that no contract will ever stipulate. As long as you're not greedy in your requests and not churlish if they're refused, you may well follow suit. What you have to gain, among other things, are the following benefits.

Office Space. Occasionally, you can arrange to use an empty editorial office, and sometimes you can manage to get access to a typewriter, a telephone and a variety of office supplies as well. If you regularly spend time in your publisher's quarters, perhaps you'll meet and make friends with employees who'll get interested enough in your project to give it special attention.

And even if you show up only occasionally, you may gain the privilege of using the company's copying machine.

Expenses. Particularly in the case of a nonfiction book that involves extensive research, it's worth asking for a supplement to your advance to cover the costs of travel, interviews, postage, copying and research materials. Unlike advances, expense allowances don't need to be earned out before you can collect royalties, and they're not taxable as income either.

Free Books. The most obvious fringe benefit for writers under contract to publishing firms comes in the form of reading matter. Don't expect to stock your library from your publisher's warehouse, but if you see a book you'd love to have, go ahead and ask for a copy of it.

Power Plays

The self-fulfilling prophecy has doomed many a book. Here's what happens: Your editor views your manuscript as nice but minor; if it breaks even on sales, everyone figures to be satisfied. Because it seems minor, the editor won't lean on anyone in marketing or publicity to produce special sales strategies or promotion campaigns to attract the attention of the buying public. And because no special efforts will be made to publicize and distribute your book, it will end up nice but minor; if it breaks even on sales, everyone will be satisfied. Except, of course, you.

This scenario—a common after-the-fact explanation of why-my-book-was-remaindered-after-three-months-and-I-never-got-a-penny-more-than-my-advance—can seem inflexible enough to convince writers that their books' failures were preordained. Feeling helpless and anguished at this realization, they'll turn on their publishers, who will respond to shrieks of outrage and demands for bigger advertising budgets with veiled (or possibly not so veiled) anger, and nothing else.

But there's no need for writers to place their books at the mercy of editors and marketing directors until it's too late to do anything about plans for them but scream. With determination, tact and knowledge, you ought to be able to steer clear of the minor-category catch. (The analogous exercise for magazine pieces would consist of working to make yours the cover story, the lead or one of the articles in the "well," or center, rather than one of those in the front or back of the book. As with contracts and payments, however, positioning is relatively unimportant for periodicals and relatively simple to fight for if you're inclined to argue.)

The first step in positioning a book with a publisher is to grasp the fact that it will be categorized very early, either in some formal way, on paper, or informally, in the minds of editorial and marketing people. The usual system involves an *A, B, C* scale, which is designed to help publishers allocate their limited supplies of staff and money. All publishers obviously want the maximum return on their efforts, so when half a dozen books on a forthcoming list seem likely to bring the house a profit if they're heavily promoted, those titles will be designated *A* books and slated to get the bulk of the promotion budget. The *B*s and the *C*s will have to compete for what's left over (which may not be much), and it's more than likely that the *C*s will end up with no budget whatsoever.

Authors today are more and more apt to ask for promotion provisions in their contracts, but since publishers aren't eager to grant such requests, most writers still have to rely on plumping for position. And the optimal time to begin doing that is immediately after you sign your contract. Normally this is the very moment when writers are most anxious to get out of business hassles and back to the business of writing. But the hours you put in now planting seeds for the full campaign to come (see "Why and How to Be Your Own Best Sales Force") can mean the difference between a book that is ignored or mishandled and one that is granted the most favorable treatment possible.

Your primary goal between the day your manuscript is accepted and the day it's published should be to get everyone—from your editor to the publicity director to the people handling all sorts of sales—involved with (and, if you can manage it, excited about) the future of your book. To make them envision that future the way you want it to happen, you'll have to reinforce and supplement the marketing suggestions you made in your original proposal through occasional short, informal notes to your editor.

Since most editors have numerous authors to deal with, an outpouring of "me first" epistles is not recommended. Just write in an enthusiastic, contributory spirit. "It's occurred to me that it might be a good idea to play up the self-improvement angle in promotions throughout California" may make an effective approach. And suggestive tones—*coulds* rather than *shoulds; we might* rather than *you'd better*—will make it clear that you're willing not only to fire off suggestions but also to do the work entailed in executing them. Each of your letters, if it's well worded, will encourage your editor to think about a new dimension of your book and provide at least one viable idea the editor can pass along to sales and publicity people. Keep copies; as publication date nears and promotion plans are firmed up, you'll want to refer back to these early memos.

Among your efforts to gain momentum for your book in its early stages, you might include the following:

* If there's anything in the news that's relevant to your book's contents, write a short piece for a newspaper's Op Ed page or letters column or for a magazine's opinion department; include a biographical note mentioning that your material comes from a book you're working on; and use the clip of the published piece as evidence to convince your publisher that you're dealing with a timely and important subject.

* If your book requires that you do research, ask for data by running an author's query in the pages of *The New York Times Book Review*. Publicly seeking information will not only help you get it but will also start people talking about your book, and it may lead to invitations to speak before groups or at conferences, which will add further to your fame and thus to your developing good fortunes.
* Keep your eyes open for gatherings relevant to your subject; volunteer to be on a panel or to participate in a series of readings. Ask for, or collect, a list of names and addresses of attendees to whom you can send notices and order blanks when your book is published, and after a successful speaking engagement drop a note to your editor about the event and the enthusiastic response you met at it.
* Once you develop the habit of thinking in terms of positioning, you'll be visited by enticing ideas at all sorts of odd moments. To keep them where you'll be able to find them, start a file that will include:

Names (and addresses if possible) of writers, critics, broadcasters and anyone else who's famous and who, because of their interest in your subject or their ideological bent, might give your book favorable advance comments for use in cover blurbs and press releases.

Names of magazines and newspapers that would have good reason to run excerpts from your book or to review it or to plug it in one of their regular columns.

Potential sales pitches. "This book is for people who . . . and we can reach them by . . ."

Appealing advertising slants. Read book ads with care and decide what, if anything, makes them effective.

Titles. Improvements in your working title are likely to occur to you as you write, and if you keep a record of them all— even those that don't quite make it in your mind—you may eventually come up with one that works beautifully.

All of these steps, along with others to be discussed in the chapters that follow and still others that you'll think of on your own, will help give your book its best chance. But that's not all the good they'll do: when you're so stymied in the actual writing that you've begun to think nothing will ever be published at all, they'll give you a psychological boost; even (and sometimes especially) when you're disgruntled, it's just plain fun to work on ways of making your book the biggest deal it can legitimately be.

Editing, Copy-editing, Design, Production and Part-and-Parcel Advertising

THE IDEAL AUTHOR, from the point of view of practically everyone in a large publishing operation, will open his or her mouth only to say thank you as a manuscript moves through the editing and production stages. Even the editor who loved a book from the start won't be eager to hear protests about the changes that seem indicated now, while the copy editor, the designer and the production manager (all of whom are highly trained in technical fields) are apt to bridle if a writer tries to tell them their business, on the entirely plausible grounds that an amateur's mistakes will cost dearly in money and time.

Partly because they are less compartmentalized and partly because their general approach assumes a partnership, people in smaller firms are far more likely to welcome an author's participation. Writers for small houses are freer to contribute ideas, to challenge preconceived plans and to involve themselves in production, sometimes by submitting their work on computer tapes or discs and helping to process it electronically. This kind of thing should be happening more and more at larger houses too, because it can cut costs for typesetting and proofreading. As Stephen F. Roth, managing editor of *Personal Publishing,* points out, authors with computers are taking over a good many tasks publishers used to handle; so far, it's not clear how much, if any, of the money that the publishers are saving finds its way into the authors' pockets.

But if the tone of the proceedings differs between larger and smaller publishers, the steps are the same; and it's important for every author (a) to have control over them and (b) to exercise that control for the good.

Groundwork

The best preparation for smooth passage through editing and production shoals is a thorough dry run through your manuscript. After it's been accepted and before editing begins, get the typescript back and go over it, marking every textual and stylistic point you care deeply about. Is it important to you that a particular example not be cut; that footnotes appear at the back of the book instead of on the bottom of each page; that section headings seem twice as powerful as chapter headings; that dialogue be punctuated exactly as you've indicated? Expressing preferences of this sort may not get you everything you want (and perhaps you'll eventually be glad if it doesn't), but it will help you avoid some conflicts, and it will maximize your influence on the outcome of others.

It's intelligent also to state clearly and in writing—before work starts—whether you want the right of approval for any or all of the following (and to insist on reviewing at least the first three):

The edited manuscript.
The copy-edited manuscript.
The title and the subtitle if there is one.
The index.
The typeface(s) and layout.
The illustrations (if there are any) and the captions.
The book cover design and copy, or the magazine cover line.
The catalog copy.

You needn't—in fact, you shouldn't—be strident or combative when you make your request. A friendly, informal note to

The Author's Basic Anti-Snafu Checklist

Date   *Milestone*

_____ Editing complete. Check edited ms.

_____ Copy-editing complete. Check copy-edited ms, including title and copyright pages.

_____ Sample pages and layout due. Check design, with special attention to headings and to illustrations and captions, if any.

_____ Ms. goes to typesetter. Check to see that copies of ms. go out for early blurbs to use in cover copy.

_____ Index due. Check index.

_____ Author's questionnaire due. Fill out and return questionnaire. (Remember: Many editors use the description called for in a questionnaire when writing promotional copy.)

_____ Catalog copy due. Offer to draft and/or ask to OK final catalog copy. (Overworked editors will be glad to have your draft.)

_____ Sales conference. Prepare materials that show your book's strengths and give them to your editor at least three weeks before sales conference begins.

_____ Cover design due. OK design; discuss use of your picture.

_____ Cover copy due. Offer to draft and/or ask to OK final front and back cover copy and flap copy, if any; submit photograph if needed; check on inclusion of blurbs on hand.

_____ Cover goes to press.

_____ Proofs due from printer. Read and OK proofs, with special attention to front and back matter.

_____ Proofs due to publisher, with all corrections.

_____ Press release due. Offer to draft and/or ask to OK final copy.

_____ Bound galleys due. Check to see that sets go to potential blurb writers and to reviewers like *Publishers Weekly* and *Kirkus* that need materials well before publication; check on copies for periodicals that publish once a month or less often and that may review your book or buy serial rights.

_____ Bound books ready. Check on copies for reviewers and serial rights buyers on weeklies and dailies and in radio and TV.

_____ Official publication date. Start collecting reviews and comments to add to cover if your book goes back to press.

your editor explaining that you want to be involved (and that you don't intend to be obstructive) should serve you well. Backstop the note, though, by becoming familiar with your manuscript's timetable.

As a first step, ask your editor to give you your book's milestone dates, which are indicated on the checklist on page 114. Then fill in the checklist's date column and rearrange the list as necessary to get the items into strict chronological order. (The sequence of prepublication activities varies somewhat from book to book, depending on a pub date's position in the publisher's seasonal cycle.) Finally, as deadlines approach, check to see that what should be done actually is being done and that material you want to OK is indeed submitted for your approval while there's still time for you to have a say about it.

Editing

Editors come in two varieties at some giant firms: acquiring and line. Acquiring editors scout for material, take authors and potential authors out for lunch or drinks to discuss projects and herd manuscripts through the acceptance stages. Line editors edit. Most companies, big and little, are set up so that every editor is an idea person and a pencil-and-paper person, but if your publisher divides the functions—or if your editor turns editing jobs over to junior colleagues—try to arrange to deal face to face with the editor who's actually working on your manuscript as well as with the one who was in charge of it to start with.

How much editing that person will do depends on how much your work needs, on individual style, on time pressures and, obviously, on ability. Ideally, an editor will clarify what you have to say, suggest cuts and additions to strengthen the impact of your work and change nothing unless change means improvement.

In fact, some editors habitually change a great deal; tackling a manuscript with scissors and stapler as well as pencil, they cut, rearrange and reword until they think they've got the material in its most effective shape. Others make virtually no alterations, sometimes because they simply don't have time to rework the text. Occupying a very large middle ground between those who overedit and those who hardly edit at all are editors who vary their activities markedly with each manuscript they handle, deleting large chunks of the flabby ones, moving sections around in the disorganized ones or suggesting two pages' worth of revisions to authors who seem capable of fixing their own text, given guidance.

If your manuscript hasn't changed much in appearance by the time an editor is through with it, you can be sure it's been edited lightly. If it's heavily pencil-marked, you're an average editee. And if it's clean, fresh, retyped copy, the editor probably rewrote the whole thing, and you probably had to wait quite some time for the results. It takes most editors a week or so to edit an average book and roughly a day to do a normal magazine piece, but with heavy rewrites these figures can easily triple.

Despite individual differences of style and speed, editors generally agree on what to do to a given manuscript (the opening should build up momentum more quickly; the mother's speech in the confrontation scene should be foreshadowed; readers ought to be told the basis for the findings in paragraph 4). And they tend to agree, too, about what not to do. Editors remind themselves and their assistants—often and with conviction—to refrain from superimposing ideas on or changing characters in an author's work. Editors are supposed to realize your story's potential; if they have tales they themselves want to tell, they should tell them on their own time and typewriters.

Good editors take pains to treat authors as carefully as they treat manuscripts. In fact, some editors are so solicitous of writers' egos that they've developed a special diction for suggesting revisions. "That's a marvelous lead," they'll say; "compelling and thoroughly apt. And your conclusion works beautifully. But I wonder whether the middle section might, perhaps, benefit from just a bit of tightening. If you don't object, I'd like to try tinkering with it a bit, being careful, of course, not to injure your style or your point in any way."

Roughly translated, this means: "I genuinely admire what you've written; I know how hard it was to write; and I don't want you to feel hurt because the final product is less than perfect. What you don't know and I do, however, is that every manuscript has notable weaknesses; for your own good, I want to correct the flaws in yours. The midsection is verbose and confusing and needs to be cut by a third."

To forestall the defensive reaction that may arise when editors come along and tell you, tactfully or not, that they can make your manuscript better than you've made it, think about these contrasts:

* Editors don't have to cope with a blank piece of paper. You've originated a story or a line of argument that's worth transmitting to readers; all they have to do is fine-tune the signals.
* Editors are intimately familiar with a wide range of literary techniques because they've worked with dozens of writers, while you've got only your own experience and learning to draw upon.
* Editors know their audiences. Sometimes, by using their hard-won knowledge of readers' predilections, they can reshape a manuscript so that it will draw a bigger and more receptive crowd.
* Your editor isn't sick of the whole damn thing. After endless rewriting, both your words and your concepts may blur and grow stale in your mind, but the material is new to the editor, who can therefore come to it clear-eyed and eager.

In spite of everything writers can do to persuade themselves to adopt a professional attitude toward being edited, some find it impossible not to bristle. If you're in this group, read your revised manuscript through once, fast, and take a breather. Go run around the lake or play a couple of sets of tennis before you look at your copy again, and then try to read it as if it were the work of a total stranger and to imagine as you read what your publisher's problems with it may have been (does the magazine have a particular tone of voice to maintain; are cuts of twenty-three pages necessary to keep your book's cost down to the point where bookstores will stock it; did that lovely descriptive section you struggled with for weeks destroy the story's pace?).

Whatever complaints survive a dispassionate reading should be taken up—calmly—with your editor. Don't squabble if you can avoid it, because you and the editor are jointly responsible for creating and nurturing a piece of writing, and creative, nurturing tasks are best performed by teammates who focus on the good of the offspring rather than on failings in each other.

Copy-editing

A mutually satisfactory working relationship with your editor is at least as important after editing is finished as it was before and during the editing phase, since from now on you'll have to rely on the editor to help settle disputes with everybody else. The odds-on favorite for most-likely-to-be-disputed-with is the individual who gets your manuscript next: the copy editor. (In smaller publishing operations your editor may be your copy editor too, which cuts down on the number of personal relationships you need to establish. And on many newspapers the editor who's called the copy editor will have general, high-level responsibilities, but you're not likely to have much direct contact with people of this stripe.)

Copy editors have a lot to put up with. Their status is low, as is their pay, and their job—which tends to be literally thankless—demands a peculiar, contradictory blend of character traits: copy editors must be highly intelligent, dazzlingly knowledgeable, keenly alert nitpickers.

To copy-edit is to be responsible for making a manuscript correct in all its details. Authors are generally disinterested when a copy editor conforms their work to house style ("theater," not "theatre"; *The New York Times,* not the *New York Times* or the

New York *Times*) and they're grateful, on the whole, when copy editors catch and correct their mistakes, by supplying appropriate double consonants in "accommodate" or "desiccate," for instance, by taking San Antonio away from the Pecos River and placing it on the banks of the San Antonio River or even by pointing out that the action in a particular story couldn't happen (take the tender scene in a leading novelist's work in which a father tiptoes in to place a goodnight kiss on the cheek of his child as she lies asleep in her crib; Listen, said the copy editor, you can't kiss a kid in a crib unless you balance on your stomach over the railing; God, how embarrassing, said the novelist; thanks very much).

It's when the copy editor presses for documentation or defines as a correction something the author sees as a distortion that trouble starts.

More and more, documentation is the author's job because fewer and fewer publishing concerns can afford to have a fact checker on the staff nowadays. To protect against lawsuits and to ensure accuracy, the copy editor must often call upon writers to cite (and perhaps to produce) their sources. Writers who have kept careful notes will naturally find the task less onerous than writers who haven't, but even the most rigorous recordkeepers may have to exert themselves considerably, because copy editors know—from long and sad experience—that what you read in print is not necessarily so. Satisfying their rule of thumb—when two out of three authorities agree, that's good enough—generally calls for additional research, which few authors undertake without grumbling.

The grumbling turns to groans, or even screeches, when writers come up against copy editors who have a context to contend with (is yours the second piece in this issue to use the Mad Hatter's tea party as a metaphor? If so, you'll probably find the allusion has been cut) or whose ideas of correctness don't jibe with their own. Robert Pilpel, who repeatedly referred to Churchill as Winston throughout his "affectionate portrait," *Churchill in America,* was furious to discover that a copy editor had laboriously changed all his "Winstons" to "Mr. Churchill,"

"Churchill," or "the PM" on the grounds that "Winston" sounded disrespectful. Pilpel thought it conveyed just the tone he wanted. He won the point.

You can win similar arguments with copy editors if you treat them with kindness and respect. In fact, you can probably have your way on most editing and copy-editing questions; after all, it's your story. It's important that you not make an issue out of everything, however, and it's vitally important that if you're going to take a stand, you take it early. After the copy-editing stage, it gets extremely expensive to fuss with the text. (To learn more about copy-editing, see the Starter Kit in "The Self-Publishing Option.")

Indexing

All too often, an author assumes that providing an index is part of the publisher's job, while the publisher assumes that an author who doesn't ask for an index doesn't want one. Since a nonfiction book with an index will sell many more copies than the same book without it, you should check your contract on this subject and take appropriate steps in good time.

Design and Production

When you and your editor and your copy editor have finished with your manuscript, it is sent off to the typesetter with a full set of specifications for typefaces, column widths, spacing and the like. The person who chooses specs is a designer; the person who supervises their execution is a production manager. The smaller the firm, the more likely it is that the designer and the production manager will be one and the same; in every firm, their functions are intimately related.

To get a firm grasp on design and production, you can turn

Editing, Copy-editing, Design, Production, Advertising

to the self-publishing Starter Kit; to learn enough about these operations so that you'll know what their effects are, read on.

At its simplest level, design has to do with how a manuscript should look in print. Given the available space, a range of type options and possibly a budget for artwork, a designer will select one or more sizes and styles of type for text and several others for headings; the designer will also devise a format and perhaps commission or secure drawings or photographs—all this with two goals in mind: making your work readable, and visually reinforcing its message. Once the basic choices are made, the designer combines text and titles and pictures to create an effective array of pages. Because most writers know little or nothing about layout and type, and because many book and periodical designers have a strictly limited range of options, there's not much an author can contribute at this stage; in fact, you should feel freer now to ignore your manuscript than you've been before or will ever be again.

With intermittent breaks for required activities, your recess period should last all through production—which consists of purchasing materials and services, scheduling and routing the manuscript, coordinating printing and binding with distribution and keeping everything straight and moving along with the help of detailed written records. A production cycle lasts several weeks at most magazines and between five and nine months for the average book, and unless you're responsible for coding and correcting your manuscript on your computer, you can safely leave it to the specialists. Do read your galley proofs, though, to catch any mistakes you and the copy editor missed and any a typesetter may have made; and return them on time because deadlines matter more now.

As publication date approaches, your manuscript's schedule gets increasingly inflexible and changes get more and more complicated and costly. There's a little bit of give at every point of every production timetable (despite what you'll hear to the contrary from people who don't trust you to meet a real deadline), but by the time page proofs are pulled, things are generally moving so fast that only minor and absolutely essential corrections can be made.

Authors don't see page proofs as a rule, so if you want to have some effect on layout and illustrations, don't wait; get involved while rough sketches are in the works. Be prepared, even that early, to meet resistance; editors and designers alike may prefer not to use pictures unless they're essential, because artwork adds enormously to expenses, and they're apt to have sharp preferences of their own about how your manuscript should look in print.

Part-and-Parcel Advertising

After a book or article is published, its author should find a variety of ways to let people know it exists and to make them want to read it ("Why and How to Be Your Own Best Sales Force" and "Managing Sales" will elaborate). There's one piece of advertising, however, that's conceived and executed well before publication because it's an integral part of your work. For a book, it's the cover; for an article or a story, it's the cover line (only a few items from a magazine's table of contents get listed on its cover; if you can come up with a phrase that will attract buyers to yours, perhaps it will be one of those that's featured).

Like coming-next-issue squibs and headnotes, magazine cover lines are presented as the publisher's work rather than the writer's. That being the case, editors frequently feel no obligation to check them with authors, and authors usually don't mind.

Almost always, however, writers want to preview their book covers and, unfortunately, almost always, they don't know how to evaluate what they see. Controversy in this area erupts when publishers define covers as point-of-purchase ads, while authors assume they should be works of art. Since the first point of view is demonstrably healthier for sales, you'd be wise to adopt it and, having adopted it, to decide then what ideas and/or sketches and/or leads to picture sources you might usefully contribute.

Out of politeness, publishing people may pay lip service to your suggestions, no matter how off-base they think you are. But if you want them to heed as well as to listen once you get into the conflict-ridden area of publicity, advertising and sales, you will have to convince them that you don't fit the conventional writer's mold. For a writer, as pictured in publishing's collective unconscious, is a babe in the business woods, an impractical type who's understandably eager to succeed and infuriatingly misinformed about how success is achieved. Because this mental image has a substantial foundation in fact, overcoming it means absorbing knowledge and terminology. You can start by realizing that your book's cover may be the only ad it ever gets, and by the time you've read the next chapter you'll have learned enough to position yourself verbally and intellectually on your publisher's wavelength. Then you can really start to fiddle with the controls.

Why and How to Be Your Own Best Sales Force

CALL IT THE curse of abundance; with roughly 40,000 new books each year, and periodicals starting up all the time, only a small percentage of what's published catches the attention of the public. This reality comes as a shock to most writers, and as an especially severe shock to authors of first books, whose expectations about sales and reviews always escalate as publication day approaches. To help cushion the inevitable blow, many editors deliver a standard prepublication speech. At small houses, the gist of it is, We hope to rack up sales over the years, but making a big splash now just isn't in the cards. And at large houses, an editor may say, in effect, Don't expect much (or, for most fiction writers and poets, don't expect anything); your book is not going to sell 100,000 copies—we'll be lucky if it sells 2,000; don't look for a display ad in *The New York Times,* because there isn't going to be one; and no, you won't get on *Today* or the *Donahue* show; in fact, unless a major book club chooses it or some publisher makes a whopping bid for reprint rights, your book will vanish without a trace three months after publication.

Fortunately, as the ghost said to Scrooge, these are the shadows of things that will be only if you don't get busy.

To promote a magazine or newspaper piece, about all you need to do is draw up a list of influential men and women who figure to comment on it and ought to get copies, draft a covering letter to them and tell your publisher about any contacts you have with media people who might focus on your story. (If you want extra copies of your piece for your friends or your files, order them before the issue they'll appear in is printed; they're cheaper that way.) To promote a book, however, you can do a great deal more, and you'd better.

Profit and Loss and the Bigbook Bind

It's part of publishing's proverbial wisdom that each book is unique and that it therefore requires individual attention—"This isn't toothpaste we're selling" is for reasons unknown the standard comparison. In fact, though, publishers generally produce and distribute their wares assembly-line fashion. For this apparent contradiction, they have a ready, and thoroughly plausible, excuse: with dozens or hundreds of titles to sell and strict limits on time, money and staff, routinization is essential.

Why do publishers continue to produce so many books if they lack the resources to sell them? Why, to put it another way, does a $12.2 billion business accept it as a fact of life that book after book after book will fail to bring in a penny of profit? A full discussion of the reasons would make a book by itself, but three of them deserve mention here.

* Even the largest, most commercial houses sometimes publish books that don't seem likely to make any money, because editors there think those books are important to contemporary thought or literature.
* There's some truth in the toothpaste analogy, not because each book is unique (most current titles have obvious counterparts in the publishing past) but because the public will greet it as if it were until they've been educated to believe otherwise. The educational process is expensive—conventional book publishing houses, after all, have no brand-name loyalties to draw upon and no subscription systems to guarantee that money they spend initially to round up an audi-

ence will be paid off over time—so large firms quite naturally concentrate on telling the world about those titles that have a huge potential readership and leave the rest to luck.

Since each book is a one-shot deal, publishing people must base initial commitments to a particular title on the rough guidelines their experience offers and on apparently unquenchable sparks of hope. Usually, though, the hope proves forlorn because in the end the routine measures that publishers have time to put into effect almost never suffice to locate and arouse a particular book's best audience, and authors, who might inject some nonroutine verve into the proceedings, don't know how to help.

* The bigbook has the industry in a bind. On the one hand, bestsellers (not unlike toothpaste) appeal to a large general market, and that enables publishers to benefit from market research (of an admittedly informal sort) and from economies of scale. On the other hand, however, they draw funds and attention away from the majority of the books on a publisher's list, and they demand a strenuous commitment to hype.

Here's how the bigbooks grow:

1. Editors at a particular publishing house get hold of a book with bestseller potential.

2. The book gets a two-page write-up in the new catalog; editors and marketing people begin to talk it up over lunch and drinks with editors at the major book clubs and other publishing insiders, and to collect ecstatic blurbs from celebrities they work with; ads are scheduled for *PW* and major metropolitan newspapers; and a cross-country tour, complete with radio and TV appearances and local press coverage, is planned for the author.

3. Booksellers, librarians, reviewers and reprint editors, seeing the catalog, the ads and the press releases and hearing the trade gossip, get the bigbook signal loud and clear and hurry to leap on the bandwagon before anyone can accuse them of not being with-it.

4. Reviewers review, bookstores and libraries buy, and the public—responding reflexively to the hoopla—decides to get with-it too, by rushing out and grabbing that book that absolutely everybody is reading.

5. Absolutely everybody reads it.

Increasing Your Influence

The bigbook bandwagon gets a considerable part of its power from implicit comparisons (this is the cream of a very large crop, goes the unstated bigbook message); thus, it can damage your chances by defining your book as inferior (it's something other than cream, quite clearly, and perhaps no more than watery milk). And, of course, the bigbooks can also hurt you (along with any publisher's overall track record) by preempting the major portion of all sales resources (that initial advertising blitz is expensive, and so is the tour, and after sales reps push a bigbook as hard as they're often instructed to do, they won't have much energy left for selling the rest of the list).

To counter the forces that will work to keep your book just one more title on "the rest of the list," you'll have to attract an audience for it, and the most efficient way to do that is by identifying the connections that already exist between you and your work, on the one hand, and classes of readers, on the other.

Try people who know you, people who share membership with you in a formal or informal group of any sort and people who will feel a sense of kinship with your characters, your settings or your subject. Is your protagonist a liberated house-husband? Tell women's organizations and men's clubs. Does your subject involve college students? Reach the campuses. Is there a scene in Chicago, a narrative account of abortion, a proposal to abolish free public education? Across the country, people who identify in some way with these areas of interest (and with almost any others you can think of) regularly convene, and communicate through newsletters; and if you use their particular concerns to provide points of entry to selected aspects of your work, the whole of what you've done will get its fair chance to capture their attention and earn their admiration.

Once you succeed in stirring up interest, you can use evidence of your success to convince the staff at your publishing house to back you. When they see signs (even small ones) that you're a winner, they'll be more likely to make your book one of the titles they urge on booksellers, librarians, reviewers and all the other intermediaries who stand between conventionally published writers and their readers.

Persuading your publisher to get out there and sell your book is a never-ending job that demands a good deal of gall (though they don't want to be quoted, publishing people all admit that demanding authors get more attention for their books). But skillful maneuvering is useful too, and for best results you'll want to devise sensible promotional plans, figure out how to fit them in with your publisher's standard operating procedures and then get up the gumption to see that they're put into effect.

The following descriptions and suggestions should tell you what you need to know to manage all three steps.

Major Departmental Development

Publicity, Promotion and Advertising

At large houses, separate departments may exist to handle each of these areas; at small firms one person is often responsible for them all, and for other things besides. In any case, though, all three are closely related and extremely important.

Probably the only request these departments will ever make of you is that you fill out a questionnaire providing them with an autobiographical sketch, a description of your book, an account of how it was conceived and written, a list of its newsworthy aspects and a roster of names and addresses of people who might provide blurb copy or otherwise help focus attention on what you've written.

In a rational world, all writers would complete these forms immediately and with care. What actually happens, however, is that publicity people have to plead for information—"We know it's a chore to fill out forms" is the way one house begins its questionnaire's covering letter, "but if you could spare a few moments to answer the attached questions, it would be a great help to us in publicizing and promoting your book"—and when they finally get writers to hand the forms in, they discover half the time that the data supplied are too sketchy to be of any use.

Bolstering this evidence of authorial sloth, there are numerous indications of authorial ignorance (writers not only have an unbounded and ungrounded faith in ads, for instance; they also seem to believe that bookstore clerks, who say they've never heard of a book are saying something true and significant). Having listened to all these stories and lived through too many of them, most publicity people don't count on much help from writers. In fact, they've been badgered so often by inappropriate demands that their automatic response to the idea of author participation is horror.

Before you can make a contribution, therefore, you'll have to demonstrate that you're different, that while others may try to nag and second-guess marketing people, what you intend to do is provide extra information and elbow grease.

Where you get your supply of elbow grease is up to you, but the bulk of your information ought to come straight from your book, which you have every reason to know intimately and which many of the people at your publishing house may never have read. All too often, publicity personnel and others in charge of selling a book have to proceed knowing nothing more about it than its central subject. Thus, if your book is called *A History of Fitness Fads,* they'll know enough to alert fitness groups and periodicals to forthcoming publication, but because they won't have read the chapter on next year's Be Fit Fair in Cleveland, they won't be able to develop potential there.

You could, though; you know every chapter, every scene, every sentence, and if you assess them as candidates for fairly standard promotional efforts, they can give you quite a lot of mileage.

Consider, for example, review copies. As a matter of course, most publicity departments send copies of every new book they handle to major review media like *Publishers Weekly, Library Journal,* American Library Association magazines, *Kirkus Reviews, The New York Times,* the Washington *Post* and the Los Angeles *Times.* Columnists and magazine and newspaper editors with large, national audiences who have expressed interest in a book (or who figure to be interested in it) will also get copies.

But small periodicals can print effective reviews too, and because the publicity department may not know the ones in your field (and surely won't have time to ferret them out), it becomes your job to get up a list. Include small-town papers and neighborhood throwaways published in places you've mentioned in your book, along with pertinent special-interest journals, and include names of contacts at these periodicals whenever possible.

As a general rule, between 100 and 500 copies of a new title go out for review. Though the press releases regularly issued by publishers vary at least as widely in number, they too constitute powerful selling tools for any sort of book. You should be able to think of good places to send them by creating appropriate conclusions for the sentence that starts, "This book will be of special interest to you because . . ."

What people or groups would be especially interested in the people or groups your book mentions? What local papers serve the places you've described? What associations care about your subject? What directories exist in the field? And how can you get your work listed? (The Bowker and Gale Research catalogs, which are listed in "The Self-Publishing Option Resources," will be helpful here.)

If you think your book would be valuable as a text or for supplementary reading in schools, draft a letter to teachers explaining how they might use it, and pass the draft along to your editor. If you know about meetings of people active in the book's field, write a memo about them. And if you've spotted the newsworthy side of what you've written, by all means develop your thoughts and share them as soon as you can.

Remember, too, that publicity departments frequently send announcements to notify friends, family and interested others that a particular author's book has just been published. This is a relatively inexpensive practice (much cheaper, for example, than mailing out review copies or scheduling ads), so you're not likely to meet much resistance if you press for its use.

The best way of all to sell a book is face to face with a prospective buyer, and the odds are 50-50 that your publisher arranges interviews and speaking engagements for nonfiction authors (the chances are somewhat less good that the publisher will manage to have promotional materials and bound books on hand to fill any demand they generate). But if no one else schedules you, you can schedule yourself.

Molly Peacock, whose books of poems include *And Live Apart* and *Raw Heaven,* does a mailing every so often to people in charge of readings. Her covering letter begins, "I hope you will consider me for a place in the [Such-and-Such] poetry reading series." Then it goes on to talk about the magazines that have published her poetry and the readings she's already given. She also sends along a copy of one of her book jackets, copies of reviews, a précis of her professional accomplishments and several poems that show the quality and flavor of her work.

Readings regularly result and Peacock reports that "the psychic rewards are terrific."

The financial rewards can be pretty good too. A poet who's "completely unabashed" about selling her books when she reads, Molly Peacock has found that giving readings plus judging poetry contests plus getting grants can propel her annual income from poetry into five figures.

Readings also work well for novelists, but the best way for nonfiction writers to meet their readers is by preparing presentations they can give before groups.

One of the greatest success stories in contemporary publishing is traceable to a series of talks initiated by an unknown author. *I'm OK, You're OK* had an advance sale of 7,433 and sold 19,843 copies during its first year. Respectable, but by no means extraordinary. Sales went up over 100,000 the next year, however, and continued to mount each year until they peaked at over a million. The publisher gave the credit to the author, Thomas A. Harris, because his talks before small audiences got sales to the point where the publicity department felt justified in planning a strong promotional campaign.

Where public appearances are concerned, your knowledge of your book is again your best asset, and you should use it to select upcoming conferences and conventions that will be worth attending. Many authors have been successful in selling their own books at conventions and fairs, so you may have no trouble getting your publisher to cover your expenses at such gatherings (if you do go, try hard to get a list of names and addresses of the attendees; it could supply productive leads for mail-order sales).

Unabashed promotional devices like posters, circulars, bookmarks and ads are useful when you speak before groups, and in theory some of your book's projected revenues will be allocated for them. In practice, though, bigbooks get much more than their share and most books get much less. If you're artistic, you may be able to compensate by designing and executing promotional materials yourself in consultation with publicity and promotion people (see the Starter Kit that begins on page 159); and if you're realistic in your suggestions about advertising, you might get some money for that too. Just don't plump for space in the standard book review media. Ads there are exceedingly expensive—a full page in *The New York Times Book Review* costs roughly $13,000—and their rate of return may be only a fraction of what you'd get from two tiny coupon ads in publications that focus on your area of interest. (See "A Foot in the Door Resources" for leads.)

The publicity department will be delighted if there's enough evidence of interest in your book to warrant keeping it alive. And when and if a book starts to take off, they may try to help it along by issuing periodic announcements to the trade journals about favorable new reviews or large new printings. The more developments there are, the better; so keep working to interest the local bank, the library, the schools or the stores in displaying your book; keep sending small periodicals material about it whenever a news event comes along to serve as a peg; keep looking for groups that might welcome you as a speaker; and above all, keep telling your publisher what you're doing. Each new sign of interest and enthusiasm you can report may stimulate still more attention.

Subsidiary Rights Sales

During the 1970s, major book clubs and mass market paperback reprinters paid so handsomely for rights in big hardcover books that many hardcover publishers didn't much mind seeing books on "the rest of the list" lose money. In the '80s, however, as economic conditions worsened in America, the sub rights picture changed. Both houses that used to do hardcovers only and houses that once did nothing but paperbacks now publish hard- and softcover books; either may sell rights in one format or the other; and either may decide to issue reprints of material they originated.

Some authors get a measure of control over reprint deals in their contracts, but in general it's hard to affect major sub rights sales. Writers can be influential, though, with regard to serial sales (of excerpts, to magazines and newspapers, before and after publication), and, once again, your intimate knowledge of your book can make the difference between getting offers and getting ignored. If you suggest that the analysis of sitcoms on pages 85 to 90 might appeal to *TV Guide,* that chapters two and three, with some connective tissue and a new lead, would work for *Rolling Stone,* or that your section on old country inns should interest *Southern Living,* your rights director (or your agent, if that's who's handling serial sales) will be delighted—and much more effective.

Left to their own devices, overworked rights directors are likely to send a complete set of galleys of your book out to a magazine that shares its general area of interest. When the galleys arrive, magazine editors will be faced with a choice: (a) to plow through three hundred pages worth of material in hopes of finding fifteen that might, with some work, make a piece; or (b) to ship the book back and risk missing a decent article. Quite often—and quite rightly, given time pressures and priorities—an editor will opt for the latter. If you want portions of your work to appear in the periodical press, therefore (and you will if you consider either the money or the publicity you can gain that way), you'll have to carve them out yourself and help direct them to the most appropriate openings you can find. Confer with your editor on timing, and consult "A Foot in the Door" and "Spinoffs" for leads.

Sales to Bookstores

The job of getting books into stores is performed by a sales force, which can number roughly one hundred at a very large publishing house. At least twice a year, salespeople at most large firms convene for a full-dress presentation of their house's new books. In the past, sales conferences were generally held in the publisher's own home territory and editors introduced their own titles; nowadays these conferences are more likely to take place at an island resort, and the editor-in-chief, along with other members of upper management, is apt to announce the entire line, describing each book and suggesting how to sell it.

It's important to get your book presented favorably at the sales conference because if the reps sense that it's a loser they'll classify it mentally as a "skip book" (one they can use to build confidence with booksellers by saying, "Between you and me, you can skip this"); and then, of course, a loser is what it will be. To avoid this fate, you should prepare a package of selling documents and pass it along to your editor in the hope that the editor, in turn, will relay copies to all the marketing people.

Consider including a list of promising markets together with notes on how to reach them, an analysis of the distinctions between your book and its competition, a particularly engaging excerpt and/or a table of contents.

In addition, you might offer to talk with the assembled sales reps if they're in your area, either by addressing them at a meeting or by attending one of the parties the house may be giving for them during a sales conference.

Since more than a hundred titles may be presented at each sales meeting and since each sales rep will have approximately twenty-nine seconds to sell a book in the stores, it's a good idea to create a tag line for yours. "What I need most," noted Nancy Taylor as a sales rep for Random House, "are key words or phrases that will be sure to catch the attention of the retailer. For instance, when *Inner Tennis* came out, I jotted down 'Zen approach to tennis' and 'meditative techniques applicable to sports.' And that's what I used to sell the book. If there's no handle, it's difficult to sell a book, no matter how good it is."

When, after close to a week, sales conferences end, each sales rep goes forth—armed with catalogs, book covers, photos of authors and a quota to meet for every title—to call on accounts (a single rep may be responsible for contacting a hundred or more booksellers). Because most books sold to stores are fully returnable and because the sales reps' bonuses are based on sales minus returns, it does them no good to load retailers up with copies of a title the stores won't be able to move. Still, once the books are on the shelves the manager will try to find customers for them (or so the theory goes), and besides, quotas help publishers provide an objective correlative for impressionistic first-printing orders.

Unfortunately, despite quotas and clever sales pitches many new books have a hard time getting into bookstores, and those that do make it onto the shelves aren't likely to stay there long. Because they know they can return most titles they stock, bookstore managers take little risk in ordering, have little incentive to sell aggressively or imaginatively and tend to go with our cultural flow toward the new, new, new and the big, big, big. Ninety days after a book's publication, booksellers who want room for other titles may simply pack it up and return it to the publisher for credit, and unless they're convinced that would be a mistake, it's just what they'll do.

Everyone agrees that present systems of distribution are unsatisfactory all around and perhaps at their worst in those moments—known to authors, publishers and booksellers alike—when it's impossible to cash in on a surge of interest in a particular book because the damn thing isn't in fact "available at your bookstore," as the ads and media coverage promised, but is, instead, stuck in the warehouse, lost in the mail or held up in its second printing by a strike at the bindery.

On the whole, the transience and unpredictability of a book's life in the stores make everybody miserable, and there's not much relief in sight. You can take a small step toward sanity, however, by reminding yourself that—just like the publicity people and the subsidiary rights people—sales reps can't be relied upon to have read your book and that they need you to tell them what's between the covers.

If you've written about patients' rights, for example, and you know that Boston, New York and San Francisco are among the cities in the vanguard of medical change, write a memo to the sales force and urge them to set high quotas for stores there. Try to isolate as many promising geographical markets as you can, whatever your subject, and prepare a list for the sales force, complete with explanations (I grew up in Newtown, Connecticut, my parents live in Boise, Idaho; chapter six is set in Helena, Montana).

Selecting three cities for special attention, Joanne Leedom-Ackerman helped propel her first novel, *The Dark Path to the River*, into a second printing shortly after its publication date. With good reviews and a schedule of public appearances in hand, she arranged to autograph books and deliver posters at chain and independent bookstores in Los Angeles (where she lives), New York (where her story takes place) and Dallas (where she comes from; where her supportive publisher, Saybrook, is based; and where her novel soon made the bestseller list, which it stayed on for weeks). "Targeting a few areas and making personal contacts with the booksellers there was one of the most successful things we did," Leedom-Ackerman reports.

Special Sales

For a variety of reasons, many people never set foot in a bookstore. They do, however, go to stores that cater to their special interests: tennis players frequent sporting goods shops, knitting enthusiasts head for the yarn department, kids hang out where toys are sold, and the list goes on. In fact, all sorts of groups not only have stores that serve their needs; they have periodicals, associations, catalogs and conferences as well. Reaching readers through these and other special-interest, "nontraditional" channels is the job of the special sales department.

A good many special sales departments have developed recently, because publishers now know that special sales can bring in sizable amounts of money—more, for some books, than bookstores ever will. Suggestions from authors are usually welcome in this area, so find out who handles special sales for your publisher and then get up a memo pinpointing the nontraditional channels the house should use to get your book directly to its natural readership. See page 187 for further guidance.

Sales to Libraries

In addition to selling directly to retailers, some salespeople call upon wholesalers, who get a large discount because they buy in bulk and who sell their inventory to retailers and libraries. Wholesalers (or jobbers, as they're sometimes called) sell books of all publishers and offer all the advantages that accrue to one-stop suppliers in any industry, including simplified ordering, billing and shipment procedures.

It's their greater efficiency and their discount policies that recommend jobbers to librarians, who order from them after studying publishers' catalogs and reviews in professional journals. Since libraries are obviously a crucial market and since books lead comparatively long lives on library shelves, you'll want to establish contact with librarians in your area, and perhaps you'll decide to include an index in your book (a "no index" note at the end of a review in a library journal can mean "no reference value" to a librarian and thus no sale to you). Otherwise, you can rely on whoever handles library promotion to do whatever is practical for your book in this area.

Fighting the Fear of Hustling

Authors rarely lobby for their books within the houses that publish them (which means less competition for you if you follow this chapter's advice), and they're even less likely to go out by themselves in search of sales. Somehow, they seem to think, it's not dignified to hustle for anything you yourself created. Well, dignified people do it, and for a dignified reason: believing that what they have to say is worth saying, they accept the responsibility of finding those individuals who will benefit from hearing it.

Dr. Wayne W. Dyer's *Your Erroneous Zones,* a book that might have been chalked up as one more self-help manual and quickly forgotten, provides a case in point. Because Dyer believed in the therapeutic value of what he'd written, he set aside a summer to acquaint the American people with his work. Loading 400 copies of his book into his car, Dyer and his wife covered 28,000 miles, visiting forty-seven of the fifty states—most of them more than once—and giving 800 interviews. *Your Erroneous Zones* subsequently made the bestseller lists, and Dyer's editor, Paul Fargis, is the first to applaud his valiant efforts. "Dyer had lots of chutzpah as far as publicity goes," Fargis explains. "He would insist that feature writers hear him out even if they didn't want to listen. And unlike a lot of authors, he didn't look down on doing interviews with small papers or local radio stations; he knew they might lead to bigger things. The publisher/author relationship is a symbiotic one, and because Dyer was working so hard, we bent over backward for him."

Dyer was an unknown who'd written a book with a lot of strikes against it, but even famous, well-established authors are not so smug or rich that they won't get out and give their latest book a nudge or two. A buyer for the Radius Book Store on the West Side of New York City, Susan Bergholz, reported that Joseph Heller, who was a neighbor of hers as well as the author of *Catch-22* and *God Knows,* periodically came into the store to autograph a few copies, to check the stock and positioning of his book and to see how many copies had been bought. And Alex Haley, who could have easily taken a long-deserved rest after sales of *Roots* skyrocketed, continued his breakneck schedule of lectures until he was forced by exhaustion to slow down.

Haley, like any author with insight, probably realized that nothing sells a book better than personal connections. To get the most from yours, with the least psychological strain, start by talking before audiences that will think of you as a neighbor or a friend. Arrange for a reading at a local library. Check with groups in your area that might sponsor meet-the-author get-togethers. See if a book shop downtown will display your book and invite people to meet with you to talk about it. And whether they'll do that or not, arrange to autograph the store's copies of your book (since autographed copies are more likely to sell and booksellers can't return them to publishers, it's smart also to sign copies in bookstores outside your area whenever you travel).

While you're stalking the home front, call the local papers and radio stations to volunteer for interviews or to see if they'd like to serialize your book. And by all means drop a note to the book reviewers of all local publications to tell them that a hometown citizen has been published. Whatever lengths you go to, it's all but impossible to overemphasize the importance of sales on your home turf. For example, Rose Naftalin sold 6,000 copies of her cookbook in her hometown—Portland, Oregon—alone.

After you've utilized every connection your personal roots suggest, you can start to develop connections through subject matter. Consider the example of Jane Seskin—author of *Young Widow, Living Single* and *A Time to Love*—who prepared a brief talk about living alone and meeting people, combined those remarks with readings of her lighthearted poems about the single life and arranged to deliver the resulting presentation at a variety of singles clubs.

Ever since Seskin heard writer Elizabeth Janeway say that she and her economist husband, Eliot, never spoke anywhere without bringing some copies of their books to sell, she has carted a supply of her own books around to meetings. Because she finds juggling money awkward, she usually takes a friend along to transact sales, but she personally autographs every copy on request. (For more information about money-making opportunities on the lecture circuit, see "Spinoffs.")

Wherever you speak and whether you bring your own personal stock or rely on your publisher to get books into the area, be sure to have a supply of flyers with order forms along for backup. Ask your editor to get the sales department to prepare some for you, and if they won't or can't, you can produce them yourself (see the Starter Kit for instructions). Be sure, too, to let the publicity department know at least six weeks in advance about any speaking engagements you've lined up so that they'll have time to alert the local press and bookstores and so that you'll have time to take advantage of any public-speaking services your publisher has to offer.

Some houses provide coaching for their authors before scheduled radio, TV and personal appearances, but whether or not lessons are available, you can always make up a list of provocative questions that an interviewer might ask, and then practice answering them fast and fully. Since the average interview lasts eight minutes, there's plenty of time to establish eye contact with your audience and to mention the title of your book with fair frequency; all you need by way of preparation is a few rehearsals.

Those of you who still feel shy may be emboldened by the story of Diana Brown, told here in her own words.

As a librarian, I was well aware of the number of titles published each year, so when my first novel—*The Emerald Necklace*—appeared, my family and I put our heads together to explore what we might do to save an entertaining book from possible oblivion. We sought out all our contacts: personal, professional, educational, ethnic, and told them of the novel's release.

Attending a political convention, my husband had "campaign" buttons made up for each of us announcing "My wife [or mommy] [or I] wrote *The Emerald Necklace* by Diana Brown." These we wore to an ever increasing number of talks I presented to local groups—friends of the library, schools, service and women's clubs.

May's birthstone being the emerald, we approached a local jeweler with a chain of stores in busy shopping centers who agreed to display my book along with his emeralds, and with a sign noting it was by a local author. We also purchased a small advertisement in a local shopping guide suggesting *The Emerald Necklace* as a May birthday gift.

I wrote a press release on the novel, its progress, and my own background for distribution to local papers. When *The Emerald Necklace* was featured in *Good Housekeeping* and later by *Buenhogar* (the Spanish-language version of that magazine) we had this release translated for Spanish-language papers and radio stations in our area.

Our summer vacation was turned into a promotion trip. Armed with the press release and copies of reviews, we called on newspapers, radio and television stations along our route. Since *The Emerald Necklace* had been chosen by the Sunday supplement *Family Weekly* as suggested summer reading, we made sure to approach each newspaper that carried that magazine. The trip resulted in numerous reviews and feature stories.

Using photocopies of the book jacket, we designed our own notepaper and envelopes. We also reprinted the publisher's catalog copy, and no bill payment or letter left our home without one of these promos being inserted in the envelope. Our Christmas card was also designed from the book jacket—which happened to have been adapted from a handsome portrait by Sir Henry Raeburn.

All of these personal and family efforts resulted in *The Emerald Necklace* going into three hardcover printings. It has since been reprinted in paperback and published in England, Argentina, and Greece. Undoubtedly its success added to the publisher's enthusiasm for my later novels—including *Come Be My Love, The Hand of a Woman,* and *The Blue Dragon.*

The Editor Exits and Other Evils

Authors are prey to strange evil forces. When the reviewer assigned by a prestigious magazine to cover your book does a lousy job and the piece gets chucked, you get no coverage there. When delays of one sort and another mean your tap-dancing guide comes out after the craze is over, you'll have lost your audience. When two books with subjects like yours suddenly fail, you'll forgo the support of the sales force. And when your editor is feuding with the publicity director, you will suffer.

But no matter how events conspire against you, if you believe in your book you can change your luck. Here's a sampling of suggestions.

* When your editor leaves the house, don't panic. As soon as you hear the news, find out who might adopt your book once it's orphaned (your original editor should be able to supply some names), and then meet with all the candidates to assess their enthusiasm for your work and their ability to do well by it. Finally, after you've been assigned a new editor, make a lunch date to explain your book's strengths in detail. (Resell your book also when a new sales manager, special sales director or other key player enters the picture.)

    If, as sometimes happens, no editor on the premises seems likely to handle your book well, then explore ways you might get the project away from its present publisher and resell it to another house (your original editor may be able to make some suggestions, and writers with agents should call on them for help).

- Authors with the money to back their convictions can hire publicists and marketing consultants (see the *Literary Market Place* listings). Some publicists won't work for a book that's already out, and no publicist or marketing consultant can promise results. Still, marketing energy and expertise have breathed new life into many a title.
- If you have plenty of convictions but very little money, try hiring an energetic student whom you can train to be your own personal publicity agent. With a week's study of the standard publicity guides (see "The Self-Publishing Option Resources"), even an amateur should be able to put ten good ideas into practice.
- At your own expense, you can place coupon ads for your book in publications read by members of your target audience, and then you can fill orders from your home with copies you've bought at a discount. (It's a good idea to insist that payment accompany orders; billing poses a host of problems.)
- To alleviate the no-books-in-the-stores problem, you can call bookstores in areas where you'll be getting publicity and explain when and why they should have your book in stock. One writer who went this route was initially afraid that bookstore managers would hang up on her, but in fact they were grateful for her calls and—more important—they did arrange to have copies of her book on sale when she was in town.
- In the unhappy event that your book goes out of print, you can revive it through *The Buckley-Little Catalogue*. Created by William F. Buckley, Jr. (the novelist, editor and talk show host) and Stuart Little (formerly editor of the *Authors Guild Bulletin*), the catalog lets booksellers, librarians and individuals order out-of-print books from the people who wrote them. All you need to do is lay in a supply of copies (negotiate a price when your publisher decides to remainder its stock), write a brief description of your book (remember to stress the benefits it offers readers) and pay a fee to get it included

(for additional fees, the catalog company will stock, ship and/or advertise your book; see "Resources"—"Tools" if you want the details).

* You can start fresh. Books get second lives all the time. Look, for instance, at remainder dealers, who buy publishers' overstock in bulk at below-cost prices, offer readers a bargain and sometimes sell so many copies of a particular title that they wind up reprinting it over and over again. Or consider the story of Feenie Ziner's *A Full House*, about her experiences as the mother of triplets. When Norton gave up on the book, Ziner resold it to The Center for the Study of Multiple Birth, which brought out a charming paperback edition.

Instead of finding a new publisher, as Ziner did and writers often do, you may decide to *become* your book's new publisher. Consult your lawyer, or your agent if you have one, about severing your current publishing ties and see the next section for guidance on how to proceed after that.

The Self-Publishing Option

✳   ✳   ✳

The Case for Doing It Yourself
OR
Don't Skip This Chapter Unless You're Willing to Let Prejudice Stand Between You and What May Be Your Best Destiny

A DEMONSTRABLY FALSE series of assumptions keeps a great many writers from seriously considering self-publishing, which is a shame because many of them could earn more money and have more fun if they brought out their own work. Compounded by one part ignorance, one part laziness and one part unadulterated snobbery, the chain of thought might be summarized as follows: I am a writer; a writer's job is to express ideas, images and information in words; after a writer has done this job, noncreative types should pronounce it good and take it over, leaving the writer free to write some more.

At first glance, the argument seems logical enough, but closer examination reveals a fatal flaw. If expression is a writer's goal, why is a publisher necessary? Why, indeed, is anything necessary besides a desk drawer big enough to hold completed manuscripts?

The answer, of course, is that expression is really only a preliminary goal, a necessary first step toward the ultimate end of writing, which is communication.

Once you accept the fact that when you write you want to communicate, you'll realize three things: (1) you need people to communicate with; (2) you're most likely to communicate effectively with people who'll be receptive to your writing's particular style and substance; and (3) finding those people is the only way to fulfill your role as a writer.

In theory, you can get a publishing company to track your audience down for you; in practice, though, busy professionals handling masses of titles are not likely to concentrate on drawing receptive readers to yours. Thus, if you want to reach as many people as possible you'll have to plan selling campaigns on your own (and maybe execute them on your own as well) whether you're self-published or conventionally published. Those who self-publish, however, will be spared one burden: they won't have to start by putting their ideas across to a publisher with an impulse to ignore them.

Looked at in this light, do-it-yourself publishing may seem a more attractive alternative than it used to. Writers who are beginning to like the idea but who are not yet convinced that they'll be able to implement it should read the next two chapters to resolve their doubts one way or the other. And writers who are troubled by the always sticky matter of money may ease their minds with the following string of comparisons.

Self-publishers pay to have their work issued. Writers who use vanity presses pay to have their work issued (though they pay much more and get much less; see "Openings"). But the group that pays the highest price of all is composed of the men and women who write bestselling books for conventional publishing houses. True, these writers don't pay to begin with. But the advances they receive can sometimes be matched by self-publishers (see "Front-end Funding"). And besides, by the time successful books go out of print at a major house, their authors will have repaid the publisher many times over, not only for their advances but also for all expenses, through the portion of their profits that the firm keeps for itself.

Therefore? Therefore, who pays what and when and to whom is not, by itself, a useful gauge of publishing worth.

Instead of allowing yourself to be diverted by quibbles about front money or picturesque notions of the cloistered literary life, why not confront the decision to self-publish by examining self-publishing's advantages, as sketched below, to see how well they would blend with both your work and your character?

Advantages

Quality Control. Self-publishing is often the only way to produce a book or periodical that will live up to your personal standards.

Photographer Bob Adelman began putting his own books out when he found that conventional houses wouldn't or couldn't meet his specifications for design and reproduction. Working closely with designers, printers and journalists whose achievements he knew and admired, Adelman put together a book he's proud of. Called *Street Smart: Adventures from the Lives of Children*, it's an unusually handsome volume.

Ron Jones, motivated by educational rather than aesthetic considerations, turned to self-publishing because he and several of his fellow teachers thought conventionally published textbooks inadequate. "During the six years I taught in city and country schools," Jones explained, "no one ever stole a textbook, and I think I know why. Every year textbooks pop out of the publishers' ovens with new covers and new titles, but the content is always the same. They encourage verbal skills and deductive paths of logic. They avoid the use of intuition, imagination, contemplation and direct action as problem-solving tools."

Jones and a loose confederation of parents and teachers decided to publish a "de-school primer" called *Zephyros* to stimulate thousands of students through projects like "Make Your Own Religion" or "Pretend You Are a Building." At a regulation-model textbook house, where editors must meticulously tailor their books for adoption by school boards, *Zephyros'* unorthodox learning experiences would have been either drastically modified or totally scrapped.

Freedom of Form. Despite the honored place of pamphlets in American history, publishers nowadays don't print them. They don't print narrative poems much, either, or novellas or nonfiction that's longer than a normal magazine article but shorter than a normal book.

If you have something important to say that can best be expressed in 15,000 words, one of two things is apt to happen: a publishing firm will buy your manuscript, in which case you'll be asked to pad it to 25,000 words (so it can count as a book) or to cut it in half (so it will fit into a standard magazine format); or you'll decide to bring it out yourself, in which case you can leave it at the length that suits it.

Self-publishers are free to vary physical dimensions other than length (small commercial firms have produced books with the dimensions of cigarette packs and Frisbees, among other things). And they are free, as well, to demarcate new literary boundaries. Tom Montag, whose review journal, *Margins*, offered incisive observations of the small press–little magazine scene, noted not long ago that hybrid crosses between books and periodicals were issuing from little literary publishing houses.

Following the lead of these innovative publishers, a self-publisher can put out magazines that resemble books because they're aesthetically unified, or books that resemble magazines because they're issued serially, or, for that matter, works of prose, poetry or pictures like nothing ever seen before on earth. In short, when self-publishing authors want to break old publishing molds and construct new ones, nobody can stop them.

Tangible Sources of Satisfaction. When a women's writing workshop began planning to self-publish an anthology of members' work and circulate it within the group, a lot of potential contributors got worried. With their poems and stories already in print, they thought, they'd be tempted to slack off, and then they'd never write anything worth offering an outside audience.

As things turned out, the anthology did nothing to depress creativity; on the contrary, it stimulated a surge of new composition. Having seen their words clothed in the dignity of bound and printed pages, the workshop writers found their energies fueled by pride. They'd picked the printer, after all, and checked galleys for typos and roughed out the cover and glued the binding on, and now they had a professional-looking edition to show for their efforts. In these pushbutton times, the pleasures of physical achievement are reserved mainly for children, but self-publishers, along with a handful of other adults who work with their hands building things they love, are privileged to share the I-made-it-myself elation.

Reader Response. Unlike a writer whose book circulates in the hands of a publishing company's sales force, self-publishing authors often deal face to face with wholesalers, retailers and members of the reading public, and thus create innumerable opportunities to converse about their work with people who have actually read it. When feedback from readers is favorable, it's a delight; and when it's unfavorable, it may still be instructive.

Ease of Entry. No preparatory rigmarole is required when you publish your own writing. You don't have to sell anyone on its merits until it's printed, and you don't have to know more about how to get it printed or about how to sell it when the time comes than you can learn from this book (in fact, many people who started out knowing far less than it explains have done just fine).

Furthermore, you can edge into self-publishing by degrees, without ever making a major commitment before hard evidence shows that the move will be wise. Suppose, for example, that you've written *The Complete Small-Engine Repair Manual*. With a modest cash outlay, you can get 1,000 copies printed up to offer local hardware stores, department stores and bookstores on consignment, and to retail personally at nearby vocational schools and continuing-education centers. Then, if those markets work well, you can go back to press, begin to experiment with mail orders and wholesale distribution over a wide geographical area and perhaps wind up selling hundreds of times as many copies as there were in your original print order.

Or suppose (to frame another example drawn from actual experience) that you've just moved to the Ozarks and that you want to share observations on your new homeland with friends you've left behind. If you begin by mimeographing reports to them, and if they pass your pieces on to friends and acquaintances of theirs, and if the chain continues to lengthen, you will have founded a newsletter or a magazine before long, and developed a mailing list that more scientific periodical publishers will envy.

Camaraderie. One of the nicest side effects of self-publishing is friendship. People working together toward a common goal often forge close personal ties, and self-publishing writers can convene as big a group of collaborators as they like. Conventional houses react badly to having more than two people on the other side of a publishing contract (both profits and decision-making powers will, they fear, be spread too wide and thin). But works produced in concert do succeed when self-publishers are in charge; consider, by way of shining example, the *Whole Earth* catalogs.

The men and women who labor along with a self-publisher on a particular project aren't the only ones who offer aid, comfort and affection, however. Members of the country's vast small-publisher network may also be ready to help. Many small publishers are generous with advice and assistance, and coming to know them by joining their associations frequently means coming to like them as well.

Longevity. Large, established, book-publishing firms, which must make room in their catalogs for hundreds of new titles twice a year, can't afford to keep a book in circulation for more than a few months unless its initial rate of sale is impressive. The life span of articles in established magazines is even more severely limited; one month after the March issue comes out, it's off the stands, no matter how many copies remain unsold or how many people are just now beginning to show an interest in the piece you wrote for it.

By contrast, a self-published work can be granted the gift of time, and with time it may well attract a following. Many books that make no splash when they're released become profitable over the years as appreciative readers begin to wield the single most powerful selling tool any publishing company ever has: word of mouth. And once word of mouth begins to operate, it's relatively simple for self-publishers to capitalize on it. When you're personally involved with your readers, you can get their names and the names of their interested acquaintances onto a mailing list that will give you a ready-made market not only for further sales of things you've already written but for all your future writing projects as well.

Natural Candidates

If a major publishing house with close ties to influential media people is going to give your book its bigbook treatment, then you will probably do better under its auspices than you would on your own. In other circumstances, it's not so easy to decide whether conventional publishing will be a better bet than self-publishing or vice versa.

As if to underline the availability of both self- and conventional publishing options for a wide variety of projects, dozens of writers have always moved back and forth between the two systems. Historically, the roster of self-publishers has included many names that now appear under publishing's most prestigious imprints. (Thomas Paine, William Blake, Washington Irving, Percy Bysshe Shelley, James Fenimore Cooper, Edgar Allan Poe, Walt Whitman, Mary Baker Eddy and Mark Twain are among those cited by Bill Henderson in his classic *Publish-It-Yourself Handbook*.) And crossovers continue in present times.

Richard Weiner, for instance, originally sold his book *Professional's Guide to Public Relations Services* to one of the largest publishing houses on the East Coast but decided to publish it himself when he found the second edition badly dated and the publishing firm reluctant to replace it with a third.

Conversely, Maggy Simony began by self-publishing three

volumes of *Traveler's Reading Guides,* which list and describe fiction and nonfiction about anywhere anyone might be going. Then, after getting excellent reviews in library media and write-ups in travel and consumer publications (including *The New York Times*), she sold rights to Facts on File, which brought out an 800-page, one-volume edition that also became available through the Book-of-the-Month Club and the Quality Paperback Book Club.

It's by no means unusual for a major house to pick up a proven self-published work; in fact, self-publishers who are tired of business aggravations and eager to devote themselves full time to new writing projects frequently go after bids from conventional houses once their books are launched—and get them. Any self-publisher who makes a deal with a big firm, though, ought to be represented by a lawyer who's thoroughly familiar with the publishing industry and who's a bit of a scrapper besides.

But if it's true that almost anything a commercial company can publish (and some things it can't) can be self-published instead, it's also true that two classes of writing are particularly well suited to the self-publishing process:

* Works that are clearly of interest to at least one well-defined, relatively large, easy-to-reach audience (because a single individual can market them as well as an established firm, and if you do it yourself you get to keep all the profits).
* Works that figure to interest a very small group of readers, at least to begin with (because established firms aren't likely to take them on, and if they do, they'll probably let them die in short order without ever giving them a decent chance to live).

Whether self-publishers sell hundreds of copies or hundreds of thousands of copies will depend on their level of skill with words and with business arrangements, as well as on what it is that they've written. Diverse kinds of material offer good self-publishing potential across a wide sales spectrum, though. For instance:

Need-to-Know Pieces. In this expensive era, factory outlet stores attract financially strapped consumers, and Joan Bird of Oradell, New Jersey, decided several years ago to publish a directory of the ones near her home. Her first edition—500 copies of a thirty-two-page pamphlet—sold out within the week, thanks in large part to coverage Bird had arranged with a local newspaper. Then she began to publish annual *Factory Outlet Shopping Guides* for New Jersey, New York, eastern Pennsylvania, New England, the District of Columbia, Virginia, Delaware and Maryland as well as a newsletter that updated the *Guides* eight times a year.

Seizing on the need for different kinds of information, John Muir sold roughly a million copies of the self-published *How to Keep Your Volkswagen Alive,* while other writers have produced substantial profits with such items as a newsletter describing job openings in the federal government, a brochure explaining how to get rid of groundhogs and a book analyzing the management of paperwork.

Local Stories. When the locality in question is a region and the self-published work is a full-size book or periodical, sales may easily mount into the high thousands (regional books pay the rent for a good many commercial publishers). But even if both the area and the self-publishing project are defined by more modest limits, success is still possible, as witness the experience of F. Alan Shirk. A lifelong resident of Berks County, Pennsylvania, he compiled a brief, illustrated hometown history he called *The Colonial Berks Sampler* and sold it by placing coupon ads in local newspapers and sending complimentary copies together with order blanks to local schools, libraries and civic organizations.

Scholarly Papers and Classroom Texts. Circulating ideas and information is essential in academia, but teachers who write or compile materials for distribution to their colleagues or their students can't rely on publishing houses to produce a book that a few hundred people figure to read. Fortunately, though teachers' markets may be small, they are solid. Thus, by computing sales accurately in advance, self-publishing scholars can arrange to keep costs down to the point where they'll surely be matched by revenues.

Special-Interest Literature. Clem Labine sells his *Old-House Journal* to 100,000 subscribers. Ruth Portis, who self-published "Step by Step Beadstringing—A Complete, Illustrated, Professional Approach," sold thousands of copies partly through the Jeweler's Book Club, the Gemological Society of America and catalogs from jewelry supply companies. Glen C. Ellenbogen, author/publisher of the satirical *Journal of Polymorphous Perversity,* made a 3,300-copy bulk sale to Smith, Kline & French Laboratories, which wanted to distribute an issue featuring its pharmaceutical products (eventually, by the way, he also made a paperback sale to Ballantine, which brought out a collection of "Readings from the *Journal of Polymorphous Perversity*" called *Oral Sadism and the Vegetarian Personality*).

Like Labine, Portis and Ellenbogen, hundreds of other self-publishers have tapped into specialized markets with gratifying consequences.

If what you've written will serve a special-interest audience, you may find it relatively easy to get financial help when you put on your publisher's hat. But even if you bear all initial expenses yourself, you shouldn't be out of pocket for long, and you should reap major rewards in the form of response quite quickly when you serve a public that's hungry for word of its avocational enthusiasms.

Novels, Short Fiction and Poems. Because more fiction and poetry seems to be written each year than existing companies of any size can handle, some novelists and poets see no alternative but to self-publish. Whether last resort or first choice, self-publishing in this area can have thoroughly agreeable results.

Harriet Herman started out with a 1,000-copy print order

when she published the first edition of *The Forest Princess*, her fairy tale about a heroine instead of a hero. Within two months she'd sold every book she had. A second printing of 2,000 copies sold out within a year, and a third (3,000 copies) followed suit. Herman then reported in the magazine *The Self-Publishing Writer* that she was planning a fourth edition of *The Forest Princess* (which she also produced and showed on television as a filmstrip); she's self-published a sequel; and she sold United Kingdom rights to both books to a British publishing firm.

Robert Lane ended up with even more overseas sales. His novel about a schizophrenic child is called *A Solitary Dance* and was published originally by Serrell & Simons (i.e., Bob and his wife, Mary). They then sold rights to Reader's Digest Condensed Books, New American Library's Signet paperback line, several foreign publishers and a couple of book clubs. At last count, more than two million copies of *A Solitary Dance* were in print in sixteen countries and nine languages.

Activist Arguments. In nonmilitary battles, the call to arms is often sounded by words on paper, which makes newsletters, pamphlets and magazines perennially popular formats for rallying supporters around a multiplicity of causes.

Not long ago, a small North Carolina collective of women who called themselves Lollipop and who shared Harriet Herman's concern with nonsexist children's literature successfully self-published a book called *Exactly Like Me*. At about the same time, the Corporate Action Program—a Washington, DC, group with "an abiding faith in the power of people to shape their own destinies, and the belief that institutions should be servants, not masters, of our social needs and goals"—offered the public its *Corporate Action Guide*; and residents of major metropolitan areas began founding papers to spread the word about apartment dwellers' rights.

Through advertising, subsidies from interested organizations or sales revenues, activist self-publishers may manage to cover expenses and perhaps to produce profits as well. But most writers who aim to change the world with their words are prepared to look elsewhere for economic sustenance. What they want from publishing is the chance to deliver a message of importance to an audience of responsive individuals, wherever they are and whatever their numbers.

If self-publishing did not already exist, such motives might suffice to create it. As matters stand, though, the option is open to all and clearly to be preferred by a good many writers for a variety of kinds of writing. Moreover, as the chapters that follow will show, it's becoming easier to exercise with every passing day.

A Complete Starter Kit of Self-Publishing Skills
With Applications for Anybody's Promotional Materials

TAKE A SIMPLE task like tying shoelaces, write out step-by-step instructions for a person who's never done it before, and the response you'll get will be, Thanks just the same but it sounds awfully complicated and I think I'll stick to moccasins.

Something similar happens when beginners read up on self-publishing. As with tying shoelaces, though, the steps involved in producing what you've written are much simpler than they sound and it's easy to get the hang of them if you just leap fearlessly into action; any mistakes you make will probably be both correctable and instructive, and they will certainly not be fatal.

Skeptics may protest that self-publishing requires mastery not of one new activity, but of a whole series of unfamiliar processes. And that's quite true. It's equally true, however, that you don't have to handle any or all of these processes completely alone. Free guidance is available (read on); paid help is not hard to find (see "Tools" and "People, Places and Programs" in this section's "Resources"); and, as you progress through production, you can effect any number of trade-offs between expenditures of your time and energy, on one side of the equation, and of money to procure professionals' services, on the other.

In fact, this chapter assumes that you'll get professional help at various points. Together with selections from "Resources," it will tell you as much as you want to know about how to create a bound book, a pamphlet, a periodical or—please note—an effective piece of promotional material for whatever you write, no matter who's publishing it. But by itself, what it will teach you is how to master those operations that any amateur can handle with a minor investment in equipment and no more than a modicum of background information.

Editing

Most writers get so heartily sick of reworking their words that they can barely get their eyes and minds to focus on the pages when the time comes to edit their manuscripts. In such a situation, it makes sense to look around for someone else who could do the job, but many self-publishing writers don't bother. Instead, they simply skip the editing stage, sometimes (1) because they believe it's of little value, sometimes (2) because they're afraid of having their work distorted and sometimes (3) because they don't know how to find a good editor.

Points one and two are debatable, although every piece of writing can benefit from sensible editing (many will be significantly improved) and good editors don't distort (on the contrary, they clarify and strengthen). If you tend to agree and decide to look for an editor who'd be right for your work, you might start by finding out who edited books you admire and asking them if they'd do yours (call or write the publishers' publicity departments to get names if the books don't supply internal evidence). In the event that the editors can't afford the time or you can't afford their fee, perhaps they'll suggest colleagues you might contact.

Alternatively, you can choose a freelance editor from those who are listed in *Literary Market Place* or enrolled as members of the Editorial Freelancers Association. See this section's "Resources" and ask for references and samples before you make a commitment.

Copy-editing

The same approaches should suffice to find a good copy editor, but because copy-editing demands an entirely different mental set than writing, even authors who've grown blind to the import of their work can copy-edit for themselves.

To copy-edit a manuscript (as the second chapter of "The Sale and Its Sequels" shows), you must make sure that it is correct and consistent fact by fact, word by word and even letter by letter; and the best way to do that is by following a copy-editing style manual (you should find at least one that's to your taste listed in "Resources"). On its simplest level, copy-editing style is what determines whether you use "blond" rather than "blonde," and no matter how complicated its prescriptions get, style's function is simply to ensure consistency in the interest of clarity.

Descriptions as well as spelling ought to be consistent throughout a manuscript (don't drive your readers to distraction by presenting them with a character who's dainty and petite on page 16 and a strapping Amazon on page 92), and what you choose to stick to matters less than choosing to stick to something.

If you imagine, all the while you're copy-editing, that your manuscript is the work of a slipshod and possibly feeble-minded soul, you'll find it easy to adopt the most effective copy-editing attitude: suspicion. Go slowly and question everything: is Wales correctly described as a peninsula; could anyone really fly to Rome in daylight all the way; does that say "dilemmma"; is "accurrate" spelled right; doesn't that plural verb refer back to a singular subject; and wouldn't the thought be clearer if it were presented in two sentences rather than one?

Though a careful copy editor will check all proper nouns, all facts (even fiction has them) and all words that look the slightest bit odd, the most important statements to verify are those that might lead to legal difficulties. If you are writing anything that is derogatory and/or untrue about real, living people or functioning businesses you may face a libel suit or a suit for invasion of privacy. Additional legal pitfalls open up when writers quote too extensively from other people's material, or when they print matter that might be adjudged obscene. Moreover, a new legal danger zone has arisen as a result of our culture's increasing emphasis on self-help; a reader with vertigo who falls off a branch and is seriously hurt while following the advice in your "Blueprints for a Treehouse" may think there are grounds to sue you.

This last trouble spot is the hardest to deal with, because no nontechnical guides on the subject exist yet, but common sense may be of some help (don't assume that your readers will realize they should unplug the toaster before they start fiddling with its innards, for example; or that they'll think to consult their doctors before embarking on a strenuous diet or exercise program). On the other fronts listed, your best course is to get hold of one of the manuals on literary property mentioned in "Resources"; after you've read that sort of guide you'll know better whether you need to call in a lawyer or take any other measures to protect yourself from legal action. In addition, as attorney Harriet F. Pilpel points out, you'd be wise always to remember that even those people who win lawsuits find litigation expensive and aggravating, which means it's sound policy to recast all potentially dangerous material in your manuscript unless doing so involves violating your principles.

Mark all changes, no matter what their purpose, with the standard proofreading symbols you'll find in your dictionary. And when your work is as correct, consistent and clear as you can make it, remember to claim your own legal rights and the status your work deserves in the eyes of librarians, booksellers and reviewers by registering your copyright and applying for a Library of Congress Catalog Number and an ISBN or ISSN. See "Resources," pages 282–84, for details on what forms to send for, and send for them early on.

Design

What your work looks like will have a good deal to do with how it's received. If it's sloppy or jumbled, if the body type is too small to read easily or the headings are so big and black that—no matter what they say—they always seem to be threats, then the power of your carefully assembled words will be vitiated.

Art school students and freelance or moonlighting book and periodical designers can help you come up with a format that will fit your work both physically and spiritually (the students, because they're seeking experience, will charge less). And a printer who has an art department or a flair for design may also be able to supply good advice. But unartistic authors can handle design well on their own so long as they keep it standard and simple.

The first standard to adhere to is that of page size. You'll save money by choosing the dimensions both paper companies and printers are accustomed to working with. For books and pamphlets, this generally means a page that's roughly 5½ by 8½ inches; and for magazines and newsletters, one that's 8½ by 11 inches. Check with printers you're considering to see exactly what sizes their equipment handles most economically.

Having chosen a size for your page, you then must decide on margins (use your own books or magazines as models, and remember that unless the bottom margin is larger than the top your page will look droopy) and on how to arrange text, heads, artwork and white space effectively within them. A smattering of technical terms should enable you to move comfortably through these decision-making points and those that will arise later:

Body type: type that's used for text rather than for headings (i.e., titles). Body type is measured in points (which are defined below) from the top of a letter like *h* to the bottom of a letter like *p*—that is, from the highest to the lowest extremities of the alphabet in a particular typeface.

Display type: type that's used for headings (or "heads") rather than for text; also measured in points.

Justification: the spacing of a line of type so that it will extend fully to both right- and left-hand margins. When lines of type do not extend to meet the right-hand margin, the copy is *ragged right*.

Layout: a plan, on paper, that shows how text, titles, artwork and all the other elements of a work to be printed should be arranged.

Leading: the space between lines of type (the term was coined in the days when printers worked with lead type and had to insert strips of lead above and below lines of text to create space between them).

Letter space: logically enough, the space between the letters of a word. Letter spaces can be adjusted to make lines slightly longer or shorter than they normally would be and are therefore useful for justification, but letter-spaced words tend to look funny. Ask to see samples before you agree to have a typesetter letter-space your work.

Pica: the printer's unit of measurement. A pica equals approximately one-sixth of an inch and is used for expressing column widths and other important dimensions of a page.

Points: divisions of the pica (12 points = 1 pica), used to express such things as body-type sizes and amounts of leading. Points are symbolized by a mark that looks like a straight, single quotation mark.

Running heads: the titles that are repeated at the top of book or periodical pages.

Typeface: a particular design of type. Each face has a name (like Helvetica or Bodoni Book) and consists of all capital and lower-case letters and a full range of numbers and punctuation marks in a variety of point sizes. Italic and boldface variations on any given face are generally available and are called Helvetica (or whatever) itals or bold for short.

Word space: just what it says, and adjustable within narrow limits to justify columns of text or to squeeze or extend headlines.

Text

Given a variety of typefaces to choose from, it's possible to select one that will make a particular manuscript fit into a particular number of pages. Copy-fitting techniques depend on simple arithmetic and are not hard to learn, but using them to good purpose requires a thorough knowledge of typography.

For a first self-publishing venture, therefore, you might as well not worry about making your manuscript into a printed work of a preordained size. If you're using a typesetter and/or a printer, find a book or periodical you'd like your work to resemble and ask for advice on specifications (or, in the trade jargon, specs). Chances are, a standard point size—10-point is usual for books, and 9- or 10-point will work nicely for newsletters and magazines—in a standard face like Baskerville or Times Roman with a standard 2 points of leading will serve you well. And if you're using typewriter type, all you have to decide is when to begin hitting the keys (see this chapter's "Typesetting" section). Those who find at the finish that they need a few extra pages to satisfy the requirements of the printing press can add material and/or blank sheets front and back.

Heads

Specs for display type are somewhat harder to arrive at than specs for body copy, but one easy solution is to use a headline face with the same name your body typeface has. On more difficult choices, your printer can advise, and your typesetter will be happy not only to make suggestions but to do the work.

Again, a printed work that you admire will make a fine model, and you can't go far wrong by sticking with a conventional face and simply varying its size to indicate relative importance (36- or 30-point might, for instance, be perfect for part titles, with 30- or 24-point chapter heads and 18- or 14-point for the subheads within chapters).

The largest display type that you use will probably appear on your cover. Don't be afraid to be splashy. If you design the front of your book as if it were a billboard, you'll stand your best chance of doing justice to what's inside.

Artwork

For some self-publishers, artwork is an integral part of the project; others want pictures to illustrate or to decorate, and sometimes they have trouble finding good ones. If you're in this second category, try the public relations departments of large organizations involved with work that's relevant to your subject (what they supply will be free); the sources of noncopyrighted drawings available in art supply shops (see "Tools" in "Resources"); appropriate governmental agencies (through their PR departments); and the picture sources listed in *LMP*.

Be sure to get permission in writing to use their pictures from people you or other individuals photograph. Perhaps you can copy the release form your local newspaper uses.

Layout

Three basic principles will stand amateur designers in good stead as they begin their first layouts: (1) The simpler the better; symmetrical and centered arrangements pose the fewest problems. (2) The fundamental unit of design is the spread—or pair of facing pages that the reader's eyes take in with a single glance. (3) White space (i.e., blank space) is important; if you don't leave enough of it or you don't arrange it well, you'll end up with dense, uninviting pages.

By drawing on published books or magazines for models (and perhaps also using some of the guides listed in "Resources"), beginners can construct layouts that range from serviceable to handsome. If you're working with straight text, you'll have only a few questions to answer. How much space should chapter heads get (for instance), or should each article start on a new page, and what should the running heads look like? After you've solved such problems, all you'll have to do is fill each succeeding page with text until it's time to repeat the opening-page format once again.

Some writers now handle page makeup with the help of software. Others stick with scissors and rubber cement, which they use to create a dry run called a dummy (see below). Don't slather the paste on, though, until, through trial and error, you've found a system of juxtaposing textual and visual elements that pleases your eye and works all the way through your book, periodical or promotional piece.

While you're sketching your layout you may be confronted with text that's too long or too short and pictures that are too big or too little. Almost any text can be cut (developing the knack of cutting copy so that no scars show is itself a rewarding activity) and pictures are easy to adjust. If they're the wrong size for the space you want them to occupy, they can usually be cropped and/or inexpensively enlarged or reduced.

For scaling pictures, there's a beautifully simple method: draw a rectangle exactly the same size as the picture you have; then draw a diagonal line across it from bottom left to top right and mark off the dimension you must satisfy on one side (i.e., if your column width is 3¼ inches and you want the picture to fit into one column, put your mark 3¼ inches from the left on the bottom of your rectangle); finally, draw a line from this mark to the point where it meets the diagonal and measure it. The figure you get is the height your picture will be when its width is 3¼ inches.

Black-and-white line drawings will reproduce as is. So will stick-on decorative borders and rules of assorted sizes (which are available on tape and used to create boxed copy, underlined heads and the like); art supply stores stock both. Photographs, however, must be processed for the press, and you should send yours out to be turned into prints called veloxes that offset presses can handle. Your printer can advise you on specifications, and you can ask the printer (or a friendly typesetter, designer or locally based publisher) for advice on what velox house to patronize. Whichever one you choose will also be able to enlarge or reduce your black-and-white line art.

Process every piece of artwork and insert it in its proper

place, so that you can really see how your pages will look and correct miscalculations if necessary.

When your layout is done and pictures are under control, stop for a minute and consider whether using one extra color would be desirable. Printing a headline in red, say, or tinting a picture or the background of a text block with a screen of color is a relatively cheap way to add life and interest to your pages. Those who want to try it should ask their printers for information about the cost.

Typesetting

Until recently, most printing consisted of direct impressions made by inked metal type on paper, and if you didn't own any metal type or any of the cumbersome machinery needed for using it, you had no choice but to take your manuscript to people who did and pay them. Today, though, offset printing—which utilizes a photographic plate—is abundantly available, with the result that what a camera sees as type can now function as type. The popularity of offset printing is responsible for flourishing new typesetting processes that also involve cameras (and laser beams and chemicals and computers), and—more important for our purposes—it enables everyone who wants work printed to set type themselves.

For full explanations of all printing and typesetting processes, turn to "Resources." To see whether you'd rather hire a typesetter or become one, read the discussion that follows.

Professional Typesetting

Although a number of publishing companies have begun using computerized equipment of their own to set type, most still hire outside typesetters; so ask nearby publishers of good but not expensive-looking books or periodicals which compositors they use and whether they'd recommend that you use them too, and then call to get estimates from at least three firms (be prepared for enormous variations—like from $7 per page to many times that—and remember that estimates can be accurate only if they're based on knowledge of the whole job).

Before you hire anybody, examine samples and references; look for evidence of pride in the work that the typesetter does; ask for an explanation of technical capabilities (if you've composed on a computer, make sure to find out whether the typesetter's equipment can make use of your floppy discs); establish clearly who's going to pay for correcting the compositor's errors and who'll pay for changes; and think twice if a prospective typesetter demands full payment in advance.

One-third up front, one-third on delivery of the job and one-third after final corrections have been made is a reasonable system for payment. At some companies, the manager may be willing to let an employee make extra money by using the typesetting equipment for personal clients after hours, in which case you could get professional-looking copy fairly cheap.

To minimize costly mistakes, make sure that the manuscript you send a typesetter is clear in every detail and that you have come to a firm agreement on all specs (should copy be justified; should heads be centered; how much space between heads and body copy; how much between words and letters?).

At the manuscript stage, mark all corrections on the manuscript itself, because that's what typesetters will be looking at as they keyboard; but later, when you note errors on galley proofs, you should indicate corrections in the galleys' margins, since they'll deal now only with lines that need to be changed. Don't forget to note which are the printer's (i.e., typesetter's) errors; mark them PE, so you won't be charged for those corrections.

The farther along you get in production, the more expensive changes become (although making a change on your original manuscript will cost you nothing, changes on galleys may run roughly $1 apiece, and your costs can mount rapidly up into the hundreds of dollars once your material gets on press). So proofread carefully and consider asking a friend to help; one of you can read aloud from the manuscript, noting punctuation and indentations and spaces, while the other follows along on the galleys, marking and correcting mistakes.

Do-It-Yourself Typesetting

Get hold of a computer, a word-processing program and a letter quality printer or—preferably—a laser printer, and you have the means to set type for your own work.

"If you're really serious about your manuscript and you want to do it over and over and you want to get it exactly right, the computer will help you," said Alvin Toffler, author of *Future Shock* and *The Third Wave*, in a conversation with novelist Gay Courter, who wrote a bestseller, *The Midwife*, on an IBM machine; Courter's own experience and reports from many other writers she queried bear Toffler out.

The other big advantage of composing on a computer is that you can use what you produce as camera-ready copy. Type created by a daisy-wheel printer will look most professional when it's reduced in size by the printer (who will almost always shrink it for you at no extra charge), so it's wise to plan margins and spacing with reductions in mind. Type created by a laser printer will be fine as is.

Even if you don't want to handle typesetting, though, using a word processor or a word-processing computer program to produce your text can still save you time and money during the production phase of the self-publishing process, because the discs your text will be stored on can be linked to compatible photo-composition machines, which can then set type without the extra round of keyboarding and proofreading that would be necessary if text had been submitted to the typesetter on paper.

Paste-up

"Paste-up" is both a verb and a noun. You are engaged in pasting up when you do a paste-up (which, if it is final, or camera-ready,

A Complete Starter Kit of Self-Publishing Skills 171

is also called a mechanical); and to perform the task and produce the result you'll need a small supply of new mental and physical equipment.

The mental equipment consists of a rudimentary understanding of what role paste-ups fulfill in production. Essentially, a paste-up functions as a photographer's model, and it should be designed to pose for a camera that registers all blacks and all whites, that isn't likely to pick up other colors well and that can't see light blue at all. In other words, it should be composed of black elements and white elements positioned exactly as you want them to appear in their portrait and accompanied by notes and guidelines in light blue for your use and the printer's.

As for physical equipment, what follows is a bare-minimums list. Any clerk in an art supply store will be happy to suggest other things you can buy.

> Paste-up boards (your printer may supply them free or sell them cheap, or you can buy white paper or Bristol board that's big enough to accommodate a spread).
> 1 pad of tissues the size of your page or your spread.
> 1 pot of rubber cement with an adjustable brush.
> Rubber-cement thinner.
> 1 roll of white tape; 1 roll of transparent tape; 1 double dispenser.
> 1 box of single-edged razor blades.
> 1 metal pica ruler, 12 inches long or longer.
> 1 good-quality 18-inch metal T-square.
> 1 plastic triangle, as high as your page is high, and preferably tinted.
> 1 can of spray fixative.
> 1 box of non-repro blue pencils.
> Scissors.
> A drawing board, preferably with a metal edge, or a flat, rectangular working surface with a thick, straight side on which to anchor your T-square (drawing tables and light tables make it easier to do a professional-looking paste-up, but they're not essential).

The Dummy

Behind every good mechanical there's the dress rehearsal known as the dummy, and it should be pasted up from galley proofs (when a typesetter is involved) or from an extra copy of finished work that you've set yourself. Writers who use professional typesetters should get three sets of galleys and dispose of them as follows:

1. Proofread and return one set with all corrections marked.
2. Keep one set as a master; mark all corrections on it too, and flag those that mean changes in line counts (when the two words that are missing from paragraph 7 are inserted, the paragraph will number ten lines instead of nine, and you'll have to allow for the extra line in arranging your copy).
3. Cut one set up for the dummy.

Writers who've typed their own text can get by with one extra copy, as long as they too proofread carefully and note all line-count changes that will result from correcting errors.

With an ordinary pen or a felt-tip marker, write the number of each galley or typed page on every sheet of cut-up copy, so that after you've moved things around to fit your layout scheme, you'll know where each piece came from. Then, with the scissors, trim the text closely on all four sides, and assemble and trim extra copies of your layout's other elements as well (including artwork, headings and borders).

Now, using your T-square as a horizontal guideline and setting your triangle on it to form a true vertical, position a piece of your paste-up paper on your working surface so that it's straight, tape it down at the corners and, using a blue pencil, draw lines to show the dimensions of your page and its internal margins (remembering to allow for reduction if that's part of your plan).

Finally, pick up whatever goes on the pages in front of you and apply generous amounts of rubber cement to the back of each element in turn (using too little paste can make copy stick before you've had a chance to position it correctly, but using too much will simply result in spillovers that will lift off easily as soon as they're dry; buy a rubber-cement pickup in your art supply store or make one out of a big, dried blob of the stuff). Use your T-square and your triangle to check alignments, and when everything's straight, press down and move on.

Precision is important in making a dummy because you'll want to know now if chapter three is going to end with half a line on the top of page 46 (cut something from the final paragraph) or if you'll need a large picture, or two or three small ones, to fill up the page with the hang-gliding story on it. Whatever adjustments are necessary should be made before final paste-up; and where they involve substituting new copy for old, making them will be good practice for doing corrections on your mechanical.

Mistakes are easily remedied. Lift one corner of your paste-up board and slip a piece of cardboard behind it (so you won't scratch your working surface on the next step). Then cut the incorrect copy out with a single-edged razor blade (cut through the pasteup board but not into neighboring lines of type) and finally, lifting one corner of the board again, insert the new copy from the back. Because large copy blocks are easier to position than small ones, in the end it will be faster to use a corrected printout of a whole paragraph in order to change Mondsy to Monday in line 3 than it would be to try to substitute an *a* for the *s*.

In addition to showing text, heads and artwork in their proper places, and alerting you to trouble spots while fixing them is still simple, the dummy should show running heads and page numbers, which are also called folios; folios can be centered below the text or placed in outside corners; they are always odd on right-hand pages and even on the left (Page 1 is the right-hand page facing the inside front cover in a periodical and the first page of chapter one or the first part-title page in a book; pages that precede a book's page 1 should get Roman rather than Arabic numerals or not be numbered at all.) Examine current books to see the proper deployment of front and back matter, and be sure—for both books and periodicals—to insert your correct copyright notice in the place prescribed by the Copyright Office.

Once you've done your dummy and solved all the problems it revealed, you can repeat the paste-up process to construct mechanicals with your perfected printout or with the corrected repro proofs your typesetter has supplied. This time, though, when you rule your paste-up paper, add crop marks in the corners (any printer will show you how), cover the finished pages with tissue (so they'll stay clean), press down (so they'll stay stuck) and proofread one last time (or ask a friend to do that; a fresh pair of eyes will be helpful now). When you've done your final correction, you can cut the spreads apart; single pages are easier to transport.

Some typesetters and some printers will do paste-ups for you (in which case you should get two proofs of the pasted-up pages—one to proofread, correct and return, and one to keep as your master), and you can also hire designers to create your dummies, and paste-up people who freelance or are willing to moonlight to prepare your mechanicals. You'll save quite a lot, though, by doing the pasting yourself (the going rate for paste-up in New York is roughly $15 an hour) and, besides, the paste-up process comes highly recommended for reaping both tactile and psychological rewards and for cutting costs and saving time when you need flyers and other promotional materials (see "Managing Sales").

Printing and Binding

Although the laser printer, which you can own, can now substitute for the printing company that you can hire, most self-publishers contract printing out to commercial offset firms.

To select a printer, get suggestions from small publishers that issue handsome books or periodicals, and consult "Resources."

Then get at least three estimates. The price for 500 copies of a 200-page 5½- by 8½-inch book that's delivered camera-ready to be printed on 50-pound white paper may range widely, from something like $1,200 up to something like $2,400 or even more. Unit costs will decline, of course, as print orders rise, and if you're ordering 5,000 copies instead of 500, you may be able to get as good a price as an established publisher would.

Certainly, with a run of several thousand copies in mind, you can approach any printer who deals with established houses. Nowadays, even the largest publishers often print fewer than 5,000 copies of a book, and new technology lets the printing industry handle these short runs economically.

Whichever printers you approach, take your time deciding whom to hire; consider the quality of each printer's work (which you can judge from samples) and the printer's geographical proximity (which will make it possible for you to oversee quality on your particular job) as well as estimated costs in making your decision.

Most printers gladly offer suggestions about paper and ink and produce samples on request. Moreover, plenty of leads to information on these subjects appear in "Resources." You won't go wrong, though, if you pick 30-pound newsprint for a newspaper, 50- or 60-pound stock for a book and 80- to 100-pound paper for softcovers, and you're safe in letting your printer choose ink for you.

Similarly, although "Resources" will direct you to several manuals that deal with binding processes, you can rely on a carefully selected printer to handle binding for you. Just remember that when printers talk about "perfect" binding they're not promising flawless work; instead, they're referring to the popular method of gluing pages together inside a square-backed cover.

The one major decision that printers can't help you with is whether to produce a book in hard or soft covers. Until recently, binding some copies (though not all) in hardcover was mandatory, because reviewers wouldn't write about paperbacks and libraries wouldn't buy them. Today, however, many magazines and newspapers review paperback books right along with hardcovers, while librarians, who used to regard paperbacks as too flimsy to be suitable for circulation, have now figured out how to strengthen them by providing thick protective jackets or by sharing the wear and tear among several copies. Thus in both libraries and book review columns, the outside of a book is increasingly irrelevant. And softcovers are favored in most stores.

Managing Sales

IF THE BIG, established publishers—with all their money, personnel and media connections—have a tough time getting most of their books and periodicals off the ground, what chance do self-publishers have? Though you may be surprised to hear it, they have a good one, and it's getting better every day.

Self-publishing writers have three important advantages over writers who are conventionally published when it comes to selling their work.

* Self-publishers get closer to their readers. Conventionally published authors are separated from their audiences by two sets of people: the publishing-house staff members, whom the author relies on; and the booksellers, librarians, interviewers and reviewers, whom the staff members rely on.

   Working through double ranks of intermediaries is seldom the most efficient way to accomplish anything, and it's especially inefficient when the goal in view is person-to-person communication, as it is for writer and reader. It is a definite plus, therefore, to eliminate these intermediaries, particularly if you have the option of getting them to work for you when you want them—which self-publishers now do. (In fact, if their budgets permit, self-publishers can hire someone to assist with or execute almost every selling task they'll confront; see "Resources.")

* Self-publishing writers don't have to sell thousands of copies in order to have their work survive in print; editions numbering in the low hundreds make splendid economic sense so long as expenses can be kept down. As a rule, you can select a size for your first printing that will virtually ensure that you break even on it. And because a small first edition can serve as a trial run, later, and perhaps larger, print orders will be less risky.
* A self-publisher has only one person's work to promote—his or her own. Thus, the energy and time self-publishers can devote to selling far exceed what big publishers could offer. And unlike conventionally published bigbook authors (who'll be sent on grueling promotional tours to face interviewers who haven't read their books and booksellers who don't have copies in stock), self-publishers can go where they know they're wanted and arrange to create and to satisfy demand for their writing as they travel.

Instead of being exhausted and frustrated by promotional activities, self-publishers are generally stimulated. Selling makes a nice change of pace from writing (which you can do for only a part of the day anyway), and it's financially and psychologically rewarding besides. When he visited bookstores all across the country to spur sales of his novel *The Grassman* and a selection of books from his own press, Len Fulton found ample confirmation of the view that "a book's best salesman is its author, that one who shares all the continuity."

Fulton conceived of his trip as part of the logical publishing sequence, in which "the artist was the bicep, the publisher the forearm, the bookstore the fingers which touch out to what will be touched." His work, he felt, deserved "a full blood-run to the ends of the fingers"; doubtless yours deserves no less.

Because self-published writers and conventionally published writers should use essentially the same techniques in reaching out toward readers, everyone who's interested in selling self-published work should read "Why and How to Be Your Own

Best Sales Force" (in "The Sale and Its Sequels") and adopt its stress on identifying connections to potential readers as a first principle. A mental blend of the information from that chapter with the self-publishing framework outlined below should then yield a fine base for self-publishing sales operations.

Print Runs and Pricing

Even economic simpletons know that what you'll net on sales of your work will be the difference between what you get for it and what you spend for it. What you get, however, will be largely determined by what you spend (on production, promotion and distribution) and by what you charge (too high a price will have just as negative an effect on your balance sheet as one that's too low); while what you spend and what you charge may be largely determined by what you think you can get.

Leading publishing firms, which have been thrashing around inside this vicious circle for centuries, have developed a system for determining the major getting and spending variables: cover price and print order. They carefully assess unit costs for assorted quantities (which they estimate fairly accurately) in the light of projected sales (which they estimate with wildly varying degrees of success) and of current dogma about cover-price ranges. Then, when the book in question is one editors really want to do, they crunch the numbers until the bottom line looks appealing.

A more rational way to proceed is by focusing first on your market. Identify the people who are most likely to want your work and then try to figure out how many of them there are, how you might reach them, how important your book could be in their lives and how much they'd pay for it (how much do they pay now for comparable sources of information and/or entertainment? what do they tell you they'd pay for your material?).

Naturally, you'll want to set a price that's high enough to let you (1) recoup your production and marketing costs, remembering that booksellers and some other intermediaries will get a big cut of the take; (2) cover your other expenses, like rent and labor; and (3) produce at least a modest profit. If readers won't pay that high a price, however, you'd better know it early on; and if they'll pay more, that's surely a useful bit of knowledge.

Many self-publishers hedge their bets to some extent by starting with small printings and asking printers to keep tapes, plates and film of their work, or by binding only part of the first edition, for instance. But essentially what's required of you at this stage is a small but sprightly leap of faith.

Self-publishing writers who take care to cushion that leap of faith with a sensible program of action will soon find enough solid information through experience to arrive at later decisions much more rationally.

Publicizing and Promoting

Some of the first people a self-publisher should become acquainted with are the editors and publishers at small publishing companies (they're reachable through their associations and various "Foot in the Door Resources," and in many cases they're eager to share their experience). And one of the first things a self-publisher will discover in conversations and correspondence with established independents is that they're often self-publishers too (though they may publish other writers' work as well as their own). Which leads to marketing tip No. 1: imitate them by choosing a name for your publishing venture. Issuing your book from the Backyard Press (instead of under your own name) will give it a certain cachet and signal its legitimacy for those people—and there still are some—who insist on equating self-publishing with vanity publishing.

Be sure to include your address along with the name of your press in the very front of your book or periodical, to make ordering easy. Putting a coupon order form on a back page may also stimulate orders.

Like a conventional publisher's staff, a self-publisher's first priority is to get momentum going in advance of publication. Everything conventionally published writers can do for their work, self-publishing writers can do too, but the former won't be primarily responsible for securing blurbs, reviews and listings, and the latter will.

Blurbs

Try the famous-name blurb tactic if (a) you have access to any well-known personalities whose praise might help attract reviewers' attention, or (b) you think that if particular celebrities read your work they'd find you one of the most exciting talents to splash on the scene in decades and agree to be quoted to that effect. For names and addresses of potential blurb writers, consult *Who's Who in America* and Gale's *Contemporary Authors* directory. And if you send your work out for advance comments, accompany it with a covering letter that explains why you think it will interest the particular person you're addressing.

Whether or not you succeed in getting quotable comments from superstars, you should request advance quotes from leading lights in your book's field whose credentials will give weight to what they say. "The most compelling account of life under the sea I have ever read" may do almost as much for sales if it's signed by Prof. John Doe, School of Oceanography, Underwater U., as it would if it had come from Jacques Cousteau.

Reviews

Once you have copies and comments to distribute, be careful not to mail them out too early or too late. Check lead times for the review organs you hope will cover your work, and arrange to deliver it a month or two before the editors finalize the issue whose publication date coincides with yours. (Remember to include a slip announcing publication date, price and ordering information, and to use the special book rate for mailing; it's cheaper.)

As to where to send review copies, you needn't be reluctant to approach prestigious national publications, which will be hospitable to any book if it's professionally produced and submitted and if it suits their readers' needs. Remember, though, to send galleys—not bound books—to *Publishers Weekly, The New York Times Book Review* and powerful monthlies that pride themselves on running reviews either before a book comes out or right around its publication date. If what editors there get from you is a finished book, they're likely to ignore it because they'll assume (a) that pub date is imminent or past and (b) that they therefore don't have the three to four months they need to get a review into print.

Self-publishers can select other standard reviewing outlets from the list in the latest *Literary Market Place* (which provides the name of the person in charge of each one), and they can draw up their own lists of potential reviewers at special-interest journals and local magazines and newspapers. On clearly outside bets, it's fine to send only a descriptive announcement—the small firm's version of the big publisher's catalog—instead of your book itself, with a note saying that review copies are available on request.

While self-publishers shouldn't count on getting reviewed in major magazines (any more than authors with established publishers should), they can anticipate a warm reception from the numerous special-interest journals. Use "Resources" to find names and addresses and then, because new review publications and departments are springing up all the time, join COSMEP—the International Association of Independent Publishers—so you can get its newsletter. In addition to listing new review media, the *COSMEP Newsletter* presents current information on upcoming book fairs, stores looking for small-press books, cooperative distribution opportunities and the like. It's a smaller publishers' grapevine, and it carries bits of news and advice that self-publishers often find helpful.

Since libraries can be a strong and supportive market for independently published books and periodicals, be sure that

Library Journal, Booklist and *Choice* receive galleys and copies of your work for review, along with a covering letter in which you explain why you think libraries should acquire it, and follow up with polite reminder letters as necessary.

It's worth working for reviews in these magazines because librarians trust them and heed their recommendations in ordering books. And today you won't have to work as hard as self-publishers once had to, since library periodicals are more and more unwilling to let review copies from little publishers get lost in the avalanche of big publishers' materials.

Listings

A number of standard reference works are used regularly by booksellers, librarians and members of the reading public, and it's to the advantage of all published authors to be mentioned in as many as the nature of their work allows. Make sure to apply for inclusion in the Bowker directories (especially the *Books in Print* volumes and/or *Ulrich's International Periodicals Directory*) and the Dustbooks skein of small-press information; go through the Bowker, Dustbooks, Gale Research and H. W. Wilson catalogs to identify the publications from these houses that should mention what you're publishing (addresses appear in "The Self-Publishing Option Resources"); and study the "Foot in the Door Resources" listings to find additional relevant directories.

Nonfiction on your subject can also serve to publicize your work. As you come across books with appropriate bibliographies, write to acquaint their authors with the work you're doing in the field, and ask them to mention it when they do revised editions.

Sales Channels

Once word is out that your work exists and is available, the next step is enabling readers to get hold of it. Several kinds of intermediaries are in business to help publishers do just that.

Bookstores

Oddly enough, considering the fact that bookstores have seldom proved satisfactory outlets for anything but hot items, many of these intermediaries focus on bookstore distribution; and—odder still—some of them seem to have met with considerable success.

Modern distributors service bookstore accounts in two ways—either by sending sales reps to visit with catalogs and book jackets in hand (in the style of large houses) or simply by mailing new catalogs several times a year. Some outfits have built up good reputations among booksellers, so that books may sell many more copies if presented through their catalogs than if introduced to store managers by the publishers themselves.

But the main advantage a good distributor offers is this: booksellers are more inclined to buy from distributors than from individuals because they trust them more to fulfill obligations and simplify procedures; and booksellers are more inclined to pay distributors than individuals because business with them is ongoing.

Not long ago, a self-publisher's chief problem with respect to reaching bookstores was the dearth of distributors; in the near future, the basic quandary may be how to choose among them. All will take a cut of your profits, of course, but some want only to make a killing with a hot commercial property, while others are game to help the cause of serious literature. Your best best, if you want to have a distributor, is to judge each one you consider according to what it can do for you.

To narrow the field, ask congenial publishers to tell you what distributors they've found reliable and effective, look through recent *COSMEP Newsletters* for recommendations, talk with local booksellers about which distributors they prefer to deal with and consult "Resources." After you have a list of names and addresses, write to each distributor you're interested in and ask for a catalog and for information about services, fees and timetables.

Every catalog you read should give you a good feel for the

kind of book that distributor represents best. Some handle ongoing presses but not one-shot self-publishers, so you may have to cross those off your list; and others will strike you as clearly inappropriate (if yours is a how-to title, a catalog in which page after page describes experimental literature is not for you).

Once you have a final roster of likely candidates, you should answer the following questions to your own satisfaction before you sign on with any of them. (If you can't find the information you want in the literature you've received, write and ask for more data.)

* Does this distributor have its own sales force, hire independent sales reps or rely exclusively on a catalog?
* What size cut does the distributor take? California-based Bookpeople, for instance, buys on consignment at 52 percent off the retail price, and in turn sells to stores at a 40 percent discount. You'll have to figure out what discount is reasonable for you.
* What territory does the distributor cover and how many accounts does it service? How does it deal with bookstore chains and wholesalers? Can it handle sales to nonbook outlets and/or sales to consumers via direct mail; and, if so, which markets do you want the distributor to represent you in and which would you rather keep for yourself?

Since many distributors service only a part of the country, you may need to contract with more than one for a book that has national appeal, or to pick just the right one if your book is designed for a particular geographic or special-interest audience. The point is to get the coverage you need.

Self-publishers who decide to approach booksellers on their own should begin by settling down in the library to study the *American Book Trade Directory*. A Bowker publication, it lists thousands of bookstores and hundreds of wholesalers in North America by state (or Canadian province) and then by city, and it has a list of bookstore chain headquarters too.

Step two is compiling your own list of booksellers and wholesalers in your area and/or in the locations appropriate for your book. And step three is getting in touch with the buyers at every place on that list (the manager or owner, whose name you'll usually find in the directory, can steer you to the proper person in a large and departmentalized operation).

Try to schedule a talk with each buyer—over the phone or, if possible, face-to-face—when things aren't too busy, and be prepared to explain why your book will sell once it's on the shelves. Booksellers, it's important to remember, generally rely on publishers to promote books, so you'll make more headway if you can talk about the publicity you'll be getting locally, the public speaking you'll be doing in the area and perhaps the in-store events you could run.

Often it makes sense to suggest a program or display that will highlight several books; for example, you might select a dozen crafts titles (including yours), arrange them in the bookstore window with samples of your handiwork and demonstrate techniques at the store one day from 4 to 6 P.M.; or you might make common cause with another author who disagrees with your book's position on mandatory retirement, create a window display featuring both books and placards revealing the crux of the argument and invite the public to an open debate on the issue inside the store.

Since one order from a large chain or wholesaler can make your book widely available throughout the country, you'll want to contact the giants (like Ingram and Baker & Taylor, among wholesalers, and Waldenbooks, among the chains) as well as local independent booksellers, smaller chains and appropriate local or regional wholesalers.

When you sell to stores on your own, get payment in advance or resign yourself to giving away a lot of copies for nothing. And try as hard as you can to sell on a nonreturnable basis. This will mean offering a bigger discount than normal—perhaps over 50 percent—but it's sound practice, because unless store managers have paid for your book, they'll have little, if any, incentive to sell it. Most sales forces are still stuck to fully returnable policies on the dubious—and incorrect—grounds that the industry has to do business this way. But that doesn't mean you have to get hamstrung by the full-right-of-return rule too. Dover Publications is one of the publishing firms that has demonstrated the benefits of a no-return system, providing a model you'd do well to emulate.

Better Stores and Other Nontraditional Outlets

Most distributors will insist on holding the exclusive rights to sell your book to bookstores, but self-publishers of both books and periodicals can do plenty of selling themselves to nonbook departments of department stores and to nonbook stores of all kinds. In fact, in imaginative marketing to nonbook outlets, small and self-publishers have taken a definite lead over big firms. What began as a necessity (because there was no effective way for little houses to get what they published into bookstores) has thus become an asset (because bookstores are such bad places to launch anything but bestsellers). Today—thanks to small-press pioneers—health food stores, craft shops, hardware stores and sidewalk vendors are accustomed to selling written work along with their other wares.

Some books succeed handsomely in outlets like these, without ever penetrating the bookstore market, and some succeed first in such "nontraditional" or "special sales" channels and then, once word of mouth has begun to build, they find favor with booksellers. Whatever the pattern, unconventional approaches to marketing are likely to serve self-publishers well.

Take the first step in exploring special sales opportunities for your work by listing the kinds of nonbookstore retail outlets your readers are likely to frequent. Then prepare a selling speech and try it out on the managers of appropriate stores nearby. If one or more of them will take some books on consignment and customers buy those books, you can set your sights on national distribution. Let's say, for example, that the local sporting goods store proves a fine outlet for your *Backpacking with Kids* guide.

Ask the manager which wholesalers service the store, contact those wholesalers; explain that you've sold your manual through the Acme Sports Emporium in Hometown, Kansas, and that you think other sporting goods stores would do well with it too; and offer to sell them as many copies as they want at a large discount—probably well over 50 percent—nonreturnable.

Next, make a list of mail-order catalogs that might offer your book in their pages ("Resources" will lead you to likely candidates), and send for copies of the ones that sound promising to see if they carry books like yours and/or other products that would obviously appeal to your readership. Mail-order catalogs of all kinds are increasingly apt to include books; so far, how-to and novelty titles have been particularly successful.

Third, look into premium sale possibilities. The hardest kind of special sale to make, a premium sale is also often by far the most lucrative kind. Premiums—in the form of toaster ovens, calculators and a wide variety of other goods besides books—are items businesses offer to attract new customers and prompt current buyers to buy more. Since a premium sale may involve tens or even hundreds of thousands of copies—and dollars—it's worth trying for if you can make a connection between your book and a product or service. One self-publisher persuaded a company that makes fondue pots to package a copy of her fondue cookbook with each order. Perhaps you can arrange for a moving company to buy your moving manual in bulk for its clients, or work a deal with a magazine whose subscribers might renew more readily if they got your book free when they signed on for another year.

Because the list of good nontraditional sales channels for your work can be very long indeed, it pays to exercise your imagination. *Cheap Chic,* a guide for dressing well on a shoestring budget, was marketed effectively in clothing and secondhand stores; *How to Make Furniture Without Tools* sold well in lumberyards; one industrious soul got beauty salons to stock books for women that they could read under the drier, and with a little ingenuity, maybe you can top that. For further stimulation, see the *Thomas Register of American Manufacturers* (listed in "Money Resources"); you'll find names and addresses of promising companies there.

Inside conventional publishing houses, mail-order sales and sales of books by writers to readers are often labeled "special sales." They shouldn't be special for you, though; they should form the core of your sales campaign; see below.

Direct Routes to Readers

Selling retail is the purpose and the promise of all publishing. It's the retail buyers, after all, who'll be your readers, and every writer's efforts are directed, in the final analysis, to reaching them.

Self-publishers have three primary ways to get in touch with the people they want as readers—via the mail, advertising and personal appearances. In planning each approach, be sure to include provisions for feedback—in the form of orders, with payment, as well as in the form of verbal give-and-take—and when you begin to get results, keep a record of the names and addresses of everyone who places an order from any source. In the event that you publish another book or periodical or issue a revised edition, you'll have a successful, free mailing list at your fingertips.

Direct Mail

As the number-one means of distribution for small publishers, direct mail offers the best way to appeal—one-to-one—to groups of people around the country who are likely to want your work and who might not ordinarily hear about it or be able to get hold of it.

Getting a direct-mail package together can be an elaborate and expensive proposition (and it is in the hands of most sizable houses), but self-publishers can keep costs down if they simply prepare a description of their books or magazines, a collection of enthusiastic (and preferably prestigious) comments and a tear-off order blank. When a table of contents says best what the work is like, it might accompany the description, and when the author's experience or credentials are relevant, they should be mentioned too. Whatever its specific content, however, mail-order copy must always answer the question potential readers will be asking themselves: What's in it for me?

You may want to use slightly different approaches to reach slightly different segments of your public, but whether you mail one letter or a variety, choosing wisely where to send them is essential. As you'll discover when you explore mailing lists (see "Tools" in "Resources"), every imaginable interest is represented. You can rent a list of people who've bought inflatable chairs as easily as you can rent one of Ph.D. holders. Prices start at about $50 for 1,000 names, and the more narrowly you can define your market the better your chances will be of getting your money's worth.

If your work focuses on a very precise subject—like directing a summer camp, say—and you know there's an association of camp directors, you can go straight to that group and ask for the use of their membership roll (you may even get the list free if you're on it yourself).

In the event that neither your background nor your subject matter leads you directly to ideal lists, you should consult the "Mailing Lists" section of *LMP* and the Standard Rate and Data Service direct-mail catalog.

After you've studied several of these sources and come up with a few lists that seem to match the audiences you want to reach, ask the broker for each list what response rate other people have gotten with it (2 percent is considered pretty good), and solicit the broker's advice on your project. Then, using common sense mixed with courage, you'll have to decide for yourself whether a mailing will be cost-effective. Remember, expenses will include preparation of copy; purchase of paper, envelopes and postage and maybe of return envelopes (possibly also with postage); along with list rental fees (using the self-publishing Starter

Kit, you may be able to keep some of these costs down). Because it's so hard to tell in advance how many orders to expect, most people start small with a test mailing of part of a list and then mail to large groups if and only if that test mailing succeeds.

Direct-Response Advertising

Nobody in the industry has any hard knowledge as to whether ads without order forms sell books. Given the inadequacy of most publishers' distribution efforts, however, it seems unlikely that they do, so use ads *with* order forms; they'll make it easy for readers to buy and for you to measure the success of your advertising.

There's no better place to run a coupon ad than in a periodical that's printing a review or an excerpt of your work. Other logical advertising outlets include magazines, newsletters and newspapers that share your area of interest. *National Wildlife,* for example, might provide a good environment for an ad about a children's book on a prairie-dog town; while the *Vassar Quarterly* could pull orders for a history of higher education for women.

Ask the advertising departments of local newspapers, magazines and radio stations where you want to run your ad for advice on how to prepare copy (it's in their interest that your ad succeed, so don't be shy). Or hire an agency. And if you plan to advertise in more than one place, key each order form (on the coupon in the *Hometown Gazette,* for instance, instruct people to address their orders to Dept. HG, and use Dept. DN as part of the address cited on the coupon in the *Doglovers' Newsletter*); that way, when only 3 orders come in on the HG blank but you get 150 marked DN, you can arrange to keep running Doglovers' ads until the response tapers off, and to pull out of your local paper.

Classified ads, which are cheap, may work for some books and periodicals; and exchange ads, which are free, can hardly fail. Magazines often swap advertising, so if you're putting one out you ought to see what kind of a deal you can arrange with kindred publishing spirits. How much room you'll be accorded in someone else's periodical will depend upon relative circulation figures and/or upon good will.

Personal Appearances

Each group you can reach by mail and through advertising you can probably also reach in person, with far more exciting results. Refer back to "Why and How to Be Your Own Best Sales Force," and please remember that almost every one of this country's thousands of organizations has scheduled meetings. Check the *Encyclopedia of Associations* to see what conventions are held in your area or might be worth traveling to.

But neither scheduled events nor the examples in this book exhaust the avenues for selling a book in person, so strive for impromptu, innovative strategies. "Sometimes, when I don't have anything pressing to do," says Russell M. Genet, a self-publisher who's an authority on astronomy, "I'll go through the journals in my field and write individual authors short notes on their papers (probably the only responses they ever get) and also pop in flyers for my books. I get about a 90 percent order rate from this."

For additional inspiration—and evidence that the strangest schemes sometimes work magnificently—note the experience of Charleen Whisnant Swansea, editor and publisher of Red Clay Books.

When Swansea's first book came off the press, she took stock of who among her friends, acquaintances and colleagues could help her sell it. Capitalizing on one of her previous jobs—she'd been a traveling sales rep for a company that made false teeth—she decided to retrace her old route and convince dentists that those dog-eared magazines in their waiting rooms were not lively enough reading for their clients. You should spruce up the reading racks by buying my book, she told them. And they did.

Libraries

Have you sent review copies to the magazines librarians trust? Have you visited the libraries in your area to acquaint the staff with what you've published and with your availability as a reader or a lecturer? If you got a good review in one of the library journals, have you reprinted it on a postcard and sent it to librarians around the country? Have you considered getting Quality Books to handle distribution to libraries for you (see "Resources," page 286, for the address and phone number)?

If so, you've done what should be done to generate sales to the library market, although you will need to take one additional step. When orders come in, either directly from librarians or via a wholesaler like Baker & Taylor, fill them promptly and make your paperwork exemplary. Many small publishers already have excellent relationships with libraries and you'll benefit by joining their ranks.

Sub Rights Buyers

With every passing year, self-publishers win new respect from the publishing establishment, partly because by now several self-published books have snagged the prize the establishment values most—space on the national bestseller lists (*The One Minute Manager* was originally issued by its authors, for instance), and partly because many self-published books have sold in numbers that make some conventional bestsellers look sick.

Nowadays, self-publishers who want to sell rights in their books to full-fledged publishing houses have precedents to point to—trailblazers like *Mary Ellen's Best of Helpful Hints* (sold to Warner, it made—and stayed on—the charts), Jennifer James's *Success Is the Quality of Your Journey* (several publishers went after it and Newmarket Press got it) and Ernest Callenbach's *Ecotopia* (a Bantam release that sold well into six figures). Citing other Bantam titles that started out as self-published books, publicity manager Richard Sandomir recently noted that *Fascinating Womanhood* by Helen Andelin had 1,371,000 copies in print, *Limbo of the Lost* by John Wallace Spencer had 1,603,000 and *The Old-Fashioned Recipe Book* by Carla Emery had 217,000.

Like well-established publishers, well-established book clubs are receptive to submissions from self-publishers. In fact, the Book-of-the-Month Club has asked for them. In a widely distributed statement, the club declared, "While many of our important titles come from the large houses, other very successful titles come from the smaller presses. So we're always interested in keeping up with what you're publishing." Be bold, therefore, and try your book on any clubs listed in *Literary Market Place* and *Book Marketing Opportunities* that seem right for it.

If you think you have a book that a bigger publisher, a foreign publisher, a book club or anybody else ought to buy rights to, but you find that potential buyers are psychologically unprepared to deal with an author, try getting an agent to represent you. See *LMP* and ask friendly small publishers if they have recommendations to offer. And for more on sub rights sales, turn to the "Money" chapter called "Spinoffs."

Money

* * *

Front-end Funding

BEFORE YOU CAN begin a major piece of writing you'll need to know how you're to support yourself while you work on it. If you're otherwise employed and writing part-time, you may not have a problem. If you're rich, there's no problem, of course. And if your publisher has provided an enormous advance, you have nothing to worry about, at least until you launch your next project. But if you're among the vast majority of writers, you'll have to scramble to make ends meet. In fact, the first rule of the writing game is: you cannot live by writing sales alone.

To supplement whatever income you derive directly from writing, tap any or all of the money sources outlined below.

Grants

Browsing through the directories that list grants available to struggling writers should prove heartening, both because you'll see how many people and groups are trying to help, and because you'll find at least one program, and probably more, for which you're eligible. Even first-time authors have grants earmarked especially for them; for instance, a number of large trade publishing houses sponsor fellowships for unpublished writers that consist of outright prize money plus advances, and some university presses offer similar programs.

You can find out who's giving what by sending for *Grants and Awards Available to Writers,* which is put out by the writers' group known as P.E.N. and which is the only annual list compiled exclusively for writers. In addition, check listings in "Resources"; read *Poets & Writers Magazine* for announcements of new awards (and reminders about deadline dates for old ones); look at preface and acknowledgments sections of books in your field to see whether one foundation or another is especially receptive to your kind of project; and write your state council for the arts and the National Endowment for the Arts to ask for information about financial aid.

As a rule, grants are designed either to support a writer's work in general—to advance his or her "career" is the usual language—or to fund a particular project. Those who apply for career-advancement money are generally judged on the basis of samples of their strongest work. Barry Targan, whose fiction was selected for Martha Foley's prestigious anthology *Best American Short Stories* for three years running, says of a National Endowment for the Arts grant that he won: "The application form itself is quite simple and straightforward, and even though it asks what you will use the grant for (you can only honestly answer—to continue to write, for support while you do write), still I think what matters most is the feeling the judges have for the samples of writing that you submit. In my own case, the fact that I'd won the Iowa School of Letters Award for Short Fiction may have helped, but many other people who received grants have published very little."

Those who want grants for particular projects have to satisfy more complicated requirements. In addition to filling out application forms, they will probably be asked to write project descriptions, estimate the budgets necessary for their execution and solicit letters of recommendation.

All this takes a good deal of time, but it's worth doing right since you're shooting for thousands of dollars. And a good way to discover what the right approach is for any specific grant is to talk with the people who've won it. The roster of previous winners that generally comes along with each application form may seem intimidatingly star-studded at first, but because many of the famous names on it got their grants while they were still unknown, they should be willing to empathize with your needs now. So mine the winners list for clues about what level of achievement is expected and what types of projects have been funded in the past, and then muster the courage to call a couple of successful grant-getters and ask for advice. Tell them about your proposal and admit it if this is your first foray into the grants game.

Susan Jacoby—who got several grants, including an Alicia Patterson Foundation fellowship, to help finance her book about new immigrants—endorses this route, as do other writers who've tried it. "Talking with someone who's recently won a grant from the foundation you're applying to gives you an insider's edge," Jacoby explains. "Each foundation has its own style: some like polysyllabic, academic presentations; others prefer it straight and simple. What's desirable and what's not changes as the composition of the selection board changes, so it's important that you talk with someone who won recently."

To go with whatever firsthand advice you can get, here are some general rules of grant-seeking:

* Incorporate selected elements of the effective book proposal (as described in "Procedures") in your project description. Emphasize the credentials and expertise you bring to your work. Explain why your project is worth undertaking and what its significance is in relation to other work in the field. If you've received an advance from a publisher, mention it, and say why you need additional funding.
* Once you've drafted a proposal you're satisfied with, circulate it among friends for suggestions; include at least one writer who has already won a grant, if you can.
* Make up a professional-looking budget. This means estimat-

ing your living expenses as accurately as possible, and in general using hard figures whenever you can, instead of guessing.
* Contact the leading authorities in your field for letters of recommendation, and try to set up meetings with them individually. If you can't arrange meetings, write and describe your project; explain what you've accomplished thus far; and ask each authority if they'd be willing to recommend you for the grants you need. If you make it clear that your work will constitute a real contribution to their field, they'll probably agree to support your applications.

    In follow-up correspondence with sponsors who seem truly interested in your work, you might ask whether they can suggest any other foundations you ought to try. And you should be sure, of course, to thank every sponsor and to apprise them of the outcome of your efforts. Whatever grants you win—or fail to win—this time around, you may need their help again.
* Don't assume that you're limited to holding one grant at a time. Having money from X rarely precludes a writer from applying for more from Y and Z.
* If there's anything on the application form that you don't understand, call and ask for clarifications and explanations.

Writers' Colonies

There's scarcely a writer alive who hasn't felt at one point or another that a little peace and quiet was the key to getting some real work done. At a dozen or so writers' colonies scattered throughout the United States, peace and quiet are abundantly available, along with free room and board in most cases (at some colonies writers are asked to contribute by buying their own groceries and preparing their own meals).

Colonies come in a wide variety of styles, from Yaddo, outside Saratoga Springs, New York—with its mansion, formal rose garden, statuary, tennis courts, swimming pool and box-lunch delivery—to Cummington Community of the Arts in Massachusetts, the only retreat that accepts writers' families too, and invites everyone to pitch in with the day-to-day chores.

Some colonies actively encourage beginners to apply (the Fine Arts Work Center in Provincetown, Massachusetts, exists for emerging writers alone), but all say that writers with talent—published or not—will be welcomed, and most accept both fiction and nonfiction writers on the basis of samples of their work. See this section's "Resources" for help in figuring out where you might best apply.

No matter how like utopia they may sound, writers' colonies are not useful for everyone. Having your own cabin in the woods will free you from the distractions of kids at home, phones in the office and other assorted turmoil, but it won't necessarily activate your muse. As one writer who has stayed at a number of colonies put it: "You don't get inspiration by looking at the trees." Nor is the problem of self-discipline any easier to handle at a colony than it is at home, although some writers do find that living in a community composed exclusively of artists shames and/or encourages them to buckle down.

Those who get the most from colony life usually arrive with a specific goal in mind: five poems; the first three chapters; a rough draft. The goals you set for yourself will naturally depend in part on how long you plan to stay (some colonies ask that you spend no less than a month on the premises, while others have more flexible residence requirements), but even if you don't have time to get a great deal of writing done, you may find colony conditions just right for making valuable discoveries, as Anne Grant, a documentary writer and director, did when she stayed at the Millay Colony for the Arts in Austerlitz, New York, for ten days to work on her study *Elizabeth Cady Stanton's Quarrel with God*.

"I had imagined I could finish my book," she said, looking back on the experience, "but I completed only twenty pages and a lengthy outline. I accomplished something else, though. For the first time in my adult life, I discovered my natural rhythms of waking, eating and sleeping, my flow of energy and thought when I am not interrupted. At home, whenever I failed to accomplish as much as I had planned, I would reproach myself and resent my family. At the Millay Colony, I found that even under the best conditions it takes time to develop an idea and even more time to create art."

With colonies as with grants, don't be dismayed if at first you don't succeed. Understandably, the waiting lists at most retreats are long, so you may very well have to try and try again.

Economic Ingenuity

Let's say you desperately need to get away right now in order to pull your manuscript into shape, and there's no room to be had at any of the colonies you applied to. What do you do? Well, you could decide that the world's an unfair place, shelve the manuscript, and sulk; or you could choose to abandon dependence on other people's largesse and substitute reliance on your own wits. One good way to keep yourself in funds, after all, is to devise clever ways to avoid giving up those you've got.

Do some friends of yours have summer homes that they're not using and that they might allow you to live in for a couple of weeks if you volunteered to paint the kitchen during your stay? Can you afford to have a neighborhood teenager sit for your preschool kids between three and six o'clock while you work in the empty apartment of a friend who's at her office?

Most writers become experts at cash-conserving improvisations of this sort out of sheer necessity. But devising money-saving moves can be pleasurable as well as practical if you enjoy the idea of outwitting such capitalist evils as inflation and planned obsolescence by reviving secondhand clothing and furniture, for instance, or by using a barter system (maybe the electrician will fix your stove for nothing if you teach his kid grammar).

Unlike local tradespeople, the IRS never accepts payment in

services, but though you can't avoid paying cash to the government, you can keep your tax bills down. Get hold of the IRS pamphlets for self-employed workers (your local office will have a list), and remember that you're personally responsible for making Social Security payments.

One other thing all writers can do to put themselves in a favorable position at tax time is keep an expenses diary. Simply carry a pocket calendar with you and jot down records of any money you spend on work-related matters (including transportation to and from editors' offices, postage and supplies, copying costs, phone calls, magazine subscriptions necessary for your project, professional membership dues and the like). Keep all receipts; mark clearly what each one is for, unless it's self-evident; and in dealing with businesses that don't normally issue them, bring your own form (you can buy a pack at any stationery store) and get it signed. Faithfully recording your expenses should help you take full advantage of applicable tax deductions and keep the costs of tax preparation down.

Some writers' organizations help their members save money by offering informational seminars, charter flights, group insurance plans and the like. And they may also provide an incidental financial benefit: membership in a national writers' group indicates to the IRS that you are indeed a professional writer and therefore entitled to all the tax breaks attendant on that occupation.

Wages

For many men and women, writing is a sometime thing, an avocation they pursue to further their goals in business or the professions. But even people whose main ambition is to write can hold down full-time nonwriting jobs that give them economic security along with other benefits.

Look at Dana Gioia, for example. Gioia, a poet who has been profiled in *Esquire* and published in *The New Yorker* and *The*

Hudson Review, found that managing new business development for General Foods didn't just let him put food on the table and a roof over his head; it also opened up new perspectives by immersing him in workaday concerns and large-scale business decisions, and it boosted his confidence besides. "Nothing, I assume, not even the Nobel Prize, would keep a real writer from feeling some anxiety about his work, but making some visible progress in a career does help give a writer, especially a beginning writer, a base of security to work from," he told Daryln Brewer of *Poets & Writers Magazine.*

Writers who work for software manufacturers, life insurance companies, stockbrokers and law firms report similar benefits.

Subsidy Publishing

Riffle through the pages of the women's magazines and you'll notice before long that the clothes and cosmetics featured in the editorial departments tend to come from the very same companies that fill the advertising columns. Almost all magazines depend on advertising revenues for economic viability, but some are more fussy than others about the nature of the links between ads and editorial attention, and a few manage to run plenty of ads that relate to articles without relinquishing control over content in any way.

A similar system exists to fund books and pamphlets. Subsidy publishing, as the practice is called, involves interesting a business, a charitable organization or any other institution that has money to spend, in financing a written work prior to publication, and sometimes giving the sponsor a say about its contents. What the company gets out of the deal is a marketing or public relations tool called a premium; what the writer gets is a sponsor, except that instead of the Medicis or the Ford Foundation, this time it's Amalgamated Widgets.

Established book publishers often make subsidy deals, but subsidy publishing is not well known among writers, most of whom discover it by accident, if at all, the way Ann Reed and Marilyn Pfaltz did as they were making the rounds of New York houses with their cookbook, *Your Secret Servant*. When a friendly editor who didn't want the book for her list suggested that it might make a good premium, Reed and Pfaltz asked her what she meant by that, and then switched targets. Instead of offering their manuscript to publishing houses, they began offering it to advertising agencies, and fairly soon they found one that wanted to use it as an incentive to draw new accounts to a banking client's offices. The bank paid enough for its copies of *Your Secret Servant* so that the authors could print and bind 5,000 extra books for their own purposes. With the finished work in hand, selling publishers was simpler. Scribner's bought the 5,000 copies and kept the book in print for a number of years.

To find the organizations that might subsidize you, figure out what institutional aims your work might serve (maybe a company that manufactures luggage would like to fund your anthology of expeditions and distribute it as its Christmas gift this year, for instance; or maybe the Lions would underwrite your history of fraternal organizations). Then call or write potential sponsors themselves, or match companies with appropriate books by using the leads you'll find in "Money Resources."

Like all forms of patronage, subsidy publishing may raise moral issues. But if you're honest with yourself, your sponsor and your public, there's nothing to stop you from having clean hands, a pure heart and a healthy bank balance all at the same time.

Spinoffs

THE SINGLE BEST key to financial success in writing is recycling. Both the materials and the skills that go into creating a piece of written work can be reused in a great variety of profitable ways, and while those who've written books have the widest range of recycling options, everyone who's written anything should be able to make it do at least double duty for pay. Or triple. Or quadruple. Or more.

Check your contract before you start the recycling processes, though, to see which rights you control and which you'll need clearance to dispose of.

Transforming the Whole

To switch from worrying about how to put a roof over your head to worrying about how to shelter your earnings, get your story made into a successful movie or television program. TV and movie people prefer to buy bestsellers, of course, because they want presold audiences for their products, but little-known books, too, have been transformed for large and small screens.

Mostly, it's a matter of luck. Who you know is crucial (is your cousin's sister-in-law an editor at Paramount? Why not ask him to ask her to call your book to the attention of a producer or two? It probably won't do any good, but it shouldn't do any harm either). An aggressive and talented agent who specializes in dramatic properties can be a great asset (you might start a data bank, like the one outlined for editors in "Openings," in order to figure out which agents would be good for, and receptive to, what you've written). And the affection approach (see "Openings" again) may be worth trying with a producer, a director or an actor whose work strikes you as similar in significant ways to your own.

Outside the glamorous world of Hollywood, luck plays a smaller part in transforming written work for profit, and you can depend upon energy and intelligence instead to help you toward your goals. Among the many routes worth traveling, several stand out. For example:

* *Export*. Some books travel well and, if you think hard about what sorts of people in which foreign countries would respond to what you've written, perhaps yours will be one of them. To get a sense of what's currently selling abroad, read *Publishers Weekly*'s articles on publishing overseas. And then consult your publisher or your agent (if you have one) or some of the exporters and export representatives listed in *LMP* about how to effect foreign sales.

Great Britain, of course, provides a promising market for many American titles because language is no barrier, but scientific (and even semiscientific) writing may draw English-speaking audiences around the world, and so might essentially visual works for both children and adults.

A writer who finds interested buyers abroad can sell them copies of an American edition or the rights to publish an edition of their own.

* *Translation*. Whether or not there's an English-speaking foreign market for an American writer's work, there may be a market—or several markets—for it in translation. Again, you ought to come up with a list of logical candidates and then discuss the possibilities with your publisher and/or your literary agent and/or appropriate agents listed in *LMP*.

Share whatever grounds for optimism you have (are books about the same subject regularly featured on French bestseller lists; has the leading English-Spanish translator in the United States agreed to do your novel if you get a buyer for it in Latin America?). No exporter can afford to take lightly the obvious hazards that come with translation rights, so they'll all be hungry for evidence that supports projections of success.

* *Videocassettes.* Translating words on paper into visual images with sounds attached is an even trickier task but it can pay off handsomely—as witness the video versions of Jane Fonda's exercise books—so it's worth exploring for certain kinds of nonfiction. Suppose, for example, that you've written a book about living with a handicapped child; the techniques and attitudes it explains would probably be clearest if they were visually depicted as well as verbally described; and visual presentations could obviously be at least as useful with instruction manuals of various sorts—how to refinish your antique furniture, care for your houseplants, understand body language.

To find likely prospects for sales of video rights to your material, canvass companies that already reach appropriate audiences. Organizations that serve nurses might adapt a book on touch therapy, for instance, and large corporations might adapt one that explains how to get the most out of meetings.

* *Audiocassettes.* As they wend their way along the country's roads and sidewalks, thousands of Americans now regularly listen to books on tape that are produced by companies founded for the purpose and by booksellers, publishers and special-interest concerns that make cassettes as a sideline. Check your publisher's capabilities and intentions in this area and see the cassettes in stock at nearby bookstores for leads to other companies you might approach.

* *Cable TV.* Paralleling the growth of small, special-interest operations in book and periodical publishing, small, special-interest television channels have been multiplying lately. Local cable programs differ widely from one another—and from the local and network programs that used to monopolize the TV dial—but they have some things in common. In general, their need for new material is insatiable, their budgets are small, and their reliance on print materials for program ideas is marked.

Check out cable shows in your area and/or study the periodicals that cover cable to identify possible buyers of rights in your work; and when you find a likely prospect, try to come up with a proposal that meets the demands of television by remembering that what people want when they open a book is not the same as what they want when they click on a TV set.

* *Awards.* Numerous cash prizes are given each year to outstanding works in a staggering variety of categories (best first novel; best book about Ohio history; best article on dental disease), and applying for them is relatively easy. Use the directories listed in "Money Resources" to see what prizes your work might win, decide how much (if anything) you're willing to pay for entry fees, and then start filling out forms. Applications for some awards will have to come from your publisher, who will probably be glad to do the necessary paperwork. Just tell your editor what you're after and what kind of help you need.

Apportioning the Parts

Sometimes a section of a book can be lifted, virtually intact, out of the rest of a manuscript and stood firmly on its own feet. In such cases, the author needs only to figure out which periodicals might like to run it and arrange to give them their chance.

More often, however, books refuse to disassemble neatly, and carving articles or stories from their pages takes careful craftsmanship.

Once you've decided which parts of your story merit publication on their own (perhaps you'll have to supply a new lead or a few passages of transition or a local news peg before any of them does), you can approach magazines, newspapers and syndicates with your selections (see "Resources" and, if you feel the need of a refresher course, "A Foot in the Door"). You should offer to sell either first serial rights (that is, the rights to the first appearance in print of this work) or second serial rights (i.e., the rights to republish, perhaps in a slightly different form). For obvious reasons, first serial rights go for more money.

Send as many different adaptations of your material as you can prepare to as many appropriate outlets as you can find, and use the biographical note that runs with them to identify yourself as the author of their parent work. You'll want readers who are enthusiastic about an excerpt to realize that they can buy a copy of its source. Ideally, you'll be able to make that easy to do; try hard to get periodicals to print full ordering information along with your pieces.

Don't stop, though, when you've gotten a bunch of excerpts into print and a bit of action going. Fan the flames by developing reprint possibilities. Should the *Reader's Digest* see the chapter of your book that appeared in *Essence*? Would airline magazines or trade journals or special-interest newsletters or local papers pick up your piece from *Savvy*?

The effort involved in sending tearsheets out to periodicals that might reprint from them is minimal, and likely to be fully repaid even if all you get is additional exposure. There'll be big money in the offing, though, for anyone who does win the vote at the *Digest*.

Deploying Writing Skills

If you decide to use your writing skills in order to earn enough money to use your writing skills the way you really want to use them, you have several interesting options.

One thing you can do is write other people's books. Celebrities and executives and experts of various sorts with good stories to tell often lack the time and talent to tell them well. As a result, they and their agents and editors frequently go looking for ghostwriters and collaborators.

When you're tapped to write for or with somebody else, you may get a flat fee or a percentage of the royalties or both. Try for the percentage, and expect to work hard for your money however it's paid. There's no such thing as "an easy book," according to William Novak, who wrote *Iacocca* and *Mayflower Madam* in collaboration with their subjects and *The Big Book of Jewish Humor* (among other things) on his own.

Novak reports that he enjoys writing as part of a team. If you think you'd like that too, ask your acquaintances in publishing about assignments, and then, once you're hired, arrange to be billed as a co-author if you can, and be absolutely certain you get credit somewhere in it. (Drawing up a written agreement at the outset about the terms of a collaboration is a good way to ensure that these and other focuses for dissension don't cause trouble later, when the project is so well launched that you're locked into it.)

Expending less effort (and no doubt earning less in the way of psychic rewards), you can take up writing fillers, short features and greeting-card verse. Successful practitioners of these and comparable minor arts have, predictably, written books that tell how you too can cash in on them, and although you can sneer if you want to, this may be your best way to pay the grocery bills.

Other opportunities to write for money exist in organizations that need newsletters, companies that need house organs, government bodies that need speech-writing staffs and myriad other concerns. Let your own ingenuity be a guide to the ones that will work well for you.

Book packagers also hire writers. Sometimes known as book producers or book developers, packagers come up with ideas for books, find people to write them and sell the finished products—in the form of fully edited manuscripts, sets of camera-ready pages or thousands of bound volumes—to publishing houses. Authors who work for packagers can negotiate a variety of deals involving flat fees and/or shares of earnings.

To get packagers to think about hiring you, write to tell them about your special expertise and your writing credits, and enclose brief samples of your best work. See "Resources" for leads to particular book producers and send for descriptive literature from those you find appealing.

Purveying Publishing Know-How

Instead of working for a packager, you may want to consider becoming one. Hundreds of people have done that during the past few years. Their ranks include Kenneth C. Davis, the author of *Two-Bit Culture* (see "A Foot in the Door Resources"), who decided to try packaging just after his first child was born. "I was home with Jenny," he recalled, "and I had lots of ideas for books but not much time to work on them."

Packaged books are usually nonfiction, with titles like *Dial an Expert: A Consumer's Guide to Free Expertise Available by Phone* (Stonesong Press) or *The Audubon Society Nature Guides* (Chanticleer Press) or *Alternatives to Drugs* (Sarah Lazin Books) or *Theme Gardens* (Regina Ryan Publishing Enterprises, Inc.) or *Good Books to Grow On,* which Davis generated. He has packaged novels too, though—specifically, a series of mysteries that feature crossword puzzles.

By turning his ideas for fiction and nonfiction into proposals and then getting other people to write, produce and distribute the books he's dreamed up, Davis created a rewarding part-time job for himself. Those of you who'd like a similar setup might seek advice from book producers in your area and review "The Self-Publishing Option" if you decide to be the kind of packager who sells finished books, not just finished manuscripts.

Arguably, of course, if you're going to produce finished

books, you might as well handle distribution too and create your own publishing company.

Your safest move in that case is to specialize. By concentrating on one subject area or one kind of writing that appeals to a particular group of people, a publisher can build a following and eventually instill a strong brand-name loyalty that will help draw readers to new books from the house.

Some firms specialize successfully in books about a geographical region; *50 Hikes in New Hampshire's White Mountains* went through two editions and four printings in its first six years and spawned a series of related books at New Hampshire Publishing Company, for instance.

Other publishers focus on topics of current concern. Bruce and Vicki Lansky, for example, founded Meadowbrook Press on books about parenting. Beginning with Vicki Lansky's *Feed Me, I'm Yours* and *The Taming of the C.A.N.D.Y. Monster,* the house went on to issue enough other books for parents and prospective parents to fill a small bookcase—which, incidentally, Bruce Lansky once arranged to supply to retailers to entice them to order and to improve the display of Meadowbrook's titles in stores.

And Garland Publishing, Inc., found a practical route to profits by specializing in short-run facsimile books, which require no typesetting. Garland's catalogs—"Fifty Classics of Crime Fiction," "The James Joyce Archive: Unpublished Notebooks, Manuscripts, Typescripts, Corrected Proofs, Etc." and "Outstanding Dissertations in the Fine Arts," among others—go to academics and to academic libraries, which are easy to reach and, given attractive materials, very apt to order.

Experienced authors can also think in terms of selling certain publishing skills and services. If you own a typesetting machine, for example, by all means use it as a source of extra income; you should have no trouble generating assignments from paying clients. If you've developed editing, copy-editing, proofreading, layout or paste-up skills, you ought to tap the ready market for them as well; try publishing houses, newspapers, ad agencies and almost any other business that involves the preparation of materials to be printed (which almost any business nowadays does). And if you've developed as much marketing expertise as self-publishers Dan Poynter of Para Publishing and John Kremer of Ad-Lib Publications, you might follow their lead by creating books, newsletters, workshops and all manner of other goods and services that show small publishers how to connect with readers. See "The Self-Publishing Option Resources" to get a better idea of their approach.

You can get advice on selling publishing know-how from independent publishers around the country (who may advise you, too, on marketing valuable artifacts—like your mailing list).

Lecturing

Lecturing is lucrative; in fact, it's what supports a good many well-known writers. For months every year, these prominent authors crisscross the country to speak before civic and corporate groups and on college campuses, and many of them earn well over a thousand dollars per speech. (The take for beginners is lower, of course.)

The lecture bureaus that schedule celebrities' talks (*LMP* has a list) are prepared to welcome new clients, but, as in any other business, a recommendation from a respected source and a strong presentation will increase the odds for acceptance.

Both in approaching lecture agents and in fulfilling the engagements they'll get you if they take you on, you should be aware that what works when you write won't necessarily work when you talk. For a piece of writing, as Bill Leigh of the Leigh Bureau explains, is directed to a class of individuals, but a speech is directed to a group; and what people in groups want to hear is the voice of authority. You should concentrate, therefore, not on your writing but on its subject; stress your theme, your points and your credentials. And use the intimate, first-person approach that's so powerful in print sparingly, if at all, on the platform.

Teaching

Though it doesn't pay as well as lecturing, teaching makes a good sideline for writers too, and draws on many of the same skills. Enrollments in writing and journalism classes are strong today, and almost every area of the country has continuing-education programs that might be hospitable to new courses. If you're interested in teaching, explore opportunities at prisons and rehabilitation centers as well as at schools in your region; and send for catalogs. Maybe one of the instructors listed will agree to advise you about drafting and submitting a course proposal.

Teaching has several attractions. Serious writers report that helping others learn writing teachniques gives them new insights into their own creative processes, and that contact with both students and fellow instructors is often stimulating. Furthermore, the pay is steady, at least as long as the semester lasts, and much longer than that in most cases.

Endnote

✻ ✻ ✻

Righting the Scales
of Success

DOWN DEEP WHERE it matters—on some subrational level—it's natural for authors to suspect that pub date constitutes the publishing industry's equivalent of the theater's opening night. And it would be nice if it did. After the long and lonely work of writing and the petty aggravations of production, there ought to come a time when the audience cheers and the critics dole out stars and a person knows for sure whether to pop open the champagne at a party or slink off to a bar all alone.

In the normal course of events, however, a writer's audience is apt to remain silent (people almost never volunteer comments on what they've read unless it made them mad); potential critics will probably pay no attention (reviewers ignore magazine pieces and the vast majority of new books); and any responses that do come an author's way are liable to be hell on the impulse that wants certainty because they'll straggle in over such a long period of time and be so liberally sprinkled with waffle words ("Despite its flaws . . ."; "Despite its promise . . ."; "Despite its very real merits . . .").

But if random reactions are imperfect indicators of accomplishment, the supposedly scientific polls known as bestseller surveys are even worse. Credited by the public with mirroring its response to what's published, all the bestseller lists actually aim to reveal is which trade books are selling well in bookstores, and they rank even that small fraction of what people read more in terms of rate of sale than in terms of sales per se. As a result, a book that sells 2,000 copies a week for ten weeks in a particular set of stores may make the list, while another book that sells hundreds of thousands of copies over a five-year period will never get near it.

Worse still, and more important, bestseller lists don't generally rank anything right. The bookstore managers who supply data to compilers have learned over the years that the bestseller label stimulates demand, and they're not above reporting inflated sales figures for a specific book simply because—having been persuaded to order large quantities of it—they want it hyped.

On at least one memorable occasion, booksellers cited a book that hadn't been written yet, let alone published and sold, as a current bestseller, and although their motivations may have been a bit obscure in that instance, it is clear enough on the whole that bookstore managers (and publishers too) can and do regularly skew bestseller standings, so that nobody knows just what they may mean.

Given this set of circumstances, most writers find that publication day comes and goes and leaves in its wake nothing but a gnawing sense of anticlimax that can lead eventually to a debilitating conviction of failure. In fact, only two kinds of authors are likely to get a fair share of pleasure from getting published: (1) those whose books the major houses, book clubs and TV and movie studios catapult to commercial success (no matter what your personal hierarchy of values is, almost everybody in our culture gets a warm feeling at some level from winning fame and money); and (2) those who've learned from this book, or from any other source, how to go where readers they respect will appreciate them and how to appreciate themselves.

Techniques for reaching appropriate and appreciative audiences have already been outlined—in "Why and How to Be Your Own Best Sales Force" and in "Managing Sales"—but techniques for arranging to appreciate yourself are harder to explain, partly because the subject is fraught with tension. In the light of our Puritan heritage, it's hard not to believe that to appreciate yourself is to be proud, and to be proud is to be vain, and to be vain is to be threatened by comeuppance.

Forget that. If you got your work published and read, you have plenty to be proud about, and the more parts of the publishing process you completed successfully, the more plaudits you've earned. Furthermore, nobody's in a better position than you are to evaluate the extent and nature of your accomplishments.

The Achievement Awards list that follows is designed as a playful first step to help people who write learn to sing their own praises. At the outset, you may feel uncomfortable claiming credit for anything on it but the items that you can recite with a faintly self-mocking air. In the end, however, perhaps you'll abandon all pretense of sophistication, add freely to the list in your mind, and accept all legitimate commendations—whatever their cultural authority—with unself-conscious joy.

Start by assuming that you're fully entitled to applause if you have:

* Had a manuscript accepted (over 90 percent of the material submitted to publishing houses is regularly turned down).
* Discovered a way to issue a book or periodical on your own.
* Produced an aesthetically pleasing piece of work.
* Elicited congratulatory letters and phone calls from family and friends (who may or may not have read whatever it was you wrote).
* Elicited congratulatory letters and phone calls from total strangers who've not only read your work but liked it enough to comment on it.
* Gotten enthusiastic and insightful reviews.
* Gotten bad reviews with good lines in them.
* Created a tangible literary object with your name on it that snuggles on the shelf between James and Kafka.
* Built friendships—with your editor, agent, art director, readers, small-press publishers, distant colleagues.
* Mastered a new skill (paste-up, proofreading, public speaking).

* Become eligible for membership in the Authors Guild and for all the grants and prizes only published writers can win.
* Found and informed the audience that will benefit by your work, even though it numbers only 2,000 readers and they're scattered all over the country.
* Furthered a cause.
* Generated interest in whatever you do next.
* Managed to escape the 9-to-5 rat race without descending to a subsistence standard of living.
* Learned a new language ("I want the picture flopped and a 9-point caption; that's the wrong font").
* Established a track record (getting published is always easier when you have a past to parade as well as a future to promise).
* Completed what you started. Now, instead of a wistful interior monologue—"Someday I've got to write that up"—you can be party to a spirited public dialogue—"Your piece [magazine, book] made me think [laugh, weep, see more clearly, want to tell you that . . ."].

And if ever you lose sight, for a moment, of the mysterious force that prompted you to sit down and write to begin with, listen to R. V. Cassill: "Writing is a way of coming to terms with the world and with oneself. The whole spirit of writing is to overcome narrowness and fear by giving order, measure, and significance to the flux of experience constantly dinning into our lives." And that's no small achievement.

Resources

* * *

✳ ✳ ✳

How to Use Resources

This next section is designed to function as a giant Swiss Army knife. There are implements in it to serve almost any purpose you can dream up, so long as you use them creatively and with care.

If you keep it somewhere handy, you can use spare moments to browse back and forth among the listings, picking out different ones to use at different times in somewhat different ways and allowing your mind to play with the possibilities.

Before you make a sizable commitment to anyone or anything mentioned here, please investigate it with your own aims in view. Obviously, you'll have to determine not only what you need at any given point but also whether, when you need it, it still fits the description it merited when its writeup went to press.

Because book prices are unstable, they're not listed, but every book recommended here was available in libraries and/or for sale at a reasonable cost when it was selected as a Resource, and many could be had either in hardcover or in money-saving paperback editions. For the ultimate in savings, be sure to see the free catalogs and pamphlets mentioned throughout the following pages.

When the star appears, it indicates goods or services that should be exceptionally valuable to authors.

Getting the Words Right Resources

SINGLY AND IN a multitude of combinations, the listings below will help you uncover fresh material and find the time, the temerity and the talent to write it up successfully.

Advice, Analysis and Reportage

Alberti, Robert E. *Your Perfect Write: The Manual for Self-Help Writers.* Impact Publishers, P.O. Box 1094, San Luis Obispo, CA 93406. 1985.

Bob Alberti knows what he's talking about; he heads Impact Publishers, which specializes in self-help books.

Atkins, Gary, and William Rivers. *Reporting with Understanding.* Iowa State University Press, 2121 South State Avenue, Ames, IA 50010. 1987.

Examples, exercises, analysis and advice on how to get and present information, with emphasis in later chapters on special interests, including political, environmental and minority affairs.

Barzun, Jacques. *On Writing, Editing, and Publishing: Essays Explicative and Hortatory.* University of Chicago Press, 5801 South Ellis Avenue, Chicago, IL 60637. Second edition, 1986.

See "Advice, Analysis and Reportage" in "The Sale and Its Sequels Resources."

Blue, Martha. *Making It Legal: A Law Primer for the Craftmaker,*

Visual Artist and Writer. Northland Press, P.O. Box N, Flagstaff, AZ 86002. 1988.

In its first incarnation, *Making It Legal* presented solid, upbeat information well seasoned with common sense and geared to artists of various sorts. Martha Blue's new version, which is in the works at this writing, will offer expanded coverage of writers' special concerns.

Bonham-Carter, Victor. *Authors by Profession.* William Kaufmann, Inc., 95 First Street, Los Altos, CA. 94022. 1978.

If you think writers today have it tough and you pine for the good old days when publishers were gentlemen who considered literary merit and never the buck, you'll have to think twice after you read Bonham-Carter's history of authorship from the beginning of printing in the sixteenth century to the introduction of the Copyright Act in 1911. It appears that publishers have always been interested in making—and keeping—as much money as possible and that authors have always cried *Unfair!* To wit: a Society for the Prevention of Cruelty to Authors was formed in 1884.

✻ **Brande, Dorothea.** *Becoming a Writer.* Jeremy P. Tarcher, Inc., 9110 Sunset Boulevard, Los Angeles, CA 90069; 1-800-221-7945. 1981.

This book aims to "teach the beginner not how to write, but how to be a writer." Focusing mainly on fiction, Dorothea Brande asserts that there really is a magic about writing and that it can be taught. What she has to say is as eye-opening today as it was when it first appeared in 1934.

Brown, Rita Mae. *Starting from Scratch: A Different Kind of Writers' Manual.* Bantam Books, 666 Fifth Avenue, New York, NY 10103. 1988.

The author of *Rubyfruit Jungle* and *High Hearts* (among other novels) has definite ideas about how writers should live and learn. Her ebullient, bossy book includes imaginative exercises.

Bryant, Jean. *Anybody Can Write: A Playful Approach.* Whatever Publishing, Inc., P.O. Box 137, Mill Valley, CA 94942. 1985.

Friendly advice and enjoyable exercises to get your creative juices flowing.

Burnett, Hallie. *On Writing the Short Story.* Harper & Row, 10 East 53rd Street, New York, NY 10022. 1983.

Teacher, editor and writer Hallie Burnett presents essays about plot, character, style and the other elements of good short fiction along with six stories that illustrate her points.

* **Burroway, Janet.** *Writing Fiction: A Guide to Narrative Craft.* **Little, Brown, 34 Beacon Street, Boston, MA 02108. Second edition, 1987.**

    A creative writing textbook that's a joy to read. Janet Burroway, whose own prose is a delight, focuses on stories by twenty-one leading modern writers—including Jamaica Kincaid, Bobbie Ann Mason, Peter Taylor and Raymond Carver—to explore form and structure, the writing process, methods of character presentation and other essential aspects of fiction.

* **Cassill, R. V.** *Writing Fiction.* **Prentice-Hall, Route 9W, Englewood Cliffs, NJ 07632. Second edition, 1975.**

    Cassill, who's written some highly acclaimed fiction himself, advocates learning to write by reading the best writing available and by comparing your writing with that by more experienced hands. He includes readings along with his text and offers a good deal of instruction about how to analyze the ways writers produce their effects. A fine book that covers all the stages necessary in writing fiction, including getting started.

Dickey, James. *Self-Interviews.* **Recorded and edited by Barbara and James Ross. Louisiana State University Press, Highland Road, Baton Rouge, LA 70893. 1970.**

A fascinating tour of the mind of a poet. In an appealing conversational voice, Dickey interweaves observations about writing poems with reportage about his life. For material about Dickey's fiction, see *Sorties* (also available from LSU Press), which presents journal entries along with a handful of essays.

First Person Singular: Writers on Their Craft. **Compiled by Joyce Carol Oates. Ontario Review Press, 1985. Distributed by Persea Books, 225 Lafayette Street, New York, NY 10012.**

An illuminating collection of essays by and interviews with more than two dozen leading writers, including Anne Tyler, Reynolds Price, Cynthia Ozick and Eudora Welty.

Fontaine, André, and William A. Glavin, Jr. *The Art of Writing Nonfiction.* **Syracuse University Press, 1600 Jamesville Avenue, Syracuse, NY 13244-5160. Second edition, 1987.**

A more accurate title for this helpful handbook would have been *The Art of Writing the Interpretive Story*, "interpretive journalism" being the authors' term for the "new journalism" pioneered by Tom Wolfe and others some decades ago.

Goldberg, Natalie. *Writing Down the Bones: Freeing the Writer Within.* **Shambhala Publications, Inc., 314 Dartmouth Street, Boston, MA 02116. 1986.**

Natalie Goldberg, a teacher of writing and a student of Zen Buddhism, offers practical advice about writing and "about using writing as . . . a way to help you penetrate your life and become sane."

Hensley, Dennis E. *Writing for Profit.* **Thomas Nelson, P.O. Box 141000, Nashville, TN 37214-1000. 1985.**

A columnist for *The Christian Writer* briskly covers the basics. His advice is occasionally simplistic but generally sound.

Holmes, Marjorie. *Writing the Creative Article Today.* **The Writer, Inc., 120 Boylston Street, Boston, MA 02116. 1986.**

The author of a good many inspirational books and articles shares her insights about creating saleable pieces.

* **Horowitz, Lois.** *Knowing Where to Look: The Ultimate Guide to Research.* **Writer's Digest Books, 1507 Dana Avenue, Dept. JA, Cincinnati, OH 45207. 1984.**

Don't dismiss the subtitle as hyperbole. This is a meaty, comprehensive and thoroughly readable guide. Sections on indexes and on looking for addresses, statistics and other particular kinds of information are especially valuable.

Jerome, Judson. *On Being a Poet.* **Writer's Digest Books, 1507 Dana Avenue, Dept. JA, Cincinnati, OH 45207. 1984.**

Straight talk about the wellsprings and consequences of poetry, with instructive examples from Jerome's own work and from work by other poets he respects or, occasionally, exposes.

* **Jerome, Judson.** *The Poet's Handbook.* **Writer's Digest Books, 1507 Dana Avenue, Dept. JA, Cincinnati, OH 45207. 1980.**

A remarkably deft tutorial, based partly on Jerome's column in *Writer's Digest* magazine, for everyone who wants to write "effective comprehensible poetry."

Kilpatrick, James J. *The Writer's Art.* Andrews, McMeel & Parker, 4400 Johnson Drive, Fairway, KS 66205. 1984.

What to do and what not to do to become a better writer. Kilpatrick is an opinionated and engaging instructor who provides wonderful examples to prove his points.

Klauser, Henriette Anne. *Writing on Both Sides of the Brain: Breakthrough Techniques for People Who Write.* Harper & Row, 10 East 53rd Street, New York, NY 10022. 1986.

First you use the right side of your brain to create; then you use the left side to edit. According to Henriette Anne Klauser, who runs Writing Resource Workshops, it's when we try to write and edit simultaneously that we run into problems. Her incisive, energizing manual explains just how you can separate the two functions and why you'll be glad you did.

Law and the Writer. Edited by Kirk Polking and Leonard S. Meranus. Writer's Digest Books, 1507 Dana Avenue, Dept. JA. Cincinnati, OH 45207. Third edition, 1985.

Essays designed to acquaint writers with the major legal issues that affect them. Note: this edition was published before the recent tax law changes.

Loring, Ann, and Evelyn Kaye. *Write and Sell Your TV Drama.* Alek Publishing Company, 147 Sylvan Avenue, Leonia, NJ 07605. 1984.

Clear, step-by-step instructions derived from a course Loring teaches at the New School in New York.

Mann, Thomas. *A Guide to Library Research Methods.* Oxford University Press, 200 Madison Avenue, New York, NY 10016. 1987.

Good solid guidance, including a chapter that shows how to get information from people outside the library and why it's important to do that.

McCormack, Thomas. *The Fiction Editor.* St. Martin's Press, 175 Fifth Avenue, New York, NY 10010. 1988.

The head of St. Martin's Press offers conceptual tools that both writers and editors can use to diagnose and solve problems with fiction manuscripts. Pungent, persuasive, engaging and edifying.

McGraw-Hill Book Company. *Guidelines for Bias-Free Publishing.* McGraw-Hill, Princeton Road, Hightstown, NJ 08520. n.d.

Short, sensible and just what the title promises. *See also* Miller and Swift's *The Handbook of Nonsexist Writing,* listed below.

Meyer, Herbert E., and Jill M. Meyer. *How to Write.* **Storm King Press/Random House, P.O. Box 3566, Washington, DC 20007. 1986.**

The authors analyze and illustrate the decisions, steps, skills and techniques that go into writing any kind of prose and come up with a tidy prescription. Brisk, clear, sound advice that's most easily applicable to nonfiction.

Meyrowitz, Joshua. *No Sense of Place: The Impact of Electronic Media on Social Behavior.* **Oxford University Press, 200 Madison Avenue, New York, NY 10016. 1985.**

Professor Meyrowitz's masterly analysis includes a fascinating discussion of the powers (and limitations) of print.

* **Miller, Casey, and Kate Swift.** *The Handbook of Nonsexist Writing.* **Harper & Row, 10 East 53rd Street, New York, NY 10022. Second edition, 1988.**

It is possible—even easy, after a bit of practice—to use nonsexist language without awkwardness or ostentation. This book shows how. Highly recommended.

Murray, Donald. *Writing for Your Readers: Notes on the Writer's Craft from* **The Boston Globe. Globe Pequot Press, Old Chester Road, Chester, CT 06412. 1983.**

Although Murray has journalists in mind, the tips he offers will prove valuable for all sorts of writers. See especially his suggestions about crafting good strong leads.

Patterson, Benton Rain. *Write to Be Read: A Practical Guide to Feature Writing.* **Iowa State University Press, 2121 South State Avenue, Ames, IA 50010. 1986.**

Good solid guidance from a pro. Pointers on finding an angle and organizing a piece are especially helpful.

Poets & Writers Magazine.

See "Advice, Analysis and Reportage" in "A Foot in the Door Resources."

The Poet's Craft: Interviews from **The New York Quarterly. Edited** by William Packard. Paragon House Publishers, 2 Hammarskjold Plaza, New York, NY 10017. 1987.

Richard Wilbur, Diane Wakoski, Erica Jong and Gary Snyder are among the twenty-five poets who talk here about their work and how they do it.

Poynter, Dan, and Mindy Bingham. *Is There a Book Inside You? How to Successfully Author a Book Alone or Through Collaboration.* Para Publishing, P.O. Box 4232, Santa Barbara, CA 93140-4232. 1985.

If you're intrigued by the question the title poses and not sure what the answer is in your case, use the exercises here to find out.

Rico, Gabriele Lusser. *Writing the Natural Way: Using Right-Brain Techniques to Release Your Expressive Powers.* Jeremy P. Tarcher, Inc., 9110 Sunset Boulevard, Los Angeles, CA 90069. 1983.

Gabriele Lusser Rico offers undergraduates and others a system designed to foster self-expression.

Rivers, William L. *Finding Facts: Interviewing, Observing, Using Reference Sources.* Prentice-Hall, Route 9W, Englewood Cliffs, NJ 07632. 1975.

A brilliant discussion—with persuasive examples—of the elusiveness of truth and the power of perception to distort, this makes an excellent complement to Alden Todd's *Finding Facts Fast* (see below).

* **Roberts, Ellen E. M.** *The Children's Picture Book: How to Write It, How to Sell It.* Writer's Digest Books, 1507 Dana Avenue, Dept. JA, Cincinnati, OH 45207. 1981.

You don't just get detailed, practical guidance from Ellen Roberts's handsome, illustrated book; you also get the heartwarming feeling that this canny, experienced children's book editor wants to see you create a picture book that's as good—and as successful—as you can possibly make it. Highly recommended.

Seuling, Barbara. *How to Write a Children's Book and Get It Published.* Charles Scribner's Sons, 115 Fifth Avenue, New York, NY 10003. 1984.

Knowledgeable, encouraging, step-by-step guidance for beginners.

Shaw, Fran Weber. *30 Ways to Help You Write.* Bantam, 666 Fifth Avenue, New York, NY 10103. 1980.

An invigorating handbook full of practical tips to put to use right now, from getting those first painstaking words on the page, to organizing your material, to learning how to be your own best editor. This is a book you'll turn to again and again; see especially "Twelve Things to Try When You're Stuck."

* **Strunk, William, Jr., and E. B. White.** *The Elements of Style.* **Macmillan, 866 Third Avenue, New York, NY 10022. Third edition, 1979.**

    By now this collection of clearly and amusingly written "rules" of style is considered virtually sacrosanct. A valuable and thoroughly enjoyable classic.

Tarshis, Barry. *How to Write Without Pain.* **New American Library/Plume, 1633 Broadway, New York, NY 10019. 1985.**

Like Herbert and Jill Meyer (see above), Barry Tarshis breaks the writing process down into steps with a view toward making it more manageable. His prescription is less precise but generally sensible and encouraging.

* **Todd, Alden.** *Finding Facts Fast: How to Find Out What You Want and Need to Know.* **Ten Speed Press, P.O. Box 7123, Berkeley, CA 94707. Second edition, 1979.**

    As this entire "Resources" section demonstrates, there's no dearth of places, people and publications to consult when you're in need of information. In fact, your major problem may be selecting wisely from among the available sources of data, and it's advice on this question that Todd gives in his remarkably thorough and readable manual. Highly recommended for anyone whose writing projects include research.

Ueland, Brenda. *If You Want to Write.* **Graywolf Press, P.O. Box 75006, St. Paul, MN 55175. Second edition, 1987.**

"Everybody is talented, original and has something important to say." That's Brenda Ueland's position, based on her experiences as a writer and a writing teacher. First published in 1938, *If You Want to Write* dispenses courage as well as advice. Most useful for fiction.

Van Til, William. *Writing for Professional Publication.* **Allyn and Bacon, Inc., 7 Wells Avenue, Newton, MA 02159. Second edition, 1986.**

A knowledgeable introduction to professional, scholarly and textbook publishing. The text is couched as dialogue and laced with examples and references.

Venolia, Jan. *Write Right! A Desk Drawer Digest of Punctuation, Grammar & Style.* **Ten Speed Press/Periwinkle Press, P.O. Box 7123, Berkeley, CA 94707. 1982.**
A chatty, well-organized handbook.

Wallace, Robert. *Writing Poems.* **Bits Press/Little, Brown, Department of English, Case Western Reserve University, Cleveland, OH 44106. Second edition, 1987.**
This rich, inventive and encouraging book is designed to "provide the circumstances" that foster learning for poets. Focusing on form, content and process, Wallace writes with grace and sophistication about work by many contemporary poets, including himself and some of his students. And he provides excellent exercises in his "Questions and Suggestions" sections.

Welty, Eudora. *One Writer's Beginnings.* **Warner Books, 666 Fifth Avenue, New York, NY 10103. 1984.**
Eudora Welty's charming memoirs illuminate a fiction writer's mind-set.

White, Stephen. *The Written Word and Associated Digressions Concerned with the Writer as Craftsman.* **Harper & Row, 10 East 53rd Street, New York, NY 10022. 1984.**
Charming, opinionated tutelage on writing expository prose from a journalist who wrote often about science.

The Writer. **The Writer, 120 Boylston Street, Boston, MA 02116. Published monthly.**
This venerable magazine features instructive essays by published writers (some of them very well known) along with editors' opinions, news tidbits and lists of special-interest markets. The Writer also publishes books for beginning writers. Send for an annotated list.

Writer's Digest.
See "Advice, Analysis and Reportage" in "A Foot in the Door Resources."

* *A Writer's Guide to Copyright.* **Poets & Writers, Inc., 201 West 54th Street, New York, NY 10019. 1979.**

A clear, concise, inexpensive guide, complete with sample forms, a bibliography and, by way of example, the standard Random House contract circa 1979.

Writers' Journal. Inkling Publications, Inc., P.O. Box 65798, St. Paul, MN 55165-0798. Published bimonthly.

A friendly, informative periodical "that strives to encourage the writers of today toward the success of tomorrow."

The Writer's Quotation Book. Edited by James Charlton. The Pushcart Press, P.O. Box 380, Wainscott, NY 11975. 1985.

Stylish insights into writing from leading writers of yesterday and today. The editor's juxtapositions add to the appeal. Consider, for instance: "Anything that is written to please the author is worthless" (Blaise Pascal) followed immediately by "Any writer overwhelmingly honest about pleasing himself is almost sure to please others" (Marianne Moore).

Zinsser, William. *On Writing Well: An Informal Guide to Writing Nonfiction.* Harper & Row, 10 East 53rd Street, New York, NY 10022. Third edition, 1985.

Zinsser, an established writer who has taught writing at Yale, explains the importance of discipline in learning to write and to self-edit. Excerpts from his own working drafts—which show just what self-editing entails—and his analyses of leads are especially valuable.

Zinsser, William. *Writing with a Word Processor.* Harper & Row, 10 East 53rd Street, New York, NY 10022. 1983.

If you're opposed to writing on a computer, let Zinsser give you the whole story of why and how even a "mechanical boob" learned to love word processing.

Tools

* Bell, Marion V., and Eleanor A. Swidan. *Reference Books: A Brief Guide.* Enoch Pratt Free Library, Publications Office, 400 Cathedral Street, Baltimore, MD 21201-4484. Ninth edition, 1987.

A superb introduction to the best of the reference books, divided into general and special subject categories. The annotated listings should give reference-room users confidence that they'll be able to ferret out whatever facts they're after.

Chase's Annual Events. Compiled by William D. and Helen M. Chase. Contemporary Books, 180 North Michigan Avenue, Chicago, IL 60601. Updated annually.

Fun to read and useful for finding news pegs on which to hang light pieces for hometown papers or small magazines. Chase's calendar will also alert you to upcoming fairs, conventions and exhibits that might be worth covering or simply attending. Over 5,000 events in all.

Directory of Accredited Home Study Schools. National Home Study Council, 1601 18th Street, NW, Washington, DC 20009. Updated periodically.

Before you sign up for a home study program, write for this free list of accredited schools.

A Directory of American Poets and Fiction Writers. Poets & Writers, Inc., 201 West 54th Street, New York, NY 10019. Updated periodically.

Unlike most directories of contemporary writers, this one is inexpensive enough that you can own it yourself. More than 6,000 writers are listed (Saul Bellow, Mary McCarthy and John Updike, among them), along with their addresses and phone numbers. A good tool for contacting professional writers.

Directory of Special Libraries and Information Centers. Edited by Brigitte T. Darnay; John Nimchuk, associate editor. Gale Research Company, Book Tower, Detroit, MI 48226. Updated periodically.

Check the subject index for troves of information on the subject you're researching.

Encyclopedia of Associations. Gale Research Company, Book Tower, Detroit, MI 48226. Updated periodically.

The roughly 20,000 organizations and reference centers listed here can supply information and leads on almost any topic. Indexed in terms of geography as well as area of interest, entries are extremely informative.

Gale Research Company Catalog. Gale Research Company, Book Tower, Detroit, MI 48226.

This free catalog will familiarize you with a wide variety of reference books that will help you in all kinds of research.

Guide to Reference Books. **Edited by Eugene P. Sheehy. American Library Association, 50 East Huron Street, Chicago, IL 60611. Updated periodically.**

The ultimate reference book: 14,000 titles are categorized and clearly described. Available at your library.

International Directory of Writers' Groups & Associations. **Edited by John Hall. Inkling Publications, Inc., P.O. Box 65798, St. Paul, MN 55165-0798. 1984.**

Entries cover some 2,000 groups in the United States and abroad. The directory lets you zero in on writers' gatherings in your area and offers basic advice on starting a group in case you can't find a congenial one nearby.

Literary Market Place. **R. R. Bowker, 245 West 17th Street, New York, NY 10011. Updated annually.**

As subsequent "Resources" entries will show, *LMP* has many virtues. In connection with writing, its most useful sections are "Courses for the Book Trade" (which lists programs that teach publishing skills along with programs that teach writing) and "Writers' Conferences & Workshops" (which provides a small list of the perennials that you should supplement with information gleaned from *Poets & Writers Magazine, Publishers Weekly* and the May issues of *The Writer* and *Writer's Digest,* all of which are described elsewhere in "Resources."

Readers' Guide to Periodical Literature. **H. W. Wilson Company, 950 University Avenue, Bronx, NY 10452-9978. Updated periodically.**

The leading bibliography of articles from mass-circulation and other fairly general magazines, the *Readers' Guide* is useful for tracking down a piece you read some time ago that's relevant now to your work; for finding out what's appeared in the periodical press about a subject you're researching; and for introducing yourself to varied angles on the same topic (see "Basics"). To get the most mileage from this guide, be sure to look under every subject heading that might possibly pertain to your needs.

Research Centers Directory. **Edited by Mary Michelle Watkins. Gale Research Company, Book Tower, Detroit, MI 48226. Updated periodically.**

A guide to university-related and other nonprofit research organizations, this directory supplies excellent leads to experts and expertise. Indexed by subject.

"Rewriting," *Literary Market Place* **(see above).**

Plenty of professional writers are ready to give you a hand in expressing what you have to say, and this list will lead you to a number of them. In approaching a potential collaborator, be sure to ask for an estimate and to get and check references.

SoftQuad Author/Editor™. SoftQuad Inc., 720 Spadina Avenue, Toronto, Ontario, Canada M5S 2T9.

A new personal computer program designed to make it easy for authors to prepare copy keyed for typesetting. Write for information.

***Statistics Sources.* Edited by Jacqueline Wasserman O'Brien and Steven R. Wasserman. Gale Research Company, Book Tower, Detroit, MI 48226. Updated periodically.**

Arranged by subject, this book will tell you where to find organizations and publications that can supply data you need.

***Subject Guide to Books in Print.* R. R. Bowker, 245 West 17th Street, New York, NY 10011. Updated annually.**

To get a good idea of what's already been written about your subject, consult this compilation. Useful for a style survey as well as for research leads, the *Subject Guide* is on hand at most libraries and many bookstores, though you may have to ask for permission to use it.

***The Writer's Advisor.* Compiled by Leland G. Alkire, Jr. Gale Research Company, Book Tower, Detroit, MI 48226. 1985.**

Annotated listings of approximately 800 books and 3,000 articles on varied aspects of writing, from "Characterization, Voice, and Viewpoint" to "Tax Considerations."

***The Writers Directory.* St. James Press, 425 North Michigan Avenue, Chicago, IL 60611. Updated periodically.**

You'll find brief biographies here—with addresses—of more than 16,000 writers who have had at least one full-length work published in English. Get hold of it at the library to track down professional writers you'd like to contact, and check its subject index to add to your list.

***The Writer's Yellow Pages.* Steve Davis Publishing, P.O. Box 190831, Dallas, TX 75219. 1988.**

In the works at this writing, Steve Davis's directory is scheduled to list names, addresses and phone numbers of approximately 25,000 companies in more than forty categories, including: writing supplies, tour escorts, book reviewers, producers, grammar hotlines and college writing departments.

People, Places and Programs

Associated Writing Programs, Old Dominion University, Norfolk, VA 23508-8510; 1-804-440-3839.

A clearinghouse for information, AWP puts out a newsletter and a catalog of writing programs, presents awards and publishes work by "the most accomplished student writers" in an annual volume called *Intro*.

Dial-a-Writer, American Society of Journalists and Authors, 1501 Broadway, Suite 1907, New York, NY 10036; 1-212-398-1934.

Ask for help in locating potential co-authors in your area if you feel sure that your own efforts at composition are bound to be inadequate for one reason or another. If writers surface whom you might like to work with, study what they've already published, ask for and check their references and draw up a written agreement specifying the terms of the deal with you.

Editorial Freelancers Association, Inc., P.O. Box 2050, Madison Square Station, New York, NY 10159; 1-212-677-3357.

You may find just the right editor, collaborator or ghostwriter by using the EFA's Job Phone. As above, remember to ask for writing samples, to get and check references and to be clear about the deal you're making.

International Women's Writing Guild, Box 810, Gracie Station, New York, NY 10028.

Describing itself as "an alliance open to all women connected to the written word," the Guild aims to encourage and support both published and aspiring writers by running conferences, offering health insurance and issuing a newsletter, among other things.

National University Continuing Education Association, One Dupont Circle, Suite 420, Washington, DC 20036.

Representing colleges and other institutions that offer continuing education programs, this association is a good source of leads for writers who can't afford to study full-time. Write for information.

* **Poets & Writers, Inc., 201 West 54th Street, New York, NY 10019; 1-212-757-1766.**

The people at Poets & Writers have figured out lots of ways to improve the quality of a writer's life. The group's publications are designed especially for writers of fiction and poetry but they're helpful to writers of all sorts. Among them are *Poets & Writers Magazine,* the *Directory of American Poets and Fiction Writers,* a sponsors list, a list of literary bookstores and a booklet about agents. Send for the publications order form and the informational brochure, and if you write fiction or poetry ask to be listed in the next edition of the directory.

Ross Book Service, 3718 Seminary Road, Seminary Post Office, Alexandria, VA 22304-0993.

One-stop mail-order shopping for many or most of the books you'll find listed below. Miriam Ross keeps more than 1,000 titles in stock and will be glad to order others that you want. Write for details.

U.S. government.

A prime source of information on countless subjects. Write to the public relations staff of appropriate departments to request help in getting the data you want.

Writers Conferences.

See "Tools" in "A Foot in the Door Resources."

The Writers Room, 153 Waverly Place, New York, NY 10014; 1-212-807-9519.

Dozens of writers rent space at modest rates in New York City's Writers Room, which functions as a support system and a grapevine as well as an office. Interested writers in the New York area are invited to send for applications. If you live elsewhere, check around for a comparable facility, and if you can't find one, think about asking the New York room's board of directors for guidance on setting one up.

A Foot in the Door Resources

SINCE MAKING SALES to publishers depends on who you know, what you know and how you present each project, many of the resources mentioned here are designed to serve as introductions not only to markets but to people and procedures that can help you gain entry to publishing firms.

Advice, Analysis and Reportage

Adams, Jane. *How to Sell What You Write.* Putnam/Perigee, 200 Madison Avenue, New York, NY 10016. 1984.

Adams advises writers to think of their work as Product created for two different markets—the publishers or producers, whom she calls Buyers, and the readers, or Customers. It's a sound schematic, well worth keeping in mind. See also her pointers on reaching many markets with variants of the same material.

Book Publishing Career Directory. Edited by Ronald W. Fry. The Career Press, Inc., P.O. Box 34, Hawthorne, NJ 07507; 1-800-CAREER-1.

Reports by insiders about what kind of work they do and about breaking in to their special areas. Informative and (if you ignore the sometimes slipshod copy-editing) generally encouraging.

Book Reviewing. Edited by Sylvia E. Kamerman. The Writer, Inc., 120 Boylston Street, Boston, MA 02116. 1978.

If you're interested in writing book reviews, Kamerman's collection of pieces by leading book editors and reviewers is a godsend. Christopher Lehmann-Haupt, senior book reviewer of *The New York Times*, explains how to get both information about the plot and opinion into a short piece. Doris Grumbach explains how she assigns book reviews and says the best approach for a first-timer might be to send a review, rather than query first. Sample reviews are included and annotated. Lively, informative reading.

Boswell, John. *The Awful Truth about Publishing: Why They Always Reject Your Manuscript . . . And What You Can Do about It.* **Warner Books, 666 Fifth Avenue, New York, NY 10103. 1986.**

A mainstream agent, packager and writer, Boswell seems to have a blind spot when it comes to small publishers and nontraditional sales channels, but he's candid and clever about the way large trade book houses operate.

Burgett, Gordon. *Query Letters, Cover Letters: How They Sell Your Writing.* **Communication Unlimited, P.O. Box 1001, Carpinteria, CA 93013. 1985.**

Burgett uses his own letters as examples in this amiable guide.

The Business of Book Publishing: Papers by Practitioners. **Edited by Elizabeth A. Geiser and Arnold Dolin, with Gladys S. Topkis. Westview Press, 5500 Central Avenue, Boulder, CO 80301. 1985.**

This anthology stems from the solid, stimulating Publishing Institute held each summer at the University of Denver.

Columbia Journalism Review, **700A Journalism Building, Columbia University, New York, NY 10027. Published bimonthly.**

You can use the reports and analyses here to get a sense of the issues that are now important to newspaper editors and to amass information about particular papers and editors. Every issue also offers a page of wonderfully funny typos.

Coser, Lewis A., Charles Kadushin and Walter W. Powell. *Books: The Culture and Commerce of Publishing.* **University of Chicago Press, 5801 South Ellis Avenue, Chicago IL 60637.**

Based in large part on interviews with eighty-five editors from fifty-six houses (most of them in the New York metropolitan area), this sociological analysis of book publishing has some interesting observations to offer—among them, the finding that only 25 percent of the new authors at trade houses in the sample studied made their initial contacts with their publishers through agents.

Curtis, Richard. *How to Be Your Own Literary Agent: The Business of Getting Your Book Published.* **Houghton Mifflin, One Beacon Street, Boston, MA 02108. Revised edition, 1984.**

Curtis, who's both an agent and an author, is spunky and candid about dealing with large mainstream book publishers. *How to Be a Savvy, Helpful Client of a Literary Agent or a Literary Property Lawyer* would be a better title for his book, though, since it isn't smart for writers to represent themselves in negotiations with big firms.

Davis, Kenneth C. *Two-Bit Culture: The Paperbacking of America.* **Houghton Mifflin, One Beacon Street. Boston, MA 02108. 1984.**

Davis blends reportage, portraiture and analysis to chronicle a revolution in trade book pricing and distribution. His lively discussion sheds a good deal of light on the public's taste in reading and on what popular books reveal about contemporary culture.

Day, Robert A. *How to Write and Publish a Scientific Paper.* **ISI Press, 3501 Market Street, Philadelphia, PA 19104. Second edition, 1983.**

Knowledgeable and readable.

Dennison, Sally. *[Alternative] Literary Publishing: Five Modern Histories.* **University of Iowa Press, University of Iowa, Iowa City, IA 52242. 1984.**

Five captivating stories of writers who succeeded without—or in spite of—the publishing establishment.

Gage, Diane, and Marcia Hibsch Coppess. *Get Published: Editors from the Nation's Top Magazines Tell You What They Want.* **Henry Holt and Company, 521 Fifth Avenue, New York, NY 10175. 1986.**

Profiles of eighty-nine national magazines plus general advice on writing for these markets, which the authors do.

Literary agents.

See Mayer, below, and listings in "Tools" and "People, Places and Programs."

Luey, Beth. *Handbook for Academic Authors.* **Cambridge University**

Press, 32 East 57th Street, New York, NY 10022; 1-800-872-7423 (1-800-227-0247 in New York State). 1987.

A readable, informative overview, although the author has blind spots when it comes to authors turning their copyrights over to publishers (don't do it unless you absolutely must) and to self-publishing as an option for academic authors (professors often self-publish successfully).

Magazines Career Directory. Edited by Ronald W. Fry. The Career Press, Inc., P.O. Box 34, Hawthorne, NJ 07507; 1-800-CAREER-1. Second edition, 1987.

Tips from people who work at magazines big and small about what kinds of jobs exist and how to get them.

Mayer, Debby. *Literary Agents: A Writer's Guide.* Poets & Writers, Inc., 201 West 54th Street, New York, NY 10019. 1988.

Based on a survey of agents listed in *Literary Market Place* and on interviews that illuminate the author-agent relationship, this is a readable, informative handbook.

Mogel, Leonard. *Making It in the Media Professions: A Realistic Guide to Career Opportunities in Newspapers, Magazines, Books, Television, Radio, the Movies, and Advertising.* Globe Pequot Press, Old Chester Road, Chester, CT 06412. 1988.

Mogel, whose own experience has been primarily with magazines, skillfully covers a broad spectrum of careers here.

Newspapers Career Directory. Edited by Ronald W. Fry. The Career Press, Inc., P.O. Box 34, Hawthorne, NJ 07507; 1-800-CAREER-1. 1987.

Like the other volumes (on books and magazines) in the Career Directory series, this one offers advice from practitioners on a wide range of job opportunities.

✳ *Poets & Writers Magazine.* Poets & Writers, Inc., 201 West 54th Street, New York, NY 10019. Published bimonthly.

Along with timely, solid information (when and how to apply for grants and awards, what various writers' colonies offer, where to find fellow writers in your area), *Poets & Writers Magazine* has feature stories that shed light both on creating prose and poetry and on attracting readers to written work. Especially appealing because, unlike some other periodicals for writers, it doesn't talk down to its audience.

Powell, Walter W. *Getting into Print: The Decision-Making Process in Scholarly Publishing.* University of Chicago Press, 5801 South Ellis Avenue, Chicago, IL 60637. 1985.

Focusing on two pseudonymous scholarly presses that he observed closely, Powell punctures publishing myths and reveals realities. His trenchant observations conclude with a skippable chapter on organizational theory.

Provost, Gary. *The Freelance Writer's Handbook.* NAL/Mentor, 1633 Broadway, New York, NY 10019. 1982.

The focus is on articles and other short prose and the discussion is rich in specific examples. Much of what's here, however, will be familiar to readers of *How to Get Happily Published.*

Sautter, Carl. *How to Sell Your Screenplay: The Real Rules of Film and Television.* New Chapter Press/Kampmann & Co., 381 Park Avenue South, Suite 1122, New York, NY 10016.

Co-author of the much-praised "black-and-white" episode of "Moonlighting," Carl Sautter offers detailed advice on how to become a screenwriter. Consistently entertaining as well as admirably instructive.

Schwed, Peter. *Turning the Pages: An Insider's Story of Simon & Schuster, 1924–1984.* Macmillan, 866 Third Avenue, New York, NY 10022. 1984.

An urbane, illustrated introduction to the people who created Simon & Schuster, the people who built it up and people who run it now.

Science Fiction Chronicle: The Monthly SF and Fantasy Newsmagazine. P.O. Box 4175, New York, NY 10163-4175. Published monthly.

Andrew Porter, who publishes and edits the *Chronicle,* packs each issue full of news and commentary and includes annotated lists of markets every four months.

Tebbel, John. *Between Covers: The Rise and Transformation of Book Publishing in America.* Oxford University Press, 200 Madison Avenue, New York, NY 10016. 1987.

In this one-volume edition of his classic four-volume *History of Book Publishing,* Tebbel starts with the seventeenth century, goes through the 1970s and focuses mainly on large trade publishing houses. A brief final chapter sketches the publishing landscape in the mid-'80s.

West, Michelle. *The No-Bull Guide to Getting Published and Making It as a Writer.* Winslow Publishing, Box 413, Station Z, Toronto, Ontario, Canada M5N 2Z5. 1986.

Zesty pointers, based on first-hand experience, about writing for magazines.

The Writer.

See "Advice, Analysis and Reportage" in "Getting the Words Right Resources."

Writer's Digest magazine, 1507 Dana Avenue, Dept. JA, Cincinnati, OH 45207. Published monthly.

Geared primarily to beginners, the articles in *Writer's Digest* sometimes promise more than they can deliver (consider, for example, a piece that tells how to propose books "to editors in such a way that they can't say no"). On the other hand, there's savvy guidance in here too. Read skeptically and you'll be able to separate the practical advice from the puffery.

The Writer's Handbook: What to Write, How to Write, Where to Sell. Edited by Sylvia K. Burack. The Writer, 120 Boylston Street, Boston, MA 02116. Updated periodically.

A raft of well-known writers, editors and agents have contributed tips to this compilation, at the back of which is a list of approximately 2,000 markets.

Writer's Northwest Handbook: A Guide to the Northwest's Writing and Publishing Industry. Media Weavers, P.O. Box 19755, Portland, OR 97219. Second edition, 1986.

Short essays on a wide variety of topics of interest to writers, plus an alphabetical annotated listing of more than 2,000 book and periodical publishers in Oregon, Washington, Idaho, Montana, Alaska and British Columbia. Resources for writers in the Pacific Northwest are listed too.

Writer's Yearbook. Writer's Digest, 1507 Dana Avenue, Dept. JA, Cincinnati, OH 45207. Updated annually.

The *Yearbook* is essentially a fatter-than-normal issue of the monthly *Writer's Digest.*

The Writing Business: A Poets & Writers Handbook by the editors of *Coda: Poets & Writers Newsletter.* Poets & Writers, Inc., 201 West 54th Street, New York, NY 10019. 1985.

Pieces published in the late '70s and early '80s, updated and intelligently arranged. Some questionable bits of advice about multiple submissions and vanity presses, but they're far outnumbered by valuable pointers on a wide range of other subjects.

Tools

Balkin, Richard. *Book Editors of North America: A Directory.* Ten Speed Press, P.O. Box 7123, Berkeley, CA 94707. 1988.

In preparation as we went to press, this directory promises to present short profiles of roughly 1,300 trade book editors and to index them according to their special interests.

The Bloomsbury Review: A Book Magazine, 1028 Bannock Street, Denver, CO 80204. Published bimonthly.

A lively periodical that provides a wider window on the world of books than more renowned review media.

Booklist. American Library Association, 50 East Huron Street, Chicago, IL 60611. Published twice monthly September–June, monthly July–August.

Together with *Choice* and *Library Journal* (both of which are listed below), *Booklist* exerts a great deal of influence on librarians as they ponder what books to buy. Skimming its reviews, you can begin to sense the patterns of public taste that libraries both reflect and help to create. A sample copy is free on request.

Book Review Digest. The H. W. Wilson Company, 950 University Avenue, Bronx, NY 10452-9978. Published periodically.

Tidbits from reviews of some 6,000 books a year appear here. Check to see (1) how critics reacted to recent books like yours and (2) which critics might be especially receptive to your work.

Boston Literary News. P.O. Box 1463, Cambridge, MA 02238. Published monthly.

Check out Bruce Morgan's newsletter if you're a writer in the Boston area.

Bowker Catalog. R. R. Bowker, 245 West 17th Street, New York, NY 10011. Free on request.

Bowker codifies and disseminates information about publishing. Simply looking at the products in the catalog should give you fresh ideas about placement, and perhaps you'll also want to get hold of some of the reference works.

Chase's Annual Events.

See "Tools" in "Getting the Words Right Resources."

Choice. Association of College and Research Libraries, American Library Association, 100 Riverview Center, Middletown, CT 06457. Published monthly except bimonthly in July–August.

See *Booklist,* above, and send for a free sample copy.

Clardy, Andrea Fleck. *Words to the Wise: A Writer's Guide to Feminist and Lesbian Periodicals & Publishers.* Firebrand Books, 141 The Commons, Ithaca, NY 14850. Second edition, 1987.

If you've written anything for a feminist and/or lesbian audience, get hold of this informative annotated guide. It covers more than 100 book and periodical publishers.

COSMEP Newsletter. COSMEP, The International Association of Independent Publishers, P.O. Box 703, San Francisco, CA 94101. Published monthly.

Some 1,200 small publishers belong to COSMEP, and its newsletter provides a window on their tastes and needs. If your library doesn't subscribe, write for information on how you can.

Directory of Poetry Publishers. Edited by Len Fulton and Ellen Ferber. Dustbooks, P.O. Box 100, Paradise, CA 95969. Updated periodically.

Detailed listings cover more than 1,500 magazines and publishing houses that welcome poetry, and there's a useful subject index.

Editor and Publisher International Year Book. Editor and Publisher, 11 West 19th Street, New York, NY 10011. Updated annually.

This directory of newspapers names department heads and gives circulation figures and other assorted bits of data for each entry. Useful for selling stories with a local slant.

Fiction Writer's Market. Writer's Digest Books, 1507 Dana Avenue, Dept. JA, Cincinnati, OH 45207. Updated annually.

Essays and profiles surround descriptions of some 1,500 markets. If you use these listings, bear in mind that the publishers labeled "commercial" may not make the most money for their authors, and ignore the advice in "How to Contact" if it conflicts with guidelines in "Procedures" (pages 77–93).

Gale Directory of Publications. Gale Research Company, Book Tower, Detroit, MI 48226. Updated periodically.

Originally the *Ayer Directory of Publications,* or *Ayer's,* this volume offers annotated listings of thousands of newspapers, magazines and trade publications. One or more of these entries may make good targets for material with a special-interest focus or a pronounced local slant.

Hudson's Newsletter Directory. The Newsletter Clearinghouse, 44 West Market Street, P.O. Box 311, Rhinebeck, NY 12572. Updated periodically.

Browse through your library's copy to see if you can find markets for your work among the thousands of subscription newsletters listed here.

International Directory of Little Magazines and Small Presses. Edited by Len Fulton and Ellen Ferber. Dustbooks, P.O. Box 100, Paradise, CA 95969. Updated periodically.

Descriptions of thousands of publishers appear in this affordable paperback, and they're indexed geographically and by subject to make it easy for writers to zero in on the appropriate ones for a particular project.

Library Journal, 245 West 17th Street, New York, NY 10011. Published twice monthly in February–June and September–November, otherwise monthly.

See *Booklist,* above.

Literary Agents of North America: The Complete Guide to U.S. and Canadian Literary Agencies. Author Aid/Research Associates International, 340 East 52nd Street, New York, NY 10022. Updated periodically.

Hundreds of agents are listed, some with richly detailed writeups; some with just the bare-bones facts.

* ***Literary Market Place.*** R. R. Bowker, 245 West 17th Street, New York, NY 10011. Updated annually.

As noted in "Getting the Words Right Resources," *LMP* is an indispensable reference work. For the purposes of getting your foot in the door, study the following sections:

"U.S. Book Publishers"; note especially the subject listing, which, although general, is handy, and the geographical location listing, which is a gold mine of good leads, particularly for regional books.

"Reference Books for the Trade"; here you'll find specialized titles that may be relevant to your current work, along with leads to books about the publishing industry.

"Literary Awards, Contests & Grants"; if you win, you'll have acquired credentials that editors will respect.

"Writers' Conferences & Workshops"; a partial but useful listing.

"Literary Agents"; with names, addresses, phone numbers and some annotations.

"Courses for the Book Trade."

"Employment Agencies" specializing in publishing positions.

* *Magazine Industry Market Place.* **R. R. Bowker, 245 West 17th Street, New York, NY 10011. Updated annually.**

The magazine world's equivalent of *Literary Market Place,* this directory lists approximately 3,500 publications, which are arranged alphabetically and indexed by type (consumer, trade, scholarly, etc.), and by subject. Sections of special interest include "Associations & Organizations" (some of which you may want to join); "Awards, Contests & Prizes" (some of which you may want to try for); and "Syndicates" (some of which you may want to contact for recycling your material).

New Pages, **4426 South Belsay Road, Grand Blanc, MI 48439. Published three times a year.**

Casey Hill's lively tabloid newspaper focuses on the alternative press.

Poet's Market: Where and How to Publish Your Poetry. **Edited by Judson Jerome, assisted by Katherine Jobst. Writer's Digest Books, 1507 Dana Avenue, Dept JA, Cincinnati, OH 45207. Updated annually.**

Unusually informative listings cover 1,500 publications. To make his directory even more enlightening, Jerome includes short, chatty "close-ups" of thirteen poetry publishers and information about poets' resources—contests, grants, conferences, colonies, organizations and the like.

Publishers' Trade List Annual. R. R. Bowker, 245 West 17th Street, New York, NY 10011. Updated annually.

Browsing through these volumes—which offer a huge collection of current book catalogs—can lead to worthwhile discoveries about the strengths, weaknesses and idiosyncrasies of individual houses. Probably the most comprehensive introduction anywhere to the personalities of individual houses and imprints.

* **Publishers Weekly.** 249 West 17th Street, New York, NY 10011.

PW, as it's familiarly known, has no equal as a source of up-to-date information about publishing facts, figures, ideas and people. You can arrange to join the insiders who read it regularly by using your library's subscription copies or by subscribing yourself. Aimed primarily at people who work with books, it frequently announces new periodicals, which provide promising markets because they're generally hungry for copy.

The Pushcart Prize: Best of the Small Presses. Edited by Bill Henderson. Pushcart Press, P.O. Box 380, Wainscott, NY 11975. Published annually.

You can look to Bill Henderson's anthology not only for fine poetry and prose but also for insight into what literary publishers are currently enthusiastic about.

Readers' Guide to Periodical Literature. The H. W. Wilson Company, 950 University Avenue, Bronx, NY 10452-9978. Updated periodically.

Available in libraries, this standard and invaluable reference tool covers nearly 200 magazines. Use the subject headings to identify those that are likely to want your work and then tap the library's resources again to read a few issues and familiarize yourself with their style and their slant.

Small Press: The Magazine for Independent/In-House/Desktop Publishing. Meckler Publishing Corporation, 11 Ferry Lane West, Westport, CT 06880. Published bimonthly.

Check the magazine's profiles of small publishers to find firms that seem likely to welcome your work and to do a good job with it.

Standard Periodical Directory. **Oxbridge Communications, Inc., 150 Fifth Avenue, New York, NY 10011. Updated periodically.**

Listings arranged by subject cover 65,000 periodicals in the U.S. and Canada.

Stories, **14 Beacon Street, Boston, MA 02108.**

If you write short fiction, you'll be interested in Amy R. Kaufman's handsome quarterly. A sample copy is free when you send an 8½″ × 11″ self-addressed envelope with 69 cents postage on it.

* ***Subject Guide to Books in Print and Forthcoming Books.*** **R. R. Bowker, 245 West 17th Street, New York, NY 10011. Updated annually.**

Try your local bookstore or library for copies of these guides. They're excellent tools both for trend spotting and for manuscript marketing.

* ***Subject Guide to Children's Books in Print.*** **R. R. Bowker, 245 West 17th Street, New York, NY 10011. Updated periodically.**

Nearly 50,000 titles—fiction and nonfiction—are indexed here. A good way to identify kindred spirits at publishing houses if you write for kids.

Utne Reader, **2732 West 43rd Street, Minneapolis, MN 55410. Published six times a year.**

Eric Utne and his colleagues cull material from nonmainstream magazines, journals and newsletters for the *Utne Reader,* which means you can use it to acquaint yourself with a host of alternative publications and to target any that should want your work.

Writers Conferences. **Poets & Writers, Inc., 201 West 54th Street, New York, NY 10019. Published annually in March.**

A guide to roughly 200 gatherings with terse, extremely informative listings.

Lists of writers' conferences also appear in the May issues of *The Writer* and *Writer's Digest,* in *Writer's Market* (the annual put out by Writer's Digest Books) and in the "Writers Conferences & Workshops" section of *Literary Market Place.*

Once you've studied listings, you can send for literature about the conferences that interest you most, and then—taking account of the topics, the speakers, the chances for getting criticism and the condition of your pocketbook—choose those that will serve your current needs best.

Writer's Digest Consumer Books Catalog. Writer's Digest Books, 1507 Dana Avenue, Dept. JA, Cincinnati, OH 45207.

As comments in these pages indicate, some Writer's Digest titles are much better than others. Get hold of the catalog to find specialized guides not reviewed here that are relevant to your work.

Writer's Market. Writer's Digest Books, 1507 Dana Avenue, Dept. JA, Cincinnati, OH 45207. Updated annually.

Writer's Market flags thousands of publishing opportunities. If you do a bit of extra investigating to learn more about the ones that interest you before you approach an editor, these leads should serve you well.

People, Places and Programs.

American Poetry Association, 1620 Seabright Avenue, P.O. Box 2279, Santa Cruz, CA 95063; 1-408-429-1122.

The American Poetry Association sponsors two contests each year for poems no more than twenty lines long. There's no entry fee. Write for information.

The CCLM Library, 666 Broadway, New York, NY 10012-2301; 1-212-614-6551.

With 16,000 volumes of more than 1,600 literary magazines available for browsing, the library at the Coordinating Council of Literary Magazines offers a fine way to target markets for poetry and short literary prose pieces. You can arrange to use it just by calling.

The Children's Book Council, 67 Irving Place, New York, NY 10003; 1-212-254-2666.

The CBC offers free brochures on "Writing Books for Children and Young Adults" (including information on where you can examine current titles for kids), "Illustrating Children's Books" and "Members' Publishing Programs" (the members are major children's book publishers and editors). Send a self-addressed envelope with an ounce's worth of postage on it for either of the first two; you'll need 2 ounces' worth for the third.

Howard University Press Book Publishing Institute, 2900 Van Ness Street, NW, Washington, DC 20008; 1-202-686-6498.

This intensive introduction to book publishing is offered during the summer. Send for a free descriptive brochure.

Independent Literary Agents Association, 55 Fifth Avenue, New York, NY 10003.

Send for the ILAA pamphlet to get a quick overview of agents' services. The group will also send you a membership list and a copy of its Code of Ethics on request.

Mystery Writers of America, 236 West 27th Street, New York, NY 10001.

Meetings, a newsletter called "The Third Degree," a mystery library and advice about contracts are among the benefits this group offers. If you write crime/mystery/suspense, you're eligible for membership, although you won't be able to vote or hold office until you've been published. Send for the MWA brochure.

Poets & Writers, Inc.

See "People, Places and Programs" in "Getting the Words Right Resources."

Publishing Institute, University of Denver, English Department, Denver, CO 80208.

The institute offers a much-praised four-week summer course of workshops and lectures about varied aspects of book publishing, with a helpful dose of career counseling. Write for details and application forms.

Radcliffe Publishing Procedures Course, 6 Ash Street, Cambridge, MA 02138.

Another well-regarded program for people interested in training for publishing jobs, this six-week summer course covers both book and magazine publishing.

Ross Book Service.

Mail-order shopping. See "People, Places and Programs" in "Getting the Words Right Resources."

Sensible Solutions, Inc., 6 East 39th Street, New York, NY 10016; 1-212-532-5280.

A consulting firm headed by Judith Appelbaum and Florence Janovic, Sensible Solutions grew out of *How to Get Happily Published*. Its marketing plans are designed to help writers approach book publishers and (once books have been placed) round up readers.

Small Press Traffic, 3599 24th Street, San Francisco, CA 94110; 1-415-285-8394.

West Coast writers of fiction and poetry can take advantage of the workshops and readings Small Press Traffic sponsors, and also of its well-stocked library of small press literature.

Society of Authors' Representatives, 39½ Washington Square South, New York, NY 10012.

The society issues a pamphlet that lists its members and briefly explains what agents do and how they like to be approached.

Society of Children's Book Writers, P.O. Box 296, Mar Vista Station, Los Angeles, CA 90066.

Through its publications and gatherings, the SCBW serves editors, agents, librarians, teachers and producers who are involved with children's books, as well as people—published and unpublished—who write and illustrate them. The group also offers insurance and grants to members.

University of Chicago Publishing Program, University of Chicago Office of Continuing Education, Liberal Education Division, 5835 Kimbark Avenue, Chicago, IL 60637.

Most courses deal with the earlier stages of the publishing process—editing, copy-editing, design. Send for a catalog to see the specifics of what's offered.

The Sale and Its Sequels Resources

TO HELP YOUR work reach its best audience, it's wise to proceed as though you were responsible for getting it out to readers. Those of you who are ambitious, therefore, will want to study and use "The Self-Publishing Option Resources."

Writers who are inclined to play a more passive role can consult the resources for this section, which explain the conventional course of publishing events and flag the easiest, most obvious marketing aids.

Advice, Analysis and Reportage

Allen, Steve. *How to Make a Speech.* McGraw-Hill, 1221 Avenue of the Americas, New York, NY 10020. 1986.
   Friendly, commonsensical guidance.

Appelbaum, Judith, Nancy Evans and Florence Janovic. *The Sensible Solutions How to Get Happily Published Handbook.* Sensible Solutions, Inc., 6 East 39th Street, New York, NY 10016. 1981.
   A companion volume to the book you now have in your hands, this is a collection of tips and worksheets designed primarily for people who are working with trade book publishers.

* *The ASJA Handbook: A Writers' Guide to Ethical and Economic Issues.* Edited by Murray Teigh Bloom, Richard Bode and Sally Wendkos

Olds. American Society of Journalists and Authors, 1501 Broadway, Suite 1907, New York, NY 10036. 1985.

    Detailed practical advice about submitting and selling pieces to periodicals.

* **Balkin, Richard.** *How to Understand and Negotiate a Book Contract or Magazine Agreement.* Writer's Digest Books, 1507 Dana Avenue, Dept. JA, Cincinnati, OH 45207. 1985.

    Candid, substantive advice from a New York literary agent. You'll benefit by following its guidelines whether you're negotiating on your own or through an agent or a literary property lawyer (see "Getting What's Coming to You" for advice on getting someone in your corner).

Balkin, Richard. *A Writer's Guide to Book Publishing.* **E. P. Dutton, 2 Park Avenue, New York, NY 10016. Revised and expanded, 1981.**

    Balkin, an editor-turned-agent, presents an honest, intelligent introduction to book publishing, including some discussion of textbooks, professional books and children's books, an informative chapter on contracts and a section on preparing a revised edition.

Barhydt, James D. *The Complete Book of Product Publicity.* Amacom, 135 West 50th Street, New York, NY 10020. 1987.

    Barhydt's frame of reference is big, big business, but most of the principles, strategies and tactics he presents clearly here are applicable to very small-scale operations—including campaigns individual authors wage for individual books.

Barzun, Jacques. *On Writing, Editing, and Publishing: Essays Explicative and Hortatory.* University of Chicago Press, 5801 South Ellis Avenue, Chicago, IL 60637. Second edition, 1986.

    Barzun's targets in these stylish pieces include over-reaching copy editors and talk show hosts. See also the essays on writing and writer's block.

Bunnin, Brad, and Peter Beren. *Author Law and Strategies: A Legal Guide for the Working Writer.* Nolo Press, 950 Parker Street, Berkeley, CA 94710; 1-800-992-NOLO (1-800-445-NOLO in California). 1984.

    Nolo Press specializes in self-help law books. This one displays a relatively amicable attitude toward publishers. •

Chicago Guide to Preparing Electronic Manuscripts for Authors and

Publishers. University of Chicago Press, 5801 South Ellis Avenue, Chicago, IL 60637. 1987.

Drawing on six years of experience, staff members at the University of Chicago Press explain how authors and publishers can take advantage of new technology as they process manuscripts. A well-organized, thoroughly intelligible and much needed guide.

Crawford, Tad. *The Writer's Legal Guide.* Madison Square Press, 10 East 23rd Street, New York, NY 10010. 1978.

Comprehensive and readable, Crawford's book covers copyright, contracts, libel, obscenity and taxes, among other things. New developments have dated a couple of chapters, but this remains a useful introduction to the laws that affect writers.

Dessauer, John P. *An Introduction to Book Publishing.* Crossroads Publishing Co., 370 Lexington Avenue, New York, NY 10017. 1988.

Now in preparation, John P. Dessauer's *Introduction* will cover all facets of publishing and analyze the way they relate to the wide world of readers. It's based in part on his earlier work, *Book Publishing: What It Is, What It Does,* a classic, comprehensive account containing sage suggestions about how book publishing practices could be improved.

Doboff, Leonard D. *The Law In Plain English for Writers.* Madrona Publishers, Inc., P.O. Box 22667, Seattle, WA 98112. 1987.

Thorough, clear, judicious advice from a practicing lawyer who is also a professor of business law and the author of a number of other *In Plain English* guides for creative people.

Dutton, John L. *How to Be an Outstanding Speaker: Eight Secrets to Speaking Success.* Life Skills Publishing Company, P.O. Box 282, New London, WI 54961. 1986.

The suggestions—which cover every aspect of public speaking—are easy to follow, and the approach makes very good sense.

Editors on Editing. Edited by Gerald Gross. Harper & Row, 10 East 53rd Street, New York, NY 10022. Revised edition, 1985.

Graceful essays on editing as it's conceived and practiced in large book publishing houses, plus nuggets of correspondence between editors and writers.

Editor to Author: The Letters of Maxwell E. Perkins. Edited by John

Hall Wheelock. Charles Scribner's Sons, 115 Fifth Avenue, New York, NY 10003. 1987.

What an exemplary editor does, as reflected in letters from the legendary Max Perkins to both well-known and little-known writers. This collection appeared first in 1950.

Glenn, Peggy. *Publicity for Books and Authors: A Do-It-Yourself Handbook for Small Publishing Firms and Enterprising Authors.* Aames-Allen Publishing Co., Inc., 1106 Main Street, Huntington Beach, CA 92648. 1985.

Glenn, who began publishing her own books in 1980, is a smart and engaging tutor. Her thoroughly practical handbook shows how books of all sorts can capture time on the air and space in the press.

"How Many Books Do You Sell in Ohio?" *A Quote Book for Writers.* Edited by Bill Gordon. North Ridge Books, P.O. Box 13401, Akron, OH 44313-8801. 1986.

Quotes from hundreds of interesting sources, organized in dozens of appealing categories, offer insights into the strange ways of the book world.

King, Larry L. *None But a Blockhead: On Being a Writer.* Viking Penguin, 40 West 23rd Street, New York, NY 10010. 1986.

A tonic for irritated authors. King's memoirs have many charms, and writers may find his splenetic accounts of conflicts with editors and publishers chief among them.

* **Kremer, John.** *101 Ways to Market Your Books—For Publishers and Authors.* Ad-Lib Publications, 51 North Fifth Street, P.O. Box 1102, Fairfield, IA 52556-1102. 1986.

Actually, Kremer explains several hundred things you and/or your publisher can do to round up readers. Indispensable.

Lee, Marshall. *Bookmaking: The Illustrated Guide to Design/Production/Editing.* R. R. Bowker, 245 West 17th Street, New York, NY 10011. Second edition, 1979.

A splendid, highly esteemed introduction to design and production processes and the way they fit into the bigger publishing picture.

Levine, Mark L. *Negotiating an Author's Book Contract: A Guide for Authors, Agents and Their Lawyers.* Moyer Bell Limited, Colonial Hill Road, RFD 1, Mt. Kisco, NY 10549. 1987.

Mark Levine leads you step-by-step through the clauses common in book contracts, explaining what you should try to delete, add or otherwise alter. Intelligent, intelligible advice.

Mathieu, Aron. *The Book Market: How to Write, Publish and Market Your Book.* Andover Press, Inc., 506 West 34th Street, New York, NY 10001. 1981.

The first half of this book, which covers publishing in large, old-line houses, offers a superb picture of life behind the scenes. Its second section, on self-publishing, will be helpful for conventionally published authors too. *See also* "The Self-Publishing Option Resources."

McCormack, Thomas. *The Fiction Editor.* St. Martin's Press, 175 Fifth Avenue, New York, NY 10010. 1988.

What to hope for from your editor if you write fiction. And if you get less than you hoped for, tools you can use to make your book better.

Meyer, Carol J. *The Writer's Survival Manual: The Complete Guide to Getting Your Book Published Right.* Bantam Books, 666 Fifth Avenue, New York, NY 10103. 1984.

Meyer is particularly informative about standard operating procedures in large New York book publishing houses.

One Book/Five Ways: The Publishing Procedures of Five University Presses. William Kaufmann, Inc., 95 First Street, Los Altos, CA 94022. 1977.

Suppose a manuscript called *No Time for Houseplants* by Purvis Mulch comes in for consideration. Would you publish it and, if so, how would you produce and market the book? Five university presses did a dry run with the ms. some years ago and this book shows how differently they handled the project. Instructive and entertaining evidence that book publishing is an idiosyncratic art.

Poets & Writers Magazine.

See "Advice, Analysis and Reportage" in "A Foot in the Door Resources."

Robotham, John S., and Lydia LaFleur. *Library Programs: How to Select, Plan and Produce Them.* The Scarecrow Press, Inc., 52 Liberty Street, P.O. Box 656, Metuchen, NJ 08840. Second edition, 1981.

Advice from and for librarians that should help you plan a practical, attractive program featuring your book for libraries in your area.

***Rotten Reviews: A Literary Companion.* Edited by Bill Henderson. Pushcart Press/Norton, Box 380, Wainscott, NY 11975. 1986.**

Are reviewers dumping on you? Are you worried that they might? Look here to see the terrible things they said about William Faulkner, John Milton, Saul Bellow, Jane Austen and a host of others who proved them wrong.

***Trade Book Marketing: A Practical Guide.* Edited by Robert A. Carter. Communications Unlimited, 29 Woods Way, Woodbury, CT 06798. 1983.**

Essays by practitioners explain how large firms market books for the general public.

Weiner, Richard. *Professional's Guide to Publicity*. Public Relations Publishing Company, Inc., 888 Seventh Avenue, New York, NY 10106. Updated periodically.

An instruction manual from a pro, with plenty of tips and examples. See also *Professional's Guide to Public Relations Services* and *Syndicated Columnists* from the same publisher; your library should have copies.

Westlake, Donald E. *A Likely Story*. Tor Books, 49 West 24th Street, New York, NY 10010. 1984.

For comic relief when you start shepherding your book through the publication process. Westlake, whose other novels include *The Hot Rock*, deftly satirizes publishers' practices in this antic tale of a bedeviled writer.

Wilder, Lilyan. *Professionally Speaking: Getting Ahead in Business and Life through Effective Communicating*. Simon & Schuster, 1230 Avenue of the Americas, New York, NY 10020. 1986.

Wilder coaches executives and others for public appearances. Her guide covers one-on-one communication as well as talks before groups, and it provides detailed instructions on how to develop a better speaking voice.

Tools

***American Library Directory*. R. R. Bowker, 245 West 17th Street, New York, NY 10011. Updated periodically.**

More than 37,000 U.S. libraries, public as well as private, are listed here by state and city.

Author & Audience: A Readings and Workshops Guide. **Poets & Writers, Inc., 201 West 54th Street, New York, NY 10019. Updated periodically.**

Groups in every state of the union sponsor programs that help poets and fiction writers connect with readers. Some 600 are listed in this handy guide, which also explains how to generate invitations to speak and round up people to listen.

Bacon's Publicity Checker. **Bacon's, 332 South Michigan Avenue, Chicago, IL 60604. Updated annually.**

Covering magazines (and some newsletters) in one volume and newspapers in another, the *Publicity Checker* is a good tool for preparing lists of reviewers and press release recipients.

Bacon's also publishes an annual *Radio/TV Directory,* sells mailing lists and has a clipping service.

The Buckley-Little Catalogue. **Buckley-Little Book Catalogue Co., Inc., Kraus Building, Route 100, Millwood, NY 10546.**

If and when a book of yours goes out of print, consider laying in a supply and buying a listing in this catalog, which goes to libraries and bookstores. A free leaflet gives all details.

Contemporary Authors. **Gale Research Company, Book Tower, Detroit, MI 48226. Updated periodically.**

A good place to get yourself listed and to find addresses of writers you'd like to get blurbs from.

Davis, Mitchell P. *Talk Show Guest Directory of Experts, Authorities & Spokespersons.* **Broadcast Interview Source, 2500 Wisconsin Avenue, NW, Washington, DC 20007. Updated periodically.**

The idea is that producers look here to find experts they can invite to appear on their shows. You can list yourself and your area of expertise in the white pages section without charge.

De La Iglesia, Maria Elena. *The International Catalogue of Catalogues.* **Harper & Row, 10 East 53rd Street, New York, NY 10022. 1982.**

Use the index to see who publishes catalogs that might include your book. Write-ups cover a wide range of special interests.

A Directory of American Poets and Fiction Writers. Poets & Writers, Inc., 201 West 54th Street, New York, NY 10019. Updated periodically.

If you want to ask particular novelists and/or poets for prepublication comments, check this affordable book for addresses and phone numbers. See *The Writers Directory,* below, for leads to other sorts of writers.

Directory of Personal Image Consultants. Edited by Jacqueline Thompson. Image Industry Publications, 10 Bay Street Landing, Suite 7K, Staten Island, NY 10301. Updated periodically.

The nearly 400 consultants profiled here are categorized under the headings "Speech Communication," "Wardrobe Analysis," "Personal Promotion" and "Motivation, Etiquette & Career Development." Consult the geographic index if you're looking for help of this sort in your area.

Directory of Special Libraries and Information Centers. Edited by Brigitte T. Darnay; John Nimchuk, associate editor. Gale Research Company, Book Tower, Detroit, MI 48226. Updated periodically.

Using the subject index, you can construct your own mailing list of libraries that should be especially receptive to your book.

* *Encyclopedia of Associations.* Edited by Katherine Gruber. Gale Research Company, Book Tower, Detroit, MI 48226. Updated periodically.

A first-class promotion tool whether you're being published or doing the publishing yourself, this is a conduit to 20,000 groups committed to all sorts of causes and activities. Get hold of it at your library and use the key word index to zero in on the people who will welcome news of your book and help you spread the word about it.

Gale Directory of Publications. Gale Research Company, Book Tower, Detroit, MI 48226. Updated periodically.

Thousands of newspapers and magazines are listed here, with indexes designed to pinpoint special-interest market segments. Your library should have a copy.

Grants and Awards Available to American Writers.

See "Tools" in "Money Resources" for this title and for *Awards, Honors, and Prizes* and *Literary and Library Prizes.* If you think you see a way to become a winner, try it out. Both the credentials and the funds should come in handy in the early stages of a writing project or a writing career.

* **Kremer, John.** *Book Marketing Opportunities: A Directory.* Ad-Lib Publications, 51 North Fifth Street, Fairfield, IA 52556-1102. Updated periodically.

Use Kremer's lists of book clubs, catalog companies, reviewers and so on to supplement your publisher's marketing efforts. Note: they're also available on disc.

Literary Bookstores: A List in Progress. Poets & Writers, 201 West 54th Street, New York, NY 10019. Updated periodically.

Here's a way to zero in on the more than 300 bookstores in the United States that are hospitable to contemporary fiction and poetry.

Literary Market Place. R. R. Bowker, 245 West 17th Street, New York, NY 10011. Published annually.

Like Kremer's *Book Marketing Opportunities* (above), *LMP* can help you add to and reinforce whatever efforts your publisher plans to make on your behalf. See especially "Book Review, Selection & Reference," "Radio & Television" and "Public Relations Services."

National Avocational Organizations. Columbia Books, Inc., 1350 New York Avenue, NW, Suite 207, Washington, DC 20005. Updated annually.

This guide to 2,500 recreational, hobby, cultural, civic and patriotic organizations that have members nationwide is indexed by subject, location and budget. A fine way to pinpoint groups that should be interested in and supportive of your work.

National Trade and Professional Associations of the United States. Columbia Books, Inc., 1350 New York Avenue, NW, Suite 207, Washington, DC 20005. Updated annually.

The 6,300 groups listed here should include some that can help you in various ways—by providing information, funding or opportunities for publicity, for example. Use the subject index, the geographic index and/or the budget index to target organizations to approach.

Speakers and Lecturers: How to Find Them. Edited by Paul Wasserman and Jacqueline O'Brien. Gale Research Company, Book Tower, Detroit, MI 48226. Revised periodically.

Writers interested in public speaking will want to be listed here. Write for information.

Ulrich's International Periodicals Directory. **R. R. Bowker, 245 West 17th Street, New York, NY 10011. Updated periodically.**

Some 70,000 periodicals published around the world are listed here in 534 subject areas. Available in libraries.

The Writers Directory. **St. James Press, 425 North Michigan Avenue, Chicago, IL 60611. Updated periodically.**

Useful for getting in touch with people who might provide blurbs. *See* "Tools" in "Getting the Words Right Resources" for a full description and *A Directory of American Poets and Fiction Writers* (above) for other good leads.

People, Places and Programs

Author/Expert Interviews, Para Publishing, P.O. Box 40500, Santa Barbara, CA 93140-0500.

You can encourage talk shows to invite you to appear by participating in Para's Author/Expert Interviews mailings, which go out four times a year to 1,300 programs. Send for details.

* **The Authors Guild, Inc., 234 West 44th Street, New York, NY 10036; 1-212-398-0838.**

It's well worth joining this group of 6,000 professional writers and getting in as early in your career as you can, so write for application forms. The Guild and its first-rate staff give writers power to deal with publishers by providing surveys of financial terms, seminars on current problems and opportunities for writers, a newsletter that disseminates solid, useful information, access to insurance and sample forms, including a model trade book contract (comparable models for textbooks and for scholarly books are in the works).

"How to Be Your Own Book Publicist." Elane Feldman, 101-A Clark Street, 17B, Brooklyn Heights, NY 11201.

Elane Feldman offers seminars at New York University, the University of Massachusetts and elsewhere. Write for information on times, places and fees.

"**Literary & Writers' Associations,**" *Literary Market Place.*

Check the listings here for groups you might join, and then write to the ones that look most interesting for detailed information and application forms. *See also* "Getting the Words Right Resources," "A Foot in the Door Resources" and "The Self-Publishing Option Resources."

PEN American Center, 568 Broadway, New York, NY 10012; 1-212-334-1660.

A writers' organization known for its social conscience and its excellent grants directory (*see* "Money Resources"), PEN has centers abroad as well as in the United States, and branches in Cambridge, Houston, San Francisco, Chicago and Washington, DC. Members can take advantage of group insurance rates as well as of panel discussions, readings and other get-togethers.

Public Relations Society of America Information Center, 845 Third Avenue, New York, NY 10022; 1-212-995-2230.

A large collection of materials for professional public relations people; open to the public for a fee.

Ross Book Service.

An easy way to get the books recommended here. *See* "People, Places and Programs" in "Getting the Words Right Resources."

Sensible Solutions, Inc., 6 East 39th Street, New York, NY 10016; 1-212-532-5280.

Founded because readers of *How to Get Happily Published* asked for advice tailored to their particular books, Sensible Solutions is a consulting firm run by Judith Appelbaum and Florence Janovic. They confer with clients and then prepare target marketing plans designed to boost books' sales without hype and big budgets.

The Self-Publishing Option Resources

ONE OF THE best ways for self-publishers to get help is by talking with other publishers, particularly smaller ones. Try your local Yellow Pages for leads to those in your area.

Other avenues to advice and assistance are described below. For additional guidance, check back through the previous Resources sections (see especially "A Foot in the Door Resources," since the directories that help writers find publishers also help publishers find people who'll publicize their work and/or buy rights to it).

Advice, Analysis and Reportage

The Art of Literary Publishing. **Edited by Bill Henderson. The Pushcart Press, P.O. Box 380, Wainscott, NY 11975. 1980.**

A collection by and about editors from small presses, large publishing conglomerates and houses in between, all of whom, Henderson says in his introduction, "still care about words and about the caring that words can encourage." Although contributors voice the usual complaints (the corporate mentality focuses on the bottom line at the expense of literary merit), they also see some hope, if only in their own concern for quality writing and editing.

Beach, Mark, Steve Shepro and Ken Russon. *Getting It Printed: How to Work with Printers and Graphic Arts Services to Assure Quality,*

Stay on Schedule, and Control Costs. Coast to Coast Books, 2934 Northeast 16th Avenue, Portland, OR 97212, 1986.

A clear, detailed primer that's applicable to books although it doesn't often focus on them. Use it to see what your options are and to get help in exercising the ones that make sense for your project.

Bodian, Nat G. *Copywriter's Handbook: A Practical Guide for Advertising and Promotion of Specialized and Scholarly Books and Journals.* ISI Press, 3501 Market Street, Philadelphia, PA 19104. 1984.

A giant smorgasbord of information and advice from a marketing manager at John Wiley & Sons.

Bodian, Nat G. *The Publisher's Direct Mail Handbook.* ISI Press, 3501 Market Street, Philadelphia, PA 19104. 1987.

The latest of Nat Bodian's detailed, meticulously organized handbooks. See especially his comments on the "echo effect" if you're selling through bookstores as well as by mail.

Book Research Quarterly. Transaction Publishing Consortium, Rutgers University, New Brunswick, NJ 08903. Published quarterly.

Scholars and others who've done some digging to find hard data about the book world report their findings here.

Brownstone, David M., and Irene M. Frank. *The Self-Publishing Handbook.* New American Library, 1633 Broadway, New York, NY 10019. 1985.

Well organized and couched in friendly tones, this handbook offers detailed discussions of money matters.

Dessauer, John P. *An Introduction to Book Publishing.* Crossroads Publishing Company, 370 Lexington Avenue, New York, NY 10017. 1988.

By the author of the classic *Book Publishing: What It Is, What It Does.* See "Advice, Analysis and Reportage" in "The Sale and Its Sequels Resources" for a fuller description.

Dill, Barbara. *The Journalist's Handbook on Libel and Privacy.* The Free Press, 866 Third Avenue, New York, NY 10022. 1986.

Both lively and informative, Dill's handbook grew out of seminars she gives for reporters and editors. See the Q-and-A section at the back for a quick fix on basic guidelines.

Direct Mail and Mail Order Handbook. Edited by Richard S. Hodgson. Dartnell Corporation, 4660 Ravenswood Avenue, Chicago, IL 60640. Third edition, 1980.

This huge book should tell you everything you'll ever need to know about reaching your readers—and enabling them to do business with you—by mail. Direct-mail pros swear by it.

Doty, Betty. *Publish Your Own Hardbound Books.* The Bookery, 8193 Riata, Redding, CA 96002. 1980.

Both an instruction manual and a kit for producing one small book (for starters), this engaging and encouraging self-published work gives you the chance to control one more phase of the publishing process.

Folio: The Magazine for Magazine Management. Folio Publishing Corporation, Six River Bend, P.O. Box 4949, Stamford, CT 06907-0949. Published monthly.

A magazine for people who publish and edit periodicals, with some articles and news items that will interest book publishers too. The Folio Publishing Corporation also issues books for magazine and book publishers. *See The Handbook of Magazine Publishing* below and send for a catalog.

Fulton, Len, with Ellen Ferber. *American Odyssey: A Bookselling Travelogue.* Dustbooks, P.O. Box 100, Paradise, CA 95969. 1975.

Fulton visited bookstores across the country in order to see what selling his own work would be like. His account of the experience is both instructive and entertaining.

Garst, Robert E., and Theodore M. Bernstein. *Headlines and Deadlines: A Manual for Copy Editors.* Columbia University Press, 562 West 113th Street, New York, NY 10025. Fourth edition, 1982.

An excellent guide to editing. The copy editors of the title are newspaper copy editors—who do far more general editing than their namesakes in book and magazine publishing—and the book discusses such matters as writing leads, developing stories and cutting copy. Use the lengthy "Headline Vocabulary" to decrease dependence on overused words.

Glenn, Peggy. *Publicity for Books and Authors.*

See "Advice, Analysis and Reportage" in "The Sale and Its Sequels Resources."

Graham, Walter B. *Complete Guide to Pasteup.* DOT Pasteup Supply Co., P.O. Box 369, Omaha, NE 68101. Second edition, 1980.

Complete it is, and lavishly illustrated. Graham, who also offers seminars on this subject (*see* Pasteup Workshop, under "People, Places and Programs" below), shows how to deal with lots of different kinds of artwork as well as with type.

The Handbook of Magazine Publishing by the editors of *Folio.* Folio Publishing Corporation, Six River Bend, P.O. Box 4949, Stamford, CT 06907-0949. Second edition, 1983.

A hefty compendium of articles from *Folio: The Magazine of Magazine Management* that covers all aspects of publishing magazines and includes twenty-five pieces on starting new ones. If you're doing that, get hold of a copy in your library.

"How to Submit Your Book to Book-of-the-Month Club." Book-of-the-Month Club, Inc., 485 Lexington Avenue, New York, NY 10017. 1987.

A two-page invitation to smaller publishers to approach the five clubs that make up BOMC.

Huenefeld, John. *The Huenefeld Guide to Book Publishing.* The Huenefeld Company, Box U, Bedford, MA 01730. Updated periodically.

John Huenefeld has been helping small publishers manage their operations for a good long time, through consulting services, through seminars and through his newsletter (see below). In this sizable volume, he discusses everything from starting a book-publishing venture to selling one.

The Huenefeld Report, The Huenefeld Company, Box U, Bedford, MA 01730. Published fortnightly.

This newsletter is virtually unique as a source of information and ideas on running a publishing business—managing money, people, sales and so on. Write for information and a sample copy.

Information Marketing, 139 G. Street, Suite 162, Davis, CA 95616. Published monthly.

Mark Nolan's newsletter is pricey but has good tips to offer.

Judd, Karen. *Copyediting: A Practical Guide.* William Kaufmann, Inc., 95 First Street, Los Altos, CA 94022. 1982.

A delightful primer. *See* "Advice, Analysis and Reportage" in "Money Resources."

Kamoroff, Bernard. *How to Start Your Own Small Business, Keep Your Books, Pay Your Taxes, & Stay Out of Trouble.* Bell Springs Publishing, P.O. Box 640, Laytonville, CA 95454. Updated periodically.

A self-publishing success story, Kamoroff's guide has well over a quarter of a million copies in print. Excellent advice on managing your financial affairs.

Kobs, Jim. *24 Ways to Improve Your Direct Mail Results.* The Dartnell Corporation, 4660 Ravenswood Avenue, Chicago, IL 60640. 1974.

Billed as "A Dartnell Report for Direct Mail and Mail Order Advertising Executives," this pamphlet focuses on what offer a direct-mail package should make and includes a worksheet you can use to determine your breakeven figure.

* **Kremer, John.** *101 Ways to Market Your Books—For Publishers and Authors.* Ad-Lib Publications, 51 North Fifth Street, P.O. Box 1102, Fairfield, IA 52556-1102. 1986.

A dazzling array of practical, specific suggestions. Read it early if you can, to get pointers on editorial and production matters as they relate to marketing; but in any event, read it.

Levinson, Jay Conrad. *Guerrilla Marketing: Secrets for Making Big Profits from Your Small Business.* Houghton Mifflin, One Beacon Street, Boston, MA 02108. 1984.

Excellent advice for people who have lots of energy and relatively little money to invest in marketing.

Mathieu. Aron. *The Book Market: How to Write, Publish and Market Your Book.* Andover Press, 516 West 34th Street, New York, NY 10001. 1981.

Mathieu's lengthy section on self-publishing is somewhat dated when it comes to names, addresses, dollar figures and the like but still valuable for its lively case histories and its hard-to-find material on college bookstore and religious bookstore markets.

McGraw-Hill Book Company. *Guidelines for Bias-Free Publishing.* McGraw-Hill, Princeton Road, Hightstown, NJ 08520. n.d.

A short, sensible guide for you to refer to and distribute to freelance editors and copy editors. *See also* Miller and Swift's *The Handbook of Nonsexist Writing,* listed below.

The McHugh Publishing Report Series: Practical Problem-Solvers for Managers. 92 Hartford Street, Framingham, MA 01701. Published periodically.

John McHugh writes and publishes short reports for small and self-publishers. Send for lists of available titles.

Miller, Casey, and Kate Swift. *The Handbook of Nonsexist Writing.* Harper & Row, 10 East 53rd Street, New York, NY 10022. Second edition, 1988.

Whoever does your copy-editing should get this book and apply the advice in it. Miller and Swift make it easy to avoid offensive sexist terms without calling attention to the fact that that's what you're doing.

Mueller, L. W. *How to Publish Your Own Book.* Harlo Press, 16721 Hamilton Avenue, Detroit, MI 48203. Revised edition, 1978.

Mueller runs Harlo Printing Company and has dealt with a great many self-publishers over the years. The book includes useful examples of artwork in a variety of colors and color combinations in its discussion of how to self-publish.

The New York Times Manual of Style and Usage, **edited by Lewis Jordan.** Times Books, 201 East 50th Street, New York, NY 10022. Revised edition, 1976.

A standard reference work. Entries are arranged alphabetically rather than topically.

Parkhurst, William. *How to Get Publicity, and Make the Most of It.* Times Books, 201 East 50th Street, New York, NY 10022. 1985.

Parkhurst specializes in getting publicity through electronic media. He doesn't usually focus here on books but the knowledgeable advice he offers is applicable to them.

Personal Publishing. The Renegade Company, P.O. Box 390, Itasca, IL 60143. Published monthly.

A handsome magazine by, for and about desk-top publishers.

Playle, Ron. *Selling to Catalog Houses: How You Too Can Sell Thousands of Books or Other Products to Large Mail Order Catalog Houses.*

Playle Publications, Inc., P.O. Box 644, Des Moines, IA 50303. 1985.

    In these forty-eight pages, Ron Playle shares what he's learned by selling how-to pamphlets to major mail-order companies. For those of you who decide to follow his lead, he also rents a mailing list of catalog houses.

* *Pocket Pal Book.* International Paper Company, P.O. Box 100, Church Street Station, New York, NY 10008-0100. Updated periodically.

    Penny for penny, this may be your best source of information about printing processes and the production steps that precede and follow them.

* Poynter, Dan. *Publishing Short-Run Books: How to Paste Up and Reproduce Books Instantly Using Your Quick Print Shop.* Para Publishing, P.O. Box 4232, Santa Barbara, CA 93140-4232. Updated periodically.

    This knowledgeable guide covers everything from composition to binding.

* Poynter, Dan. *The Self-Publishing Manual: How to Write, Print & Sell Your Own Book.* Para Publishing, P.O. Box 4232, Santa Barbara, CA 93140-4232. Updated periodically.

    This is the best self-publishing manual on the market. Poynter offers more information per paragraph than many handbooks put on a page, and it's all clear and easy to follow. Highly recommended.

* *The Publish-It-Yourself Handbook: Literary Tradition and How-To.* Edited by Bill Henderson. Pushcart Press, P.O. Box 380, Wainscott, NY 11975. Revised edition, 1980.

    By now a classic, this collection of spirited essays by self-publishers and their supporters should serve to embolden authors considering the self-publishing option and to entertain and inform readers of all sorts.

Ross, Marilyn and Tom. *How to Make Big Profits Publishing City & Regional Books: A Guide for Entrepreneurs, Writers and Publishers.* Communication Creativity, P.O. Box 213, Saguache, CO 81149. 1987.

    Ringing changes on their *Complete Guide to Self-Publishing* (see below), Marilyn and Tom Ross provide an array of examples here that's wondrous to behold. Obviously, lots of people now realize that it's easier to publish for limited geographical markets than for the widely dispersed (and probably mythical) general reader.

Ross, Tom and Marilyn. *The Complete Guide to Self-Publishing.* **Communication Creativity, P.O. Box 213, Saguache, CO 81149. 1985.**

A retitled, updated version of the Rosses' *Encyclopedia of Self-Publishing*, which supplies sound, detailed advice on a wide range of topics.

Roth, Stephen F. *The Computer Edge: Microcomputer Trends/Uses in Publishing.* **R. R. Bowker, 245 West 17th Street, New York, NY 10011. 1985.**

How publishers can and do use computers to run their businesses and process copy. A useful introductory overview.

Scholarly Publishing: A Journal for Authors and Publishers. **University of Toronto Press, Toronto, Canada M5S 1A6. Published quarterly.**

Consistently interesting and well edited, this journal has new ideas, new information and new perspectives to offer publishers whether they're scholarly or not.

Schuchat, Theodor. *The Library Book.* **Madrona Publishers, Box 22667, Seattle, WA 98112. 1985.**

Facts and figures about a sizable market that doesn't always get its share of attention from self-publishers.

Shatzkin, Leonard. *In Cold Type: Overcoming the Book Crisis.* **Houghton Mifflin, One Beacon Street, Boston, MA 02108. 1982.**

Provocative analyses of the trade book business by an imaginative industry gadfly.

Shinn, Duane. *How to Write and Publish Your Own Book, Course, Song, Slide Chart or Other Printed Product, and Make It Go!* **Shinn Music Aids, P.O. Box 192, Medford OR 97501. 1976.**

The title accurately conveys the flavor of this looseleaf work, which offers advice for go-getters about marketing and other business aspects of publishing.

* *Small Press: The Magazine for Independent/In-House/Desktop Pub-*

lishing. Meckler Publishing Corporation, 11 Ferry Lane West, Westport, CT 06880. Published bimonthly.

Useful for its practical guidance, its profiles of kindred spirits and its review coverage.

Stone, Bob. *Successful Direct Marketing Methods.* Crain Books, 4255 West Touhy Avenue, Lincolnwood, IL 60646-1975. Third edition, 1984.

A recognized expert presents a detailed instruction manual designed for people with a heavy commitment to direct mail but useful to anyone who's involved in the area. Solid and readable.

Stone, Bob, and John Wyman. *Successful Telemarketing: Opportunities and Techniques for Increasing Sales and Profits.* NTC Business Books, 4255 West Touhy Avenue, Lincolnwood, IL 60646-1975. 1986.

Like the authors (high-level executives at Young & Rubicam and AT&T), the examples come from the big leagues, but the advice proffered here is applicable to small-scale operations as well.

Strong, William S. *The Copyright Book: A Practical Guide.* MIT Press, 28 Carleton Street, Cambridge, MA 02142. Second edition, 1984.

A thorough, orderly introduction to copyright by a lawyer whose specialty it is.

Wills, F. H. *Fundamentals of Layout, for Newspaper and Magazine Advertising, for Page Design of Publications and Brochures.* Dover Publications, Inc., 31 East 2nd Street, Mineola, NY 11501. 1965.

The focus is on ads, but the principles and techniques revealed are applicable to the design of books and magazines. A thorough and readable primer with a wealth of captioned illustrations that teach important lessons pleasurably.

Wilson, Adrian. *The Design of Books.* Peregrine Smith, Inc., P.O. Box 667, Layton, UT 84041. 1974.

Although it's now out of date on the technology of typesetting and printing, this remains a good tool for understanding and mastering basic design procedures. Heavily illustrated.

Words in Our Pockets: The Feminist Writers Guild Handbook on How

to Gain Power, Get Published & Get Paid. Edited by Celeste West. Dustbooks, P.O. Box 100, Paradise, CA 95969. 1985.

A fine source of energy. Celeste West's anthology covers writing, getting a publisher, being a publisher and related topics from a feminist point of view. Contributors are sometimes bellicose, sometimes beleaguered and sometimes wrong (especially about the publishing establishment) but always attractive for their strong sense of camaraderie.

Tools

AAFES Facts for Vendors. Army and Air Force Exchange Service Headquarters, Attn.: Public Affairs Division, Information Services Branch, P.O. Box 660202, Dallas, TX 75266-0202; 1-214-780-2763.

AAFES sells books—among many, many other things—to seven million people in the U.S. armed forces. If you're willing to thread your way through a lot of red tape, you could make sizable sales under its auspices.

Advertising and Publicity Resources for Scholarly Books. Association of American University Presses, Inc., One Park Avenue, New York, NY 10016. 1988.

Entries describe 3,200 periodicals, arranged in forty-eight broad subject categories, that can serve as conduits to readers. This is an expensive book, so try the library if you want to consult it.

All TV Publicity Outlets—Nationwide. Public Relations Plus, Inc., P.O. Drawer 1197, New Milford, CT 06776. Updated periodically.

A useful guide if you're trying to get publicity in particular geographic areas. Your library may have a copy.

American Bookseller, 137 West 25th Street, New York, NY 10001. Published monthly.

This lively magazine comes from the American Booksellers Association and lets you see what's on booksellers' minds.

American Book Trade Directory. R. R. Bowker, 245 West 17th Street, New York, NY 10011. Updated periodically.

An alphabetical listing, by state (or Canadian province) and city, of approximately 20,000 book outlets in North America, plus listings of wholesalers, importers, exporters and others who provide conduits to readers. This is invaluable if you use it to identify stores where your work figures to sell well. Try your library for a copy; use the "Types of Stores" index, and pay particular attention to large wholesalers and small bookstore chains.

American Library Directory. R. R. Bowker, 245 West 17th Street, New York, NY 10011. Updated periodically.

These lists of libraries and library schools in the United States, Canada and some overseas locations make a fine basis for compiling your own library mailing list. Available in most libraries.

Bayan, Richard. *Words That Sell: A Thesaurus to Help Promote Your Products, Services, and Ideas.* **Asher-Gallant Press, 201 Montrose Drive, Westbury, NY 11590. 1984.**

Just what the title says. Bayan, a copywriter, lists words and phrases that should come in handy as you prepare promotional materials.

"Book Review, Selection & Reference," *Literary Market Place.* **R. R. Bowker, 245 West 17th Street, New York, NY 10011.**

Use this list to make sure your book gets to appropriate journals in the right form at the right time.

Bowker Catalog. R. R. Bowker, 245 West 17th Street, New York, NY 10011. Free.

Like its counterpart from Gale (see below), this should get you thinking about promotional possibilities.

The Chicago Manual of Style, for Authors, Editors, and Copywriters. The University of Chicago Press, 5801 South Ellis Avenue, Chicago, IL 60637. Thirteenth edition, 1982.

The aristocrat of style manuals, this one is favored by many academics and professional copy editors.

CMG Mailing List Catalog. College Marketing Group, 50 Cross Street, Winchester, MA 01890.

The CMG lists—of teachers, administrators and librarians at roughly 3,000 colleges and universities and of roughly three million mail-order book buyers—are organized in 3,500 subject categories. Check the catalog to see if they'll lead you to your readers.

Directory of College Stores. B. Klein Publications, P.O. Box 8503, Coral Springs, FL 33065. Updated periodically.

Annotated, and probably available at your nearest university bookshop and/or your library.

Directory of Mail Order Catalogs. Grey House Publishing, Inc., Bank of Boston Building, Sharon, CT 06069. Updated periodically.

You'll find descriptions here of roughly 6,000 mail-order companies that sell products of every sort. Try your library for a copy.

Dover Pictorial Archive Book Catalog. Dover Publications, Inc., 31 East 2nd Street, Mineola, NY 11501. Free.

The 300 volumes in Dover's Pictorial Archive series consist of pictures you can cut out and use on your pages free of charge (except that you pay a modest amount for each book) and free of copyright worries.

Dustbooks, P.O. Box 100, Paradise, CA 95969.

Get your publications listed in the Dustbooks Small Press Information Library (which includes *The International Directory of Little Magazines and Small Presses*), and use these volumes to identify small publishers in your area who might be willing to give you advice and moral support.

"Editorial Services," *Literary Market Place.* R. R. Bowker, 245 West 17th Street, New York, NY 10011.

A list you can use to find editorial aid nearby. Be sure to get samples, check references and compare prices before you make a deal.

✽ *Encyclopedia of Associations.* Gale Research Company, Book Tower, Detroit, MI 48226. Updated periodically.

A stellar source of leads to people who will want your work. *See* "Tools" in "The Sale and Its Sequels Resources."

Follett, Robert J. R. *The Financial Side of Book Publishing.* Alpine Guild, P.O. Box 183, Oak Park, IL 60303. Second edition, 1988.

President of the Chicago Publishers Association and former president of the Follett Publishing Company, Bob Follett has created a textbook/workbook that helps people without financial expertise understand and deal with the money side of the book business.

Gale Research Company Catalog. Gale Research Company, Book Tower, Detroit, MI 48226. Free.

First-rate stimulation when you need ideas about getting in touch with readers.

Guide to American Directories. B. Klein Publications, Inc., P.O. Box 8503, Coral Springs, FL 33065. Updated periodically.

Since this directory is designed to help businesses locate new markets through the mailing lists of national organizations, it may have information on groups and reference materials relevant to your marketing efforts. Arranged by subject.

International Literary Market Place. R. R. Bowker, 245 West 17th Street, New York, NY 10011. Updated periodically.

Listings include publishers, booksellers, libraries, book clubs, literary agents and organizations in 160 countries outside the United States. Go through the book at your library if your work might sell overseas.

B. Klein Publications Catalog. B. Klein Publications Inc., P.O. Box 8503, Coral Gables, FL 33065. Free.

This annotated listing of books available by mail through B. Klein includes many titles that may help you sell your work. Some should be available in your library and perhaps some will strike you as useful enough to order.

Kremer, John. *Book Marketing Made Easier.* Ad-Lib Publications, 51 North Fifth Street, P.O. Box 1102, Fairfield, IA 52556. 1986.

A compendium of basic forms for publishers to use in acquiring books and shepherding them through conventional book trade marketing channels.

✻ **Kremer, John.** *Book Marketing Opportunities: A Directory* and *Book Marketing Opportunities: A Database,* with Marie Kiefer and Bob McIlvride. Ad-Lib Publications, 51 North Fifth Street, P.O. Box 1102, Fairfield, IA 52556. 1986.

In its print version, the directory is an even more valuable resource for book publishers than *Literary Market Place*; as a database it's better still (call for details if you have an IBM-PC or a compatible computer; 1-800-624-5893). Conceived and organized by people who clearly understand how publishing currently works, both formats provide information on wholesalers, retailers, catalogers, sales reps, publicity and marketing services, reviewers, radio and television shows and on and on.

✻ **Kremer, John.** *Directory of Short-Run Printers.* Ad-Lib Publications,

51 North Fifth Street, P.O. Box 1102, Fairfield, IA 52556. Updated periodically.

This extremely useful, intelligently indexed directory covers roughly 400 printers and tells you how to approach them. Ads and tips are interspersed among the listings.

Kremer, John. *The Independent Publisher's Bookshelf.* Ad-Lib Publications, 51 North Fifth Street, P.O. Box 1102, Fairfield, IA 52556. Updated periodically.

Kremer concentrates on books about self-publishing and marketing. This annotated bibliography also includes information about publishers' associations and periodicals for publishers.

Literary Bookstores: A List in Progress. Poets & Writers, 201 West 54th Street, New York, NY 10019. Updated periodically.

See "Tools" in "The Sale and Its Sequels Resources."

* *Literary Market Place.* R. R. Bowker, 245 West 17th Street, New York, NY 10011. Updated annually.

Spend an hour or two browsing through *LMP* to see how it can be helpful to you and then use the Index to Sections to find help of some specific sort as you need it. It's worth owning, but if you can't see your way clear to buying a copy, get hold of one in your library and study it there.

National Radio Publicity Outlets. Public Relations Plus, Inc., P.O. Drawer 1197, New Milford, CT 06776. Updated periodically.

If your work has local angles you can play up, try your library for a copy of this hefty directory. Entries are arranged geographically.

Palder, Edward L. *The Catalog of Catalogs: Where to Get Information about Almost Anything for Almost Nothing.* Woodbine House, 10400 Connecticut Avenue, Suite 512, Kensington, MD 20895. 1987.

An affordable introduction to thousands of special-interest mail-order operations. Look under the subject(s) your work treats to find catalogs that might sell it to potential readers.

Poynter, Dan. *Book Fairs: An Exhibiting Guide for Publishers.* Para Publishing, P.O. Box 4232, Santa Barbara, CA 93140-4232. Updated periodically.

Detailed practical information on where and how to use book fairs to best advantage.

Poynter, Dan. *Business Letters for Publishers.* **Para Publishing, P.O. Box 4232, Santa Barbara, CA 93140-4232. 1987.**

Don't-reinvent-the-wheel department: Here are seventy-four letters you can load into your computer and use to answer complaints, generate sales, collect payments and otherwise run your publishing business. A print version is available too.

Poynter. Dan. *Publishing Forms: A Collection of Applications and Information for the Beginning Publisher.* **Para Publishing, P.O. Box 4232-62, Santa Barbara, CA 93140-4232. Updated periodically.**

If you apply common sense in deciding when and how to use these forms and if you update names of contacts, reviewers and so on before you use them, they should serve you well.

Poynter, Dan, and Charles Kent. *Publishing Contracts: Sample Agreements for Book Publishers on Disk.* **Para Publishing, P.O. Box 4232, Santa Barbara, CA 93140-4232. 1987.**

Prepared by a lawyer-publisher team, this collection includes twenty-two forms you can use on a computer to structure agreements with authors, fellow publishers, graphic artists and rights buyers, among others.

Pressing Business: An Organizational Manual for Independent Publishers. **Volunteer Lawyers for the Arts, 1285 Avenue of the Americas, Third Floor, New York, NY 10019. 1984.**

A brief, clear discussion of options for structuring a small publishing business, particularly one devoted to literary books and/or magazines.

Publishers Weekly, **249 West 17th Street, New York, NY 10011.**

If you have arranged to distribute your book to stores around the country, send a review copy to *PW* at least three months before its official pub date. Check the masthead at the beginning of the "Forecasts" section to find the proper editor, and be sure to include information about your distribution setup along with other background data in your covering letter. *PW* is also a window on publishing events and trends; a subscription will keep you up to date, and if you can sell one of the magazine's departmental editors on a story idea you'll boost your book's chances in bookstores.

Radio-TV Interview Report. **Bradley Communications, 312-B West**

Montgomery Avenue, P.O. Box 299, Haverford, PA 19041; 1-215-896-6146. Published monthly.

A compendium of pitches that goes to 4,500 people who might book you on radio, as well as to 350 TV talk-show producers and 350 newspaper feature editors. Rates are reasonable. A similar periodical aimed at nearly 11,000 newspapers is in the works.

Specialty Booksellers Directory. Edited by Melinda-Carol Ballou, Marie Keifer and John Kremer. Ad-Lib Publications, 51 North Fifth Street, P.O. Box 1102, Fairfield, IA 52556-1102; 1-800-624-5893. 1987.

Useful for zeroing in on booksellers who should be especially responsive to your book, this directory lists more than 2,000 bookstores which specialize in dozens of different subject areas.

Weiner, Richard. ***Professional's Guide to Public Relations Services.*** **Public Relations Publishing Company, Inc., 888 Seventh Avenue, New York, NY 10106. Fifth edition, 1985.**

A goldmine of leads to assistance with every aspect of a publicity campaign.

Weiner, Richard. ***Syndicated Columnists Directory.*** **Public Relations Publishing Company, Inc., 888 Seventh Avenue, New York, NY 10106. Updated periodically.**

Entries, arranged under two dozen subject headings, include column titles and columnists' addresses and phone numbers.

The H. W. Wilson Company Catalog. **H. W. Wilson Company, 950 University Avenue, Bronx, NY 10452-9978.**

Reference books by the dozens, some of which may be grist to your mill.

Words into Type. **Prentice-Hall, Route 9W, Englewood Cliffs, NJ 07632. Third edition, 1974.**

Long a favorite of many professional copywriters, *Words into Type* is clear, comprehensive and easy to use. A first-rate guide for self-publishers, particularly if you self-edit.

Working Press of the Nation. **National Research Bureau, Directory Division, 310 South Michigan Avenue, Chicago IL 60604. Updated annually.**

The subject indexes and the amount of information included in each listing make this five-volume set valuable. Explore it at your library for leads to receptive people in radio and TV as well as in periodical publishing.

People, Places and Programs

Adams Press, 30 West Washington Street, Chicago, IL 60602.
A well-established printer of short-run books for self-publishers and others, the Adams Press also does typesetting and binding and produces jackets. Send for the "Book Printing" brochure and the price list.

Bacon's, 332 South Michigan Avenue, Chicago, IL 60604.
See "Tools" in "The Sale and Its Sequels Resources" under *Bacon's Publicity Checker*.

BISAC (Book Industry Systems Advisory Committee), 160 Fifth Avenue, New York, NY 10010.
BISAC works to streamline ordering and fulfillment procedures. Write for information about the group and its activities.

Book Industry Study Group, Inc., 160 Fifth Avenue, New York, NY 10010; 1-212-929-1393.
Publishers, booksellers, manufacturers, librarians and others who work with books come together through BISG to gather and disseminate hard data about the book business.

Cataloging-in-Publication Division, Library of Congress, Washington, DC 20540.
Send for the form called "Request for Preassignment of Library of Congress Catalog Card Number" well in advance of publication.

CCLM (Coordinating Council of Literary Magazines), 666 Broadway, New York, NY 10012-2301; 1-212-614-6551.
The Council offers practical guidance as well as financial and moral support to publishers of literary periodicals.

Copyright Office, Library of Congress, Washington, DC 20559; 1-202-287-9100.
Send for the "Copyright Basics" pamphlet (Circular R1) and for

Form TX—the application for copyright registration for a nondramatic literary work—as early as possible. (If you need applications for other kinds of creative work, the Copyright Office will supply them too.)

* **COSMEP, the International Association of Independent Publishers. P.O. Box 703, San Francisco, CA 94101.**

The *COSMEP Newsletter* is itself worth the price of admission, and the organization functions as a highly effective channel of communication. Its 1,200 members work with both books and magazines.

William H. and Gwynne K. Crouse Library for Publishing Arts, The Graduate School and University Center of the City University of New York, 33 West 42nd Street, New York, NY 10036; 1-212-764-6338.

More than 3,000 books about book publishing are available here, along with selected periodicals, clippings and more. The library's admirable collection is open to the public. Call or write for the latest word on hours.

John Daniel, P.O. Box 21922, Santa Barbara, CA 93121.

John Daniel, who publishes belles lettres under his John Daniel Publisher imprint, also provides production services for small and self-publishers. Use an imprint of your own, though, instead of his Fithian Press label, which may make your book register with booksellers and others as a vanity press release.

Distributors.

See Book Marketing Opportunities and *Literary Market Place* in "Tools," above, and consult the *Subject Guide to Books in Print* to find publishers who might function as distributors for you because they issue books like yours.

DOT Pasteup Supply Company, 1612 California Street, P.O. Box 369, Omaha, NE 68101; 1-800-228-7272.

DOT's paste-up catalog is more than 100 pages long. Its cost—$1—is refunded when you order from it.

Editorial Freelancers Association, P.O. Box 2050, Madison Square Station, New York, NY 10159; 1-212-677-3357.

If you call the Editorial Freelancers Job Phone (given above) to describe the services you need, you'll hear from experienced people who want the work. As you would with any job applicant, ask for samples and check references.

GRT Book Printing, 3960 East 14th Street, Oakland, CA 94601; 1-415-534-5032.

GRT specializes in small editions—up to 2,000 copies—for writers and publishers in California. Send for "A Closer Look at GRT Book Printing"; it presents a great deal of sensible advice as it spells out the company's capabilities.

Indexers.

If your book is nonfiction and you'd like to maximize library sales, make sure it has a good index. Leads are available through the Editorial Freelancers Association (see above), through *Literary Market Place* and through the American Society of Indexers, 1700 18th Street, NW, Washington, DC 20009.

Interpub, P.O. Box 42265, Portland, OR 97242.

Run by Cliff Martin, Interpub offers seminars and consulting services for small and self-publishers, along with a monthly distillation of advice and news called *BookNotes*.

ISBN [International Standard Book Number], R. R. Bowker, 245 West 17th Street, New York, NY 10011.

By assigning a unique number to each published book, the ISBN system simplifies ordering, shipping and billing. To get your number as soon as possible, send the agency the data on your title page along with the name and address of your press and a SASE; they'll send you the proper forms.

ISSN [International Standard Serial Number], Library of Congress National Serials Data Program, Washington, DC 20540; 1-202-287-6452.

The periodical world's equivalent of the ISBN.

Mailing lists.

See *Book Marketing Opportunities* and *Literary Market Place* in "Tools," above, and Standard Rate and Data Service, below.

Marin Self-Publishers Association, Box 1346, Ross, CA 94957; 1-415-454-1771.

Members, who come from fifteen states besides California, share

The Self-Publishing Option Resources

information and the fruits of experience at monthly meetings, through publications and otherwise.

Maverick Mail Order Bookstore, Box 213, Saguache, CO 81149.
The catalog, which is free, offers a range of useful materials.

National Association of Independent Publishers, P.O. Box 850, Moore Haven, FL 33471; 1-813-946-0293.
Headed by Betty Wright, this group issues a newsletter, runs workshops and displays books at exhibits. A free brochure is available.

The Newsletter Clearinghouse, 44 West Market Street, P.O. Box 311, Rhinebeck, NY 12572; 1-914-876-2081.
The Clearinghouse puts out a *Newsletter on Newsletters,* runs seminars, sells books about buying and selling newsletters and otherwise aims to be useful to newsletter publishers.

Para Publishing, P.O. Box 4232, Santa Barbara, CA 93140-4232.
Dan Poynter's Para Publishing supplies an ever-expanding collection of clever, practical services for book publishers, including weekend workshops in a hilltop home overlooking the Pacific Ocean. *See* "Resources" passim and write for information on current offerings.

Pasteup Workshop. Walter B. Graham, Idea Seminars, P.O. Box 369, Omaha, NE 68101; 1-800-228-7272; (1-402-342-4221 outside Nebraska).
A one-day workshop offered around the country throughout the year. Send for details and a current schedule.

Poets & Writers, Inc., 201 West 54th Street, New York, NY 10019.
See "People, Places and Programs" in "Getting the Words Right Resources."

Publication Specialist Program, The George Washington University, 801 22nd Street, NW, Suite T409, Washington, DC 20052; 1-202-676-7273/4.
Courses run for eight weeks and there are more than thirty of them, as you'll see if you send for the handsome descriptive brochure.

Publishers Marketing Association, 2401 Pacific Coast Highway, Suite 206, Hermosa Beach, CA 90254.
PMA is a vital, growing group whose members advertise, publicize

and promote their books cooperatively. Meetings, a newsletter and medical plans are among the other benefits it offers.

Publishing Center for Cultural Resources, 625 Broadway, New York, NY 10012; 1-212-260-2010.
The Publishing Center will help nonprofit educational groups and institutions with planning, production, cooperative printing and distribution.

Quality Books, Inc., 918 Sherwood Drive, Lake Bluff, IL 60044-2204; 1-312-295-2010.
Quality Books specializes in getting adult nonfiction from small publishers into libraries. They're selective; call or write to find out how to submit a review copy.

Ripinsky & Company, Production Services, Obtuse Road, Newtown, CT 06570; 1-203-426-1650, 1-212-529-3600.
Harriet Ripinsky (whose experience includes a tour of duty as director of production at Simon & Schuster) now provides production services to small and self-publishers through her own company.

Ross Book Service.
To order books reviewed here, *see* "People, Places and Programs" in "Getting the Words Right Resources."

Sensible Solutions, Inc., 6 East 39th Street, New York, NY 10016; 1-212-532-5280.
Based on the principles enunciated in *How to Get Happily Published*, Sensible Solutions is a consulting firm that helps attract readers. *See* "The Sale and Its Sequels Resources."

SISAC (Serials Industry Systems Advisory Committee), 160 Fifth Avenue, New York, NY 10010; 1-212-929-1393.
SISAC is to periodicals as BISAC (see above) is to books.

Small Press Center, 20 West 44th Street, New York, NY 10036.
A mid-Manhattan site that small publishers and self-publishers can use to exhibit their books for very low fees. Titles must have "literary, artistic or social value."

Small Press Traffic, 3599 24th Street, San Francisco, CA 94110; 1-415-285-8394.
West Coast writers and publishers of fiction and poetry can take

advantage of the workshops and readings Small Press Traffic sponsors, and also of its well-stocked library of small press literature.

Standard Rate and Data Service, Inc., 3004 Glenview Road, Wilmette, IL 60091.

Several SRDS publications are designed to give people the facts they need to proceed intelligently when they want to place ads with newspapers, magazines, shopping guides, buses and radio and TV stations. Call 1-800-323-4588 for a free brochure.

Stanford Publishing Course, Bowman Alumni House, Stanford, CA 94305; 1-415-725-1083.

The two-week Stanford Publishing Course, held every year in July, is designed to give people already in publishing a broad overview and new insights.

The Town House Press, Inc., 28 Midway Road, Spring Valley, NY 10977.

Alvin Schultzberg, who runs The Town House Press, will handle all aspects of production for small editions and, if you like, will steer you toward help in the areas of sales and publicity.

Volunteer Lawyers for the Arts.

See "People, Places and Programs" in "Money Resources."

Wholesalers.

See Book Marketing Opportunities and *Literary Market Place,* and pay special attention to the national giants, Baker & Taylor and Ingram.

Women's National Book Association, 160 Fifth Avenue, New York, NY 10010; 1-212-675-7805.

Men can belong too, and the organization is open to librarians, agents, artists, educators, critics and booksellers as well as to writers and people in publishing. Write for information and see if there's a nearby WNBA chapter you might join.

Money Resources

TO EARN MORE money from writing, first figure out how to recycle material for multiple markets; then use the resources in previous sections to attract as many different buyers as you can. To win money, save money and stretch the dollars you have, see the resources listed below.

Advice, Analysis and Reportage

Adams, Jane. *How to Sell What You Write.* Putnam/Perigee, 200 Madison Avenue, New York, NY 10016. 1984.
   Look here for sprightly, incisive tips on recycling.

Barbara Brabec's National Home Business Report, P.O. Box 2137, Naperville, IL 60566.
   Advice and encouragement. Send for the free "Homemade Money" brochure to get a sense of what Brabec's quarterly compendium offers.

Burgett, Gordon, and Mike Frank. *Speaking for Money.* Communication Unlimited, P.O. Box 1001, Carpinteria, CA 93013. 1985.
   Burgett covers seminars and Frank covers speeches in considerable detail.

Crawford, Tad. *The Writer's Legal Guide.* Madison Square Press, 10 East 23rd Street, New York, NY 10010. 1978.
   Crawford, a lawyer-writer, offers some good advice on money mat-

ters and presents a sample ledger you can use to get into the habit of recording your expenses so you're prepared at tax time. *See* "Advice, Analysis and Reportage" in "The Sale and Its Sequels Resources."

Edwards, Paul and Sarah. *Working from Home: Everything You Need to Know about Living and Working Under the Same Roof.* Jeremy P. Tarcher, Inc., 9110 Sunset Boulevard, Los Angeles, CA 90069. 1985.

Commonsensical guidance on setting up and managing any kind of home-based business.

Hanson, Nancy Edmonds. *How You Can Make $20,000 a Year Writing (No Matter Where You Live).* Writer's Digest Books, 1507 Dana Avenue, Dept. JA, Cincinnati, OH 45207. 1980.

A peppy, can-do guide to the kinds of writing you do primarily for money. Hanson makes the very good point that writers outside New York have at least as much chance of making it as writers in the city.

Judd, Karen. *Copyediting: A Practical Guide.* William Kaufmann, Inc., 95 First Street, Los Altos, CA 94022. 1982.

Speaking from experience at Random House and elsewhere, Karen Judd shows how to get manuscripts ready for publication. A delightful, effective primer for anyone who'd like to make money polishing other people's prose.

Kamoroff, Bernard. *Small-time Operator: How to Start Your Own Small Business, Keep Your Books, Pay Your Taxes, & Stay Out of Trouble!* Bell Springs Publishing, P.O. Box 640, Laytonville, CA 95454. 1981.

Besides sounding like a genuinely nice guy, Kamoroff has years of experience as a financial adviser and tax accountant to small businesses and two small businesses of his own to provide plenty of case histories and advice. He covers everything from getting started (figuring out how much money you need and then getting your hands on it) to bookkeeping to the legal and financial technicalities of partnerships and payrolls and, yes, taxes. In addition, there's a fine resources section and a sheath of ledgers for your own use. Next to the usual how-to-get-rich tone of books on this subject, *Small-Time Operator* comes as a breath of down-to-earth fresh air.

Lant, Jeffrey. *The Unabashed Self-Promoter's Guide: What Every*

Man, Woman, Child and Organization in America Needs to Know about Getting Ahead by Exploiting the Media. JLA Publications, 50 Follen Street, Suite 507, Cambridge, MA 02138. 1983.

Following his own advice, Lant unabashedly uses his books as tools for promoting himself. Fortunately, he also supplies canny tips and he's able to poke fun at his own audacity. If the brashness doesn't turn you off, this guide may embolden you to spot and pull all the strings you can for your book, magazine or whatever.

Lant's other publications include *Money Talks: The Complete Guide to Creating a Profitable Workshop or Seminar in Any Field* and a free quarterly called *Sure-Fire Business Success Catalog* that has a section on publishing and promoting books.

Levinson, Jay Conrad. *Guerrilla Marketing: Secrets for Making Big Profits from Your Small Business.*

See "Advice, Analysis and Reportage" in "The Self-Publishing Option Resources."

Messman, Carla. *The Art of Filing: A Tax Workbook for Visual, Performing, Literary Artists and Other Self-Employed Professionals.* Volunteer Lawyers for the Arts/United Arts, 1285 Avenue of the Americas, Third Floor, New York, NY 10019. 1987.

Because tax laws are constantly changing and because interpreting provisions that apply to writers is a tricky business, there's no such thing as a simple, definitive guide to coping with your IRS forms. *The Art of Filing* comes close, though. It'll give you the ground rules and it'll probably convince you that if writing is your primary source of income you should hire an accountant posthaste.

Poet's Market: *Where and How to Publish Your Poetry.* Edited by Judson Jerome, assisted by Katherine Jobst. Writer's Digest Books, 1507 Dana Avenue, Dept. JA, Cincinnati, OH 45207. Updated annually.

See "Tools" in "A Foot in the Door Resources."

Rubin, Mary, and the Business and Professional Women's Foundation. *How to Get Money for Research.* The Feminist Press, 311 East 94th Street, New York, NY 10128. 1983.

The advice in Rubin's short primer is directed to women and people doing research about women but it can be applied to a variety of projects.

Seltzer, Michael. *Securing Your Organization's Future: A Complete Guide to Fundraising Strategies.* The Foundation Center, 79 Fifth Avenue, New York, NY 10003. 1987.

Because it's so comprehensive, so imaginative and so well written, Michael Seltzer's handbook can help individuals (including writers) as well as groups (for which it's designed) to amass the funds they need.

Smith, Peggy. *Mark My Words: Instruction and Practice in Proofreading.* Editorial Experts, Inc., 85 South Bragg Street, Alexandria, VA 22312-2731. 1987.

Those of you who like catching typos and other errors can upgrade proofreading skills through the exercises in here. Editorial experts also publishes a newsletter called *The Editorial Eye,* which covers a wide range of topics—"How to Abstract a Scientific Paper," "Checking Out Grammar Hotlines" and "Successful Newsletters," for example.

Spinrad, Norman. *Staying Alive: A Writer's Guide.* The Donning Company, 5659 Virginia Beach Boulevard, Norfolk, VA 23502. 1983.

Spinrad's scrappy, incisive observations about "how commerce relates to art" will open your eyes whatever you write, although most of these essays started out as columns for a science fiction trade magazine and some of them are now a bit dated.

Towers Club USA Newsletter, P.O. Box 2038, Vancouver, WA 98668-2038. Published monthly except in August and December.

Through this newsletter and the books he writes and distributes, Jerry Buchanan advises and informs writers whose primary goal is making money.

Tools

Author and Audience: A Readings and Workshops Guide. Poets & Writers, 201 West 54th Street, New York, NY 10019. Updated periodically.

The listings here will help you pinpoint places to give your own readings and/or workshops, and the advice in the book will be helpful too. Poets & Writers also periodically issues a list of poetry and fiction workshops in the New York metropolitan area. Send $2 and a self-addressed, stamped envelope for a copy.

Awards, Honors, and Prizes. Edited by Gita Siegman. Gale Research Company, Book Tower, Detroit, MI 48226. Updated periodically.

This is a two-volume general reference work about all kinds of awards in the United States and abroad. Its subject index will lead you to those for which you're eligible. Entries are sensibly annotated.

Grants and Awards Available to American Writers. P.E.N. American Center, 568 Broadway, New York, NY 10012. Updated periodically.

An indispensable—and inexpensive—reference for writers in search of funds. Well worth perusing whether you write fiction, non-fiction, poetry, children's books, plays or all of the above.

"Journalism Career and Scholarship Guide." The Dow Jones Newspaper Fund, Inc., P.O. Box 300, Princeton, NJ 08543-0300. Updated annually.

A copy will be sent to you, free, on request.

Lesko, Matthew. *Getting Yours: The Complete Guide to Government Money.* Viking Penguin, 40 West 23rd Street, New York, NY 10010. Third edition, 1987.

Good leads to state and federal funds. Be sure to check the lengthy index for the subject(s) your work covers.

Literary and Library Prizes. Edited by Olga S. Weber and Stephen J. Calvert. R. R. Bowker, 245 West 17th Street, New York, NY 10011. Updated periodically.

Although this is not comprehensive (most journalism awards are not included; little-known prizes have been omitted; and only a handful of awards designed for people who write short prose are mentioned), what it does cover it covers admirably (all major literary prizes, including fellowships for the Bread Loaf Writers Conference and the National Endowment for the Arts fellowships). Best of all, you'll find all previous recipients of each award listed chronologically, which should make it easy for you to get in touch with the people who can help you win what you want.

Literary Market Place. R. R. Bowker, 245 West 17th Street, New York, NY 10011.

LMP comes in handy in two ways where money is concerned: it has lists that you can consult to find funding, and it has lists that you can get on to earn fees.

To consult: "Literary Awards"; "Literary Fellowships"; "Employment Agencies" (the ones that specialize in publishing); "Prize Contests."

To get on (given relevant skills): "Composition"; "Computerized Typesetting"; "Copy Editing"; "Editorial Services"; "Proofreading"; "Rewriting"; "Special Assignment Writing."

Million Dollar Directory. **Dun's Marketing Services, A Division of Dun & Bradstreet, Three Century Drive, Parsippany, NJ 07054. Updated periodically.**

Businesses often need writers—to prepare annual reports, speeches, feature stories, newsletters and manuals. Try using the geographic and industry classification indexes in this multivolume work to zero in on companies that might hire you. Entries cover more than 160,000 U.S. businesses with net worth over $500,000.

Research Centers Directory. **Edited by Mary Michelle Watkins. Gale Research Company, Book Tower, Detroit, MI 48226. Eleventh edition, 1987.**

By becoming affiliated with appropriate institutions, individuals can become eligible for some of the many desirable grants offered to nonprofit groups. To find the centers most likely to take you under their wing, look up your project's subject in the directory's index and then study the description of each group listed under that heading.

Thomas Register of American Manufacturers. **Thomas Publishing Company, One Penn Plaza, New York, NY 10119. Updated periodically.**

A great source of leads to companies that might buy your work in bulk. The *Thomas Register,* a twenty-one-volume set, is available in libraries.

People, Places and Programs

American Book Producers Association, 319 East 52nd Street, New York, NY 10022; 1-212-982-8934.

If you have enough expertise and writing credits to work for a book packager, or if you think you'd like to become one, get in touch with this group. Its members package all sorts of titles.

Associated Writing Programs, Old Dominion University, Norfolk, VA 23508; 1-804-440-3839.

For a small membership fee, the creative writer can take advantage of a number of income-generating services sponsored by AWP. The organization runs placement services for writers interested in teaching on the college level. It issues a catalog of writers available for readings and lectures; a calendar of poetry festivals, conferences and the like; and a lively newsletter, which keeps its readers posted on new workshops, projects and publications of special interest to them.

CCLM [Coordinating Council of Literary Magazines], 666 Broadway, New York, NY 10012.

A number of money-granting programs for literary magazines are administered by CCLM. Write for information.

Dial-a-Writer, American Society of Journalists and Authors, 1501 Broadway, Suite 1907, New York, NY 10036.

Some people ask the Dial-a-Writer referral service to find them collaborators and ghosts. A writer who pays the price of admission to the ASJA can see who candidates are, what they want and whether any of their projects is likely to augment his or her income.

Editorial Freelancers Association, P.O. Box 2050, Madison Square Station, New York, NY 10159; 1-212-677-3357.

Members have access to information about job opportunities through a telephone bulletin board. The EFA also offers a newsletter, a directory and insurance at group rates, plus educational and supportive meetings.

The Foundation Center, 75 Fifth Avenue, New York, NY 10003, 1-212-620-4230; 1001 Connecticut Avenue, NW, Suite 938, Washington, DC 20036, 1-202-331-1400; 312 Sutter Street, San Francisco, CA 94108, 1-415-397-0902; 1442 Hanna Building, 1422 Euclid Avenue, Cleveland, OH 44115, 1-216-861-1933.

With national offices in New York and Washington, field offices in San Francisco and Cleveland and cooperating collections in libraries throughout the United States and abroad, the Foundation Center is a splendid source of information about 24,000 foundations that offer grants to individuals and groups.

The Center also publishes books, which are addressed primarily to nonprofit groups but may be helpful to individuals too. Send for a catalog.

Poets & Writers, Inc., 201 West 54th Street, New York, NY 10019.
Through their publications and referral services, Poets & Writers can boost the income as well as the spirits of people who write fiction and poetry.

State councils for the arts.
The best way to find out whether your state has an arts council is by writing your governor's office. If it does, ask for full information about the council's programs.

U.S. government.
Federal agencies engaged in all sorts of activities have libraries and issue press releases about where funds are going and what they've been earmarked for. There's grist for sales and promotion plans when and if money is allocated to a particular region for study of the particular subject you've written about, so ask to be put on the mailing lists of agencies whose bailiwicks are relevant to your writing/publishing efforts. And find out if they have special-interest libraries that might buy your book.

Volunteer Lawyers for the Arts, 1285 Avenue of the Americas, Third Floor, New York, NY 10019 and other locations (see below).
Founded in New York to provide legal services for artists who can't afford lawyers' fees, Volunteer Lawyers for the Arts has chapters across the country—in California (San Francisco, Los Angeles and La Jolla), Colorado (Denver), Connecticut (Hartford), the District of Columbia, Florida (Clearwater, Fort Lauderdale, Miami and Tallahassee), Georgia (Atlanta), Illinois (Chicago), Iowa (Cedar Rapids and Dubuque), Kentucky (Lexington and Louisville), Louisiana (New Orleans), Maine (Augusta), Maryland (Baltimore), Massachusetts (Amherst and Boston), Minnesota (Minneapolis), Missouri (St. Louis), Montana (Missoula), New Jersey (Trenton), New York (Albany, Buffalo, Huntington and Poughkeepsie, as well as New York City), North Carolina (Raleigh), Ohio (Cleveland and Toledo), Oklahoma (Oklahoma City), Pennsylvania (Philadelphia), Rhode Island (Narragansett), South Carolina (Greenville), Tennessee (Nashville), Texas (Austin and Houston), Utah

(Salt Lake City) and Washington (Seattle). There's a chapter in Toronto as well.

Write or call the chapter nearest you to find out about services and costs, or send $2 to the NYC chapter for a list of all chapters that tells what each one offers.

Writers' groups.

The Authors Guild, PEN and more specialized organizations help writers save money by, for example, offering medical insurance at group rates. Be sure to find out how groups you belong to can help your dollars stretch.

Index

AAFES (Army and Air Force Exchange Service), 275
Access to publishers, 71–74
Acquiring editors, 115
Acquisition decisions, 64–65, 78
Activist arguments, self-published, 157–58
Adelman, Bob, 149
Ad-Lib Publications, 214
Advance quotes, 181
Advances, 45, 84, 103–4
Advantages of self-publishing, 149–53, 177–78
Advertising, 122–23, 129, 132, 143; budgets, 107–8; direct-response, 191–92; information, 287; and placement of manuscript, 66
Advice, resources for: financial, 288–91; marketing of book, 255–60; sale of manuscript, 240–46; writing, 225–34
Agency critics, 31–33
Agents, 42–46, 84, 100–102; information, 242, 243, 248; and spinoffs, 207; and subsidiary sales, 104, 194
Airline magazines, 210
Alden, Todd, *Finding Facts Fast*, 232
Alumni magazines, 74–75
American Book Trade Directory, 185, 275–76
Andelin, Helen, *Fascinating Womanhood*, 193
Announcements of publication, 131, 182
Appelbaum, Judith, 29–30, 265

Application for publication, 78
Appreciation of self, 220–22
Approval rights, 113
Arabian Horse, 88
The Art of Literary Publishing, Henderson, ed., 266
Art school students, 163
Artwork, 121, 122, 167–68; sources of, 166, 277
Associated Writing Programs, 294
Associations, directory of, 262, 277
Auction of manuscripts, 91
Audience of writing, 12–13, 85, 127–28; reaction of, 219–22; and self-publishing, 148
Audiocassettes, 208
Auel, Jean, 43
Authors: and book publishers, 97–98; and editing of manuscript, 113–14; and publication process, 1–2, 6–7; and sales of book, 124–44
Authors Guild, Inc., 102, 106, 264
Autographed copies, 139, 140
Awards, 198, 209, 292

Backlist policies, 98–99
Baker & Taylor, 186
Baldwin, Christina, 47–48
Banks, Ann, book proposal, 86–87
Barber, Virginia, 42
Barzun, Jacques, *Simple and Direct*, 35
Becoming a Writer, Brande, 35
Bellow, Saul, 20
Bergholz, Susan, 139

298 Index

Bernstein, Meredith, 47–48
Bestsellers, 126–27, 219–20
Bibliographies, listings in, 183
Bigbooks, 126–27, 132
Binding, self-publishing, 175–76
Bird, Joan, 166
Bliss, Edwin C., *Getting Things Done,* 14
Blurbs, 181
Body type, 163
Book clubs, 104, 193–94
Book covers, 122–23
Book fairs, information, 279
Booklist, 183, 246
Book Marketing Opportunities, 194, 263
Book-of-the-Month Club, 194, 269
Book packagers, 211–13, 294
Bookpeople, 185
Book proposals, 83–87
Book publishers. *See* Publishers
Book Review Digest, 246
Book reviews, 72–73, 181–83, 240–41
Books: free, from publisher, 107; about writing, 34–37. *See also* Resources
Books in Print, 62, 183
Bookstores, 263; sales to, 134–37, 184–87
Borchardt, Georges, 106
Bowker Catalog, 246, 276
Bowker directories, 183
Brande, Dorothea, *Becoming a Writer,* 35
Brewer, Daryln, 204
Brickner, Richard P., 27–28
Brown, Diana, 141–42
Brownmiller, Susan, 15
Buchanan, Cynthia, 20
Buckley, William F., Jr., 143
The Buckley-Little Catalogue, 143–44, 261
Business management, 270, 280, 289, 290

Cable television, 208–9
Callenbach, Ernest, *Ectopia,* 193
Calligraphy, 76
Camaraderie of self-publishing, 152
Camera-ready copy, 170
Campus publications, 74–75
Careers, 240, 243; and writing, 203–4
Cassidy, Robert, 72
Cassill, R. V., 222; *Writing Fiction,* 34–35
Catalogs, 184
Celebrities, ghost-writing for, 210–11
Chabon, Michael, 46

Chase's Annual Events, 69, 235
Checklist for publication, 114
Cherry, Rona, 80
The Chicago Manual of Style, 276
Children's Book Council, 252
Children's books, 89, 231
Choice, 183, 246, 247
Choices in writing, 12–13
Classes in writing, 24–28
Classified ads, 191
Classroom texts, 155–56
CMG mailing lists, 276
Co-authors, sources, 238
Cohen, Carol, 98–99
Collaborators, 16, 50, 54, 211; sources, 238, 294
College stores, directory, 276–77
Color, in self-published work, 168
Commissions of agents, 43
Communication, 37, 147, 177
Community newspapers, 73
Company magazines, 73
Compositors, 168–69
Computer technology, 112, 273; composition, 168 169, 170; database, 278; software, 33–34, 237, 280
Conferences, 46–48, 251
Connections in publishing, 41–42
Construction, literary, 35
Consulting firms, 265
Contests, 74
Contracts, 44, 97, 100–102, 103; forms, 280; information, 256, 258
Conventions, personal appearances, 192
Copy-editing, 118–20, 161–62, 289; guidebooks, 268–69, 270–71
Copy-fitting, 164–65
Copyright, 162, 174, 233–34, 267, 274, 282
Corporate Action Program, 157
Correspondence courses, 28–31
COSMEP (International Association of Independent Publishers), newsletter, 67–68, 182, 184, 247, 283
Coupon ads, 191
Courses: on publishing, 253, 285, 287; on writing, 23–31, 46
Courter, Gay, 170
Cover letters, manuscript submission, 90
Covers of books, 122–23
Creative Writers Workshop, 21
Creativity, books about, 35

Index

Critical feedback, 17–22
Criticism services, 31–33
Cummington Community of the Arts, 201
Current subjects, 58

Database, for publishing information, 278
Data gathering, research tools, 36
Davis, Kenneth C., 212
Deadlines, 15, 121
DeRosis, Helen, 50
Descriptive announcements, 182
Design of book, 120–21, 162–64, 258, 274
Diaries of writers, 11–12
Diction, books about, 35
Dillard, Annie, 19
Direct mail sales, 189–91, 267, 268, 270
Directories, 234–38, 246–52, 275–78; for marketing of book, 260–64
Directory of Accredited Home Study Schools, 30
Direct-response advertising, 191–92
Discounts, 185, 186
Display type, 163, 165
Distribution, 98, 136, 143, 184–86; information, 283; by vanity presses, 75
Documentation, 119
Do-it-yourself typesetting, 170
Dover Pictorial Archive Book Catalog, 277
Dover Publications, 187
Drafting of manuscript, 14–16
Dummies, 172–74
Duncan, David James, *The River Why,* 68
Durrell, Lawrence, 24
Dustbooks, 183; Small Press Information Library, 277
Dyer, Wayne W., *Your Erroneous Zones,* 138–39

Ease of entry, self-publishing, 151–52
Economics: of publishing, 125–27, 148; of self-publishing, 178, 179–80; of writing, 197–205
Editing of manuscript, 113, 115–18, 257–58; self-publishing, 160
Editing skills, income from, 213–14
Editorial Freelancers Association, Inc., 160, 238, 283–84, 294
Editors, 2, 4–5, 18, 41, 65, 112, 115–16, 142; acquisition decisions, 64–65; application to, 77–78; comments from, 32; information about, 65–67, 259; mistakes by, 5–6; personal visits to, 82–83; reading of manuscripts, 44; relationships with, 92, 97–100, 118–20; writing by, 65
Education, part-time courses, 238–39
Eisenheimer, Lisel, 80
The Elements of Style, Strunk and White, 232
Ellenbogen, Glen C., 156
Emery, Carla, *The Old-Fashioned Recipe Book,* 193
Employment in publishing, 49–50
Encouragement, 19–20
Encyclopedia of Associations, 69, 192, 235, 262, 277
Enthusiasm for project, 81
Ephron, Delia, 82
Excerpts of books, periodical publication, 209–10
Exchange ads, 191
Expense allowances, 107
Expenses diary, 203
Experiences, shared, 55–56
Export market, 207–8
Eyewitness accounts, 70

Facsimile books, 213
Factory Outlet Shopping Guides, Bird, 155
Failure of publications, 1, 107–8
Farbow, Norman, 56
Fargis, Paul, 138–39
Feedback from readers, 151
Feminist literature, 56–57, 247
Feminist publishing, 274–75
Fiction, 79, 156–57, 277
Fiction Writer's Market, 247–48
Figman, Elliot, 18
Files of subject material, 12
Fillers, 211
Financial management, 125–27, 270, 277
Financing of writing, 197–205, 288–96; of activist publications, 157–58
Finding Facts, Rivers, 36–37
Finding Facts Fast, Alden, 232
Fine Arts Work Center, 201
First serial rights, 104, 210
Fischer, John, 5
Flexibility in subject development, 61
Focus of subject matter, 61
Foley, Martha, *Best American Short Stories,* 198

Folios, 173
Follow-up to manuscript submission, 91–93
Foreign rights, 99, 207–8
Form of writing, freedom of, 149–50
Forms, legal, 280
Formulas for writing, 35–36
Forthcoming Books, 58
Foundations, 198, 294–95
Freelancers, 283–84; designers, 163; editors, 160
Friendships, from self-publishing, 152
Fringe benefits, 106–7
Front matter, 174
Frye, Northrop, 16, 37
Fulton, Len, 178
Fundraising, 290
Future, predictions of, 58–60

Galassi, Jonathan, 88
Gale Research, 183, 235–36, 277
Galley proofs, 121, 169, 172, 182
Garland Publishing, Inc., 213
Genet, Russell M., 192
Geographical targeting, 136–37
George, Wayne B., 32–33
Ghost writers, 16, 210–11, 294
Gioia, Dana, 203–4
Glamour, 72, 80; "Viewpoint," 72
Gollob, Herman, 64
Gordon, Elizabeth, 89
Government: funding, 292, 295; information from, 239
Grant, Anne, 201–2
Grants, 197–200, 292
Grants and Awards Available to Writers, 198, 262–63
Graphic illustrations, 61
Great Britain, as market, 207
Greeting-card verse, 211
Group membership, 56–57
Groups, publications by, 68–69
Guest, Judith, *Ordinary People,* 6

Hahn, Hannelore, 47
Haley, Alex, 139
Hancock, Elise, 73–75
Hardcover binding, 175
Harkness, James, 19
Harper's Weekly, 72
Harris, Art, 70–71
Harris, Macdonald, 46

Harris, Thomas A., *I'm OK, You're OK,* 132
Heads (typography), 165
Heller, Joseph, 139
Hemingway, Ernest, 16
Henderson, Bill, *Publish-It-Yourself Handbook,* 153
Herman, Harriet, *The Forest Princess,* 156–57
Hirschman, Susan, 89
History of writing, 226
House organs, 211

Illustrations, 61, 89
Independent distributors, 98
Indexing, 120, 284
Ingram, 186
Institute of Children's Literature, 29–3
Instruction in writing, 23–37
Instruction videocassettes, 208
International Association of Independent Publishers. *See* COSMEP
The International Directory of Little Magazines and Small Presses, 59, 66
Internship programs, 49
Interviews, 55, 131
ISBN, 162, 284
ISSN, 162, 284

Jacoby, Susan, 199
James, Jennifer, *Success Is the Quality of Your Journey,* 193
Janeway, Elizabeth, 140
Janovic, Florence, 265
Jerome, Judson, 88
Jobbers, 137–38, 186
Jobs in publishing industry, 49–50
Jones, Mimi, 6
Jones, Ron, 149
Jones, Tony, 72
Journals, 13–14
Justification (typography), 163

Kahn, Joan, 65
Katz, Herb, 47
Kavanagh-Smith, Margaret, 59–60
Keyes, Ralph, 85
Kidd, Elisabeth, 21
Knowledge, shared, 54–55
Korda, Michael, 50
Kremer, John, 214, 263
Kruchkow, Diane, 88

Index   301

Labine, Clem, *Old-House Journal,* 156
Lane, Robert, *A Solitary Dance,* 157
Language, use of, 16
Lansky, Bruce and Vicki, 213
Large publishers, 62–63
Laser printers, 174
Lawrence, Seymour, 65
Lawyers, for contracts, 100–101
Layout, 163–64, 166–68
Leading (typography), 164
Lecturing, 214
Leedom-Ackerman, Joanne, *The Dark Path to the River,* 136–37
Legal advice, 154, 256–57, 259, 288–89, 295–96
Legal problems, copy-editing, 161–62
Leggett, John, 25
Leigh, Bill, 214
Leishman, Katie, 25–26
Letters to the Editor columns, 72
Libraries, 137–38, 182–83, 192–93, 276; children's books, 89; sales to, 99, 273
Library Journal, 183, 246, 248
Library of Congress Catalog Number, 162, 282
Line drawings, reproduction of, 167
Line editors, 115
Listings, 183
Literary magazines, reading fees, 88
Literary Market Place (LMP), 65, 67, 72, 82, 194, 207, 236, 248–49, 263, 276, 277, 279, 284; financial information, 292–93; freelance editors, 160; lecture bureaus, 214; reviewing outlets, 182; writers groups, 265
Little, Stuart, 143
Local-interest subjects, 56–57, 155
Local publications, 272–73; reprints of excerpts, 210
Lollipop, 157
Longevity of self-published work, 152–53
Lunches, 4

McCall's, gazette pages, 72
McLaughlin, Mary, 59
Magazine articles, 97, 108, 122, 134; promotion of, 124–25; queries, 78
Magazines, 71–72, 102–3, 268, 269; excerpts published in, 209–10; poetry publication, 88; writing assignments, 80

Mailing lists, 153, 189, 190–91; information, 276, 278
Mail order, 99, 271–72; catalogs, 188, 277, 279
Manuscript, submission of, 62–93
Marek, Richard, 50
Margins, 150
Margins (book page), 163
Marketing information, 255–65, 270, 274, 278, 285–86
Markets for manuscripts, 62–64, 179; identification in proposal, 85; information, 235, 247–48, 252
Mary Ellen's Best of Helpful Hints, 193
Meadowbrook Press, 213
Mechanicals, 170–71, 174
Medina, Kate, 64
Milestone dates, 114, 115
Millay Colony for the Arts, 201–2
Money-saving ideas, 202
Montag, Tom, 150
Morrison, Toni, 50
Morrow, William, Publisher, 66
Motion picture rights, 104
Movements, prediction of, 59–60
Movies, 206
Ms., gazette pages, 72
Muir, John, *How to Keep Your Volkswagen Alive,* 155
Multiple submissions, 91, 98–100

Naftalin, Rose, 139
Naggar, Jean, 43
Name for self-publishing venture, 180
National Endowment for the Arts, 198
National University Continuing Education Association, 31
Need-to-know pieces, 155
New Hampshire Publishing Company, 213
Newman, James R., *The World of Mathematics,* 5–6
Newsletters, 73, 211, 269, 285
Newspaper pieces, promotion of, 124–25
Newspapers, local, 73
Newsweek, "My Turn," 72
Newsworthy events, 70
New York Public Library, Allen Room, 15–16
The New York Times, "Living," 72
The New York Times Book Review, 182;

advertising rates, 132; author's query, 110
Nonfiction, 79, 83–84
Nonsexist writing, 230, 270–72
Nontraditional outlets, 187–89
Novak, William, 211
Novels, self-published, 156–57

O'Connor, Flannery, 15
Office space, 106–7
Offset printing, 168
On Writing Well, Zinsser, 35
Op Ed pages, 72
Opening paragraphs, 17
Order forms, with ads, 191
Ordinary People, Guest, 6
Organizations, 252–54, 263, 264–65
Out-of-print books, 143–44, 261

Packagers, 211–13, 294
Page numbers, 173
Page proofs, 122
Page size, 163
Paper, choice of, 175
Paperback binding, 176
Para Publishing, 214, 285
Paris Review Interviews, 12
Pasteup, 170–74, 269, 285
Payment: from bookstores, 186; for ghost writing, 211; for manuscript, 102–6; for proposed books, 84; for typesetting, 169
Peacock, Molly, 131
Pellegrino, Victoria Y., 50
PEN, 198, 265
Perfect binding, 175
Periodicals. *See* Magazines
Permissions, for photographs, 166
Perseverance, 6–7
Personal connections, and sales, 139
Personal experiences of writers, 11–12
Personal image consultants, 262
Personal publishing, 65–66
Pfaltz, Marilyn, 205
Physical situation for writing, 15–16
Pica, 164
Pictorial archives, 277
Pilpel, Harriet F., 162
Pilpel, Robert, 119–20
Pirsig, Robert, *Zen and the Art of Motorcycle Maintenance,* 66
Placement, by agents, 44–45

Poetry, 87–89, 156–57, 228, 230–31; markets, 249–50; readings, 131
Poets & Writers, Inc., 18, 239, 295
Poets & Writers Magazine, 198, 243
Points (type size), 164
Political statements, 157–58
Portis, Ruth, 156
Positioning of books, 108–11
Poynter, Dan, 214, 285
Premium sales, 188, 204–5
Press releases, 130
Pricing, 179–80
Printers, 175–76, 278–79
Printer's errors, 169
Print runs, 179
Prizes, 292
Production managers, 120–21
Production process, 121, 258, 266–87; services, 286
Projects, funding for, 198–200
Promotion, 108–11, 132, 276, 290; by big publishers, 63; of self-published works, 178, 180–81
Proofreading, 169–70, 291
Proposals for books, 83–87
Public appearances, 132, 136, 139–42, 192, 214, 291
Publication of book, responses, 219–20
Publicity, 128–33, 186, 258, 260, 264; by author, 143; information, 271, 275; radio, directory, 279; for self-published works, 180–81; for speaking engagements, 140
Public relations, 281
Public speaking, advice, 257
Publishers, 3–5, 59, 62, 67–69, 240–54; contracts, 97; public-speaking services, 140
Publishers' Trade List Annual, 67, 250
Publishers Weekly, 43, 57, 65, 67, 182, 207, 250, 280
Publishing Institute, Denver, 253
Publishing memoirs, 65
Publishing personnel, contacts, 48–51
Publishing procedures, 259
Publishing skills, income from, 213

Quality Books, Inc., 193, 286
Quality control, self-publishing, 149
Queries, 78–82, 89
Quinn, Alice, 88
Quotations, books of, 234, 258

Index

Radio publicity directory, 279
Ragged right margins, 163
Rasmussen, Mark, 55–56
Readers, feedback from, 151
Reader's Digest, 210
Reading, learning from, 11–12
Reading fees, 88
Recycling of works, 206
Reed, Ann, 205
Reference books, 36
Regional publications, 155, 272–73
Reiss, Eric L., *The Compleat Talking Machine,* 54
Rejections, 92–93
Remaindered books, 143–44
Repayment of advances, 103–4
Reporting assignments, 70
Reprints, 104, 133, 144, 210
Reproduction of artwork, 167
Research, 36, 54–55; books about, 228, 229, 231; financing of, 107, 290
Resources, 224; financial, 288–96; publication of book, 255–65; sale of manuscript, 240–54; self-publication, 266–87; writing skills, 225–39
Retail outlets, nonbookstore, 187–89
Return policies, 135–36, 186–87
Review copies, 130, 181–82
Reviews, 181–83, 260
Revision of writing, 16–18, 35, 90
Reynolds, David K., 56
Rice, Anne, 47
Rights, 99, 102–3, 104, 206, 210
Rivers, William L., *Finding Facts,* 36–37
Robben, John, *Coming to My Senses,* 4–5
Roth, Stephen F., 112
Royalties, 104–6
Running heads, 164, 173

Sales conferences, 134–35
Sales of book, 124–44, 177–94
Sales representatives, 49, 98, 134–35, 184
Sandomir, Richard, 193
Sangrey, Dawn, 15
Scaling of artwork, 167
Scholarly publications, 273, 275; self-published, 155–56
Schwed, Peter, *Turning the Pages,* 65
Scientific works, export market, 207
Second serial rights, 210
Self-appreciation, 220–22

Self-editing, 17–18, 234
Self-publishing, 74, 75–76, 147–48; advantages of, 149–53; candidates for, 153–58; reprints, 144; resources, 266–87; skills for, 159–76
Seminars on publicity, 264
Sensible Solutions, Inc., 253–54, 265, 286
Serial rights, 210
Serial sales, 133
Service pieces, 54
Seskin, Jane, 140
Shirk, F. Alan, *The Colonial Berks Sampler,* 155
Short features, 211
Simons, Carol Lew, 27–28
Simony, Maggy, *Traveler's Reading Guides,* 153–54
Simple and Direct, Barzun, 35
Small periodicals, review copies, 130
Small Press, 58, 67
Small publishers, 59, 62–63, 88–89, 103, 112, 128, 152; contracts, 100; information, 248, 250, 277, 286
Smith, Lisa, 49
Speaking engagements, 110, 131, 140–42; information, 288
Special-interest publications, 59, 70; journals, reviews, 182; newsletters, 210; self-published, 156
Specialized publishers, 59, 62–63, 88, 213
Special sales, 99, 137, 189
Specialty bookstores, directory, 281
Specifications (typography), 165
Speculation submissions, 79–80
Speeches, 214
Speech-writing, 211
Spencer, John Wallace, *Limbo of the Lost,* 193
Spinoffs, 206–15
Spread (book page), 166
State councils for the arts, 295
Stringers, 70
Style guides, 161, 232, 271, 276
Style of writing, 13–14
Subject Guide to Books in Print, 68, 237, 251
Subject matter, 12–13, 52–61
Submission of manuscript, 62–93
Subsidiary rights, 99, 133–34, 193–94
Subsidiary sales, 104

Subsidy publishing, 74, 204–5
Success in publishing, 7
Support groups, 238–39
Surveys, for topic interest, 60
Swansea, Charleen Whisnant, 192

Talent, search for, 4–5
Targan, Barry, 198
Tauber, Peter, 48
Taxes, 203
Taylor, Nancy, 135
Teachers of writing, 24–28, 46
Teaching, for income, 215
Telemarketing information, 274
Telephone calls to editors, 82–83
Television, 206, 208–9, 275
Thomas Register of American Manufacturers, 69, 189
Time for writing, 14–15
Timetable of publication, 115
Timing of manuscript, 69–71
Titles, ideas for, 110
Todd, Alden, *Finding Facts Fast,* 60
Toffler, Alvin, 170
Tools: financial, 291–93; for marketing of book, 260–64; for sale of manuscript, 246–52; for self-publishing, 275–82; writing skills, 234–38
Toys "R" Us Magazine, 88
Trade journals, 210
Translations, 207–8
Trends in publishing, 57–58
Triegel, Linda, 21
Typefaces, 164
Typesetting, 168–70

Ulrich's International Periodicals Directory, 183
Unconventional marketing, 187–89
Unit costs, 179
Unpublished writers, grants for, 197

Unsolicited manuscripts, 71–74, 79

Vanity presses, 74–76, 148
Veloxes, 167
Videocassettes, 208

Wages, 203–4
Waldenbooks, 186
Walker, Scott, 89
Weiner, Richard, *Professional's Guide to Public Relations Services,* 153
Wholesalers, 137–38, 186
Wilson, H. W., catalogs, 183, 281
Women in Writing Conference, 47–48
Word-of-mouth, 153
Word processors, 33–34, 170, 234
Working space, 15–16
Workshops, 46, 291
The World of Mathematics, Newman, 5–6
The Writer, 233
Writers: contacts with, 46–48; critical feedback from, 18–21. *See also* Authors
Writers' colonies, 200–202, 243
Writers Conferences, 251
Writer's Digest, 75
Writers' groups, 21–22, 203, 296
The Writers Room, 239
Writing Fiction, Cassill, 35
Writing jobs, sources of, 293
Writing process, 14–37
Writing skills, 11–22, 225–39; earning from, 210–12
Writing software, 33–34

Yaddo, 200–201
Yellow Pages, local, 266

Zephyros, Jones, 149
Ziner, Feenie, *A Full House,* 144
Zinsser, William, 25–26; *On Writing Well,* 35